THE MEASURE OF OUR DAYS

Jerome Groopman

THE MEASURE OF OUR DAYS

New Beginnings at Life's End

VIKING

VIKING
Published by the Penguin Group
Penguin Putnam Inc., 375 Hudson Street,
New York, New York 10014, U.S.A.
Penguin Books Ltd, 27 Wrights Lane,
London W8 5TZ, England
Penguin Books Australia Ltd, Ringwood,
Victoria, Australia
Penguin Books Canada Ltd, 10 Alcorn Avenue,
Toronto, Ontario, Canada M4V 3B2
Penguin Books (N.Z.) Ltd, 182–190 Wairau Road,
Auckland 10, New Zealand

Penguin Books Ltd, Registered Offices:
Harmondsworth, Middlesex, England

First published in 1997 by Viking Penguin,
a member of Penguin Putnam Inc.

3   5   7   9   10   8   6   4   2

A portion of this work first appeared in *The New Yorker*.

Grateful acknowledgment is made for permission to reprint excerpts from the following
copyrighted works:
"Tell Me" from *Collected Poems* by Langston Hughes. Copyright © 1994 by the Estate of
Langston Hughes. Reprinted by permission of Alfred A. Knopf, Inc.
Tanakh: A New Translation of the Holy Scriptures According to the Traditional Hebrew Text,
Jewish Publication Society. Used by permission of the publisher.
The Tao of Healing by Haven Trevino. © 1993. Reprinted with permission of New World
Library, Novato, California.

LIBRARY OF CONGRESS CATALOGING–IN–PUBLICATION DATA
Groopman, Jerome E.
The measure of our days : new beginnings at life's end / Jerome Groopman.
p.   cm.
ISBN 0-670-87570-8 (alk. paper)
1. Terminally ill. 2. Death. 3. Terminal care. I. Title.
R726.8.G77   1997
362.1'75—dc21   97-11693

This book is printed on acid-free paper.
∞

Printed in the United States of America
Set in Bembo
Designed by Pei Koay

In memory of my father,

who taught me how to love.

Contents

THE MEASURE OF OUR DAYS

Prologue

IN THE SPRING OF 1974, I was awakened by a phone call in the middle of the night from my mother. My father, the person I loved and admired most in the world, the person who had centered and guided my life, had had a massive heart attack. He was in a small community hospital in Queens. I was living in Manhattan, a second-year student at Columbia College of Physicians and Surgeons, still learning medicine from books and in laboratories. I rushed from my dormitory, arriving in time to see my father in the final throes of cardiac shock. He was attended to by a general practitioner unknown to my family, who offered no special medical expertise or emotional comfort. My father died before my eyes. He died before his time, and without time—time for him, his family, and his friends to prepare for his passing.

This experience explains in part my powerful commitment to care for patients and their loved ones in a way that my father and my family were not cared for—with genuine compassion and scientific excellence. And it provides a very personal point of reference for why I find the time before death so precious, so worth fighting for.

We feel both a deep attraction and a powerful resistance to thinking about the biological and emotional circumstances surrounding death. Until recently, it was nearly taboo to discuss the subject of death frankly in our society. Now issues of illness and mortality are being debated even in our courts and legislatures. When I listen to such discussions, I realize how distant law and precept are from the turmoil and struggle that occur at each patient's bedside. In this book I seek, above all, to capture and illuminate that complexity, not by academic analysis, but by way of true stories, told as they unfolded before my eyes, as medical mysteries and human dramas. Some of the stories I tell here come to resolution and provide answers; others raise questions that still await a response.

After two decades of caring for people with cancer, blood diseases, and AIDS, I am often asked if I am "burned out" or depressed. The opposite is the case, despite the suffering and loss I witness and absorb. I experience my work as remarkably inspiring and gratifying.

I identify several elements that give me hope and strength in the cold company of death. One is modern science and the potential for change it offers. Another is the wisdom and solace found in faith. And, perhaps most important, as the following stories reveal, I draw on the particular lessons—of courage and endurance—gained from my patients.

I am fortunate to be a clinician who also is a researcher actively engaged in scientific discovery. At my laboratory bench I see the world of disease through a very different lens from that at the patient's bedside. It is a view of the universe of molecules and genes, a universe rapidly yielding its secrets before the power of modern molecular biology, protein chemistry, and high-performance computing. When I am worn down by the anguish and frustration of fighting a battle that I know cannot be won against a disease for which there is no cure, I take refuge in laboratory work. The idea that I am actively participating in the discovery of new therapies rejuvenates my spirit in the face of so much loss. I look to science to change the world, to make the fatal one day curable.

When I was in the fifth grade at Public School 187 in Queens, my friend and classmate Eric Gold was stricken with acute lymphoblastic leukemia, the most common form of the disease among children. I did not know what he had at the time—none of us in Mrs. Lavin's class did, because his diagnosis was unspeakable in 1960. I vividly remember how Eric changed, how his sandy brown hair was gradually shed, how his eyes became sunken and yellow, and his exuberant smile lost in a tired mask of sadness. During this transformation, Eric's parents tried to buoy his spirits with gifts, buying him the first ten-speed bike seen in our working-class neighborhood. Eric would spend his afternoons riding in slow, deliberate circles around the schoolyard, we, his friends, watching in ignorant envy.

One day Eric disappeared. Our class was told he had fallen to "blood poisoning." We sat in shock, wondering what mysterious poison had caused our playmate's death.

Today, Eric Gold would be cured. Childhood lymphoblastic leukemia was conquered for most of its victims during the twenty-five years that followed his death. Painstaking research, in the laboratory and in the clinic, led to the development of effective treatments that, when used in combination, eradicate the cancerous blood cells and allow the normal cells to thrive. For those few who do not respond to now standard therapies, there are active experimental programs aimed at cure, including bone marrow transplantation.

Such clinical triumphs have happened not just once but several times during my life, and are in the process of happening now, most dramatically for AIDS. Because of this knowledge, I do not accept the term "hopeless" applied to any illness. This tenet of a medical scientist's faith—that with enough will and wisdom, diseases which are now fatal can be cured—drives me forward when I find myself slowing from the pain. I work to have my patients also adopt this faith in medical science, and to derive new strength from it.

Although I am a scientist who draws sustenance from a rational understanding of the natural world, I am also a person who views life in deeply spiritual terms. I perceive in the intricacy and beauty of science the wonder and gifts of God. I see in the patient's struggle to reclaim and reconstruct his life a process that enhances the sanctity of that life.

I was raised in a traditional Jewish home. Much of my mother's extended family, Hasidim living in the Carpathian region of eastern Hungary and Romania made famous by Elie Wiesel, perished in the Holocaust. The few Bruckensteins who survived the hell of Auschwitz were sponsored by my maternal grandmother and came to live near us in New York. I grew up pondering the hollow light in their eyes, wondering what meaning could be found in their hushed stories, told in Yiddish, at family gatherings. From them, I became acutely aware of the special evil that can exist in man's world, the evil that marked millions as "different" and undeserving of life. I realized from some of their experiences that the very opposite of this behavior existed as well, an extraordinary kindness and caring which can flourish even under the most extreme circumstances.

When I learned in Hebrew school the stories of the Bible and the rabbinical colloquy of the Talmud, I wondered how they explained the experiences of my Bruckenstein cousins. I concluded that there were important moments in personal and world history when the face of God appears hidden, when religious doctrine does not readily provide answers. Still, faith can be called upon for strength in these moments.

I have discovered the same to be true with severe illness. I derive insight and comfort from my heritage, its knowledge of joy and suffering, its wisdom that belief is linked to questioning.

How can I understand the fear and anguish of my patients? I look back to a defining period in my life when I was not in the role of the doctor. Shortly after my marriage in 1979, while training for a marathon, I suffered an injury to my back. Anxious for a quick fix that would return me to my training and the upcoming race, I opted for surgery rather than nonsurgical rehabilitation. The operation was a failure. I awoke with my legs frozen in excruciating pain. My physicians were unsure what had occurred. I was unable to walk, uncertain if this agonizing condition would ever change.

The physical and emotional devastation of this event, and the resources I called upon to overcome it, have provided me with a perspective that few doctors share. I know myself as the patient, vulnerable, confused, and suffering, struggling to cope with a shattered world that appears out of control, told that there is no certainty that a normal life will return. I ultimately regained function by undergoing arduous physical therapy over the course of several years.

Why, with this background, did I choose to be a specialist in blood diseases and cancer, and then extend my work to AIDS?

First was the great intellectual attraction of the study of cancer. The normal physiology of the cell reveals a highly ordered program of growth and maturation, proceeding in a tightly regulated fashion. Recapitulated in the history of a single cell is the story of the greater organism: birth, reproduction, maturation, and death. The cancer cell rebels against this order. It loosens its restraints and reproduces uncontrollably, without maturing. It also mysteriously seeks other venues for its mad orgy of reproduction, leaving its proper niche in tissues and wildly invading body spaces where it does not belong—the process called "metastasis."

AIDS is the biological mirror image of the process of cancer. Instead of the cell's unregulated growth, there is its untimely death. HIV, the virus that causes AIDS, targets the T cell, which is central to the immune defense system. HIV hijacks this defender by inserting its viral genes into the T cell's nucleus. The poisonous program of the virus then mixes with the DNA that we inherit from our parents. The T cell is subverted from a key part of our immune defenses into a factory for producing new HIV, leaving us vulnerable to otherwise innocuous microbes that now cause life-threatening infections.

But it was more than the wonder of biology, the intricacies of cellular and viral DNA and proteins, that captured my imagination and my heart. It was the intricacies of the patient's condition as he faced his mortality, the efforts of his soul as he struggled to adapt to the vicissitudes of his disease.

I had the unique experience of seeing the very first cases of AIDS. These were diagnosed in Los Angeles in 1981. After finishing my fellowship training in blood diseases and cancer, I left Harvard to take a junior faculty position at the University of California at Los Angeles. During my first year at UCLA, the medical center was abuzz about the perplexing case of "Queenie," a young male prostitute who used that name. He had been living a life of humiliation and abuse on the streets of Hollywood and came to UCLA with a strange and new disease that would later be known as AIDS.

Over the ensuing year we saw many cases of this new and uncharacterized disorder among young gay men. Our ignorance of the disease and how to treat it gave these patients little time. I was deeply disturbed by their mysterious, untimely deaths, and committed myself to begin research and clinical care of people with the disease.

I was attracted to these frightened and alienated patients for the very reasons many doctors shunned them. I realized that I could lift some of the weight they carried. I found that as with those suffering from cancer, I could stand at the bedside, without flinching or retreating, and open my heart. It was at such moments I knew I had additionally relieved suffering with the medicine of friendship.

My journey, then, as a physician-scientist has been made with two companions. One is cancer, which I had chosen during my specialty training. The second is AIDS, which arrived without invitation and shrouded in mystery. I realized early in my career that similar strengths and knowledge were needed to endure the company of each. As the stories that follow illustrate, these companions have taught me more powerful lessons about life than about death.

Kirk

"*I WON'T TAKE NO* for an answer. It's bullshit. I'm fifty-four. I'm not ready to just pack it up and die. I'm a fighter. I don't buy that *nothing* can be done."

As he spoke, Kirk Bains leaned far forward in his chair, tightly locking his jaundiced eyes on mine. He was obviously studying my face, looking for clues, trying to read in advance my response. I imagined it was a style he adopted in his business meetings, where he would face down clients and look hard into their eyes, gauging whether the project and the persons before him were worth his resources. Only this time, the roles were reversed.

"You've seen my records from Yale and Sloan Kettering and M. D. Anderson. They think I'm too sick for their research studies. So you cook up some new magic. Make me a guinea pig. I take risks all the time. That's my business. I won't sue you. My cousin Grant says you're a medical genius, a wizard."

"That's kind of Grant to say, but I'm not a genius or a wizard, Mr. Bains."

"Well, Dr. Groopman, I need you to be. Because you're my last hope."

• • •

I HAD READ KIRK BAINS'S RECORDS, all ninety-six Xeroxed pages, and had no thoughts of magic, just cold despair. I had searched for some detail that had been overlooked or incompletely investigated, hoping it might guide me to devise a rational and possibly effective treatment. But each lifeless copy of CAT scans, operative reports, and blood tests was another stone in what seemed an impenetrable dense wall of facts. The oncologists at Yale, Sloan Kettering, and M. D. Anderson had quickly reached their conclusions, telegraphed in the records in disinterested clinical syntax: "Diffusely metastatic renal carcinoma. Multiple sites including liver, bones, and lungs involved. No effective therapy. Palliative care advised."

I imagined how they had gravely translated this in private to his wife, Catherine, to dissuade him from pursuing treatment: The kidney cancer has spread throughout his body; the few drugs we have don't work at this stage; he will only be hurt by their toxicities; his survival is no more than several weeks; it's best for your husband to be at home, made comfortable, and allowed to die.

I looked at Kirk Bains—his jet black hair, sharp aquiline nose, and square jaw, a handsome and decisive face—and wondered how long it would take him to accept his condition. My eyes moved away and focused on the stacked pile of his records. I found them distracting, and pushed them to the far side of my desk, dismissed like an interloper who had disturbed an intimate conversation between two friends. I took an unused tablet of lined white paper from my desk drawer, placed it where the records had been, and sat poised to write.

"I've read the reports, Mr. Bains . . ."

"Call me Kirk, Dr. Groopman."

"Then call me Jerry. Let's start fresh. I want to hear the story directly from you, not from the records, and in detail, from the time you first noticed something was wrong. Then I'll examine you. From top to bottom. After that we'll think this through together."

Kirk Bains nodded, exhaled a long, slow breath, and settled back in his chair as he began to recount the history of his illness.

In having him repeat his medical history and physical examination now for the fourth time, I wasn't merely performing a perfunctory ritual so I could justify another denial to his plea. If I were to care for him properly, first I had to confirm the accuracy of the information abstracted in his records. And even if I discovered no new fact or physical finding, there was a journey taken when I listened to a patient recount his story and I palpated his body. It was a journey of the senses—hearing, touching, seeing—that carried me to the extrasensory dimension of intuition.

I planned to walk deliberately through the milestones of Kirk's life—the character of his parents and his siblings, the extent of his education, the nature of his occupation, the details of his travel, the status of his personal relationships, the vicissitudes of his prior and current illnesses and treatments—and for brief but illuminating moments I became integrated into his experience.

After imagining his past through his retold history, I would be prepared to enter his present through the physical examination. My hands would press deeply into his abdomen to outline the breadth and texture of his inner organs; my eyes would peer behind his pupils to read the barometers of cerebral pressure and blood flow displayed on his retinas; my ears, linked by the stethoscope, would hear the timbre of his heart.

But I feared that in Kirk's case I might not reach this dimension of intuition, because medical science seemed to have locked me in a cell with no exit. The CAT scans and blood tests and operative findings were like steel bars, the consensus of my colleagues in New Haven, New York, and Houston tight shackles that restrained my mind and heart from traveling into his.

"I was on the golf course in Palm Beach. The morning of September twentieth. With two Jap investors. They had come in from Osaka. They were considering buying out my share in a refinery in the Gulf, off Galveston. I'm the lead investor. The refinery is expanding operations, betting that oil will recover. Good time to get in—early, before it becomes obvious to every maiden aunt with a pension fund. Anyway, we got up early to play and beat the heat. Japs are crazy for golf. Did you know that? If you ever want something from a Jap, first play golf with him. It doesn't hurt if you let him win, either."

I nodded uncomfortably, disturbed by his brazen attitude but considering how it might prove useful in the fight against his cancer.

"And at the first tee I felt this . . . this tug in my back. It wasn't really a pain. Not like sciatica, which I had once years ago. Not sharp like a knife cutting into me. But more a dull, heavy ache, like a charley horse that wouldn't let up. It was on my right side. I tried to ignore it, but it pulled at me through the morning. A lot of my shots went wide, into the rough. I played all eighteen holes. This time I didn't have to let the Japs win."

Kirk stopped for a moment in order to regain his breath. I noticed that his lips had assumed a faint bluish tinge, cyanosis, an indication that even the minimal exertion of speaking entirely consumed the limited oxygen carried by his blood.

"Did they buy out your share in the refinery?"

"Not yet. But they will. They're coming back after Christmas. Actually after the New Year, which is a big deal in Japan. So by January you have to have this fucking tumor gone. I'll take them out again. Depending on the final terms of the buyout, I'll beat them or let them win—but only by a few strokes either way."

Kirk smiled a sly, knowing smile, counting me as a co-conspirator in his plan.

There was no clue in his past medical history to explain why Kirkland Bains developed kidney cancer at the age of fifty-four. He had been born and raised on an estate in Newport, Rhode Island. No one in the family was known to suffer from diseases of the kidney or bladder. The Bainses, over several generations, had owned shipbuilding plants along the southern New England coast, but his father and Kirk rarely visited them. They were managed by intermediaries, and so long as the balance sheets were in their favor, with healthy yearly profits, his father was content to live the detached life of a man born to considerable wealth. Kirk and his mother moved in tow with his father through the ebb and flow of the social seasons: autumn in Manhattan, summer on Mount Desert Island in Maine, and a spring tour through the Continent.

Kidney cancer is known to be associated with a variety of environmental toxins. Cadmium, the metal used in batteries, is one of the best known of these pollutants. It had contaminated the water table surrounding many factories that carelessly dumped their spent charges into nearby rivers or buried them in the earth without sealed containers. Cadmium precipitated in the kidney and traces of the metal could be found in the malignant cells that formed the initial seed of cancer. Other factory materials, including petroleum products and asbestos, the insulating material used in the construction of ships and homes, are also associated with cancer of the kidney. But Kirk reaffirmed when I asked him about such exposures that he had never "dirtied his hands" in his father's factories. His father had instructed him in how the business was financed, its margins and beneficial capital depreciations, asserting it was "foolish to pretend to be a worker when you're the owner's son." Anyway, Kirk further recounted, after his father's death in the late 1950s his estate had liquidated the shipbuilding factories, which was fortunate, since the industry in New England crashed shortly thereafter.

Cadmium, asbestos, and petroleum products had become unusual causes of kidney cancer, with stricter regulation of their industrial uses. Tobacco was now the most common predisposing factor, increasing the risk for the disease two- to threefold. The tars from cigarette smoke leached from the lungs into the bloodstream, and then, like cadmium, asbestos, and petrochemicals, were deposited in the kidneys. Kirk told me he had smoked, but only for a short time at boarding school, and just a few cigarettes a day.

"Everyone did in the fifties at Saint Grotlesex," he admitted.

"Where is Saint Grotlesex?" I hadn't heard of this prep school.

"It's not in one place. Really, it's not *a* place. It's more like a state of mind. It refers to the snobbiest of the boarding schools, a notch above Andover and Exeter. Saint Grotlesex is a contraction of Saint Paul's, Saint Mark's, Saint George's, Groton, and Middlesex. You got in because of family and old money. Now they talk about 'diversity.' When I was at Groton, we talked about perversity. Which boy was getting buggered.

"But I stopped smoking when I left for Dartmouth. Which is a bit of a blur really. Because I majored in drinking. The diploma said 'economics,' but it was really beer. Beer doesn't cause kidney cancer, does it?"

"Not to my knowledge."

"Too bad. We could short the beer companies, then let out the bad news, and make a bundle."

"And go to jail together."

"Hospital. Jail. Not much difference that I can see."

He had traveled all over the world, using the funds he inherited after his father's death to establish an independent investment company that focused on venture capital and commodities trading. Kirk had first worked out of Lagos, in the early days of Nigerian oil, when "anyone who didn't leave Africa with a few gold bars in his luggage had to be an idiot." He had spent time in Egypt and the lower Nile valley but did not contract schistosomiasis, a parasite that infests the genitourinary system, causing inflammation and scarring of the tissues and predisposes to bladder cancer. He had never had radiation exposure or even kidney stones. He disliked medicines, and avoided over-the-counter analgesics for headache, which could accumulate in the kidney and had been linked, when used regularly and in high doses, with kidney cancer.

"We Bainses are disgustingly hardy. Good protoplasm. That's why it's worth trying some magic on me," Kirk affirmed in as forceful a voice as his limited breathing would allow.

But much "magic" had been tried for this particular cancer, and none of it worked well. I could not keep that knowledge from clouding my mind as I listened to Kirk's story. Every known chemotherapy drug had been tested against the disease at one time or another, and the "response rates," meaning the percentages of treated patients who had meaningful shrinkage of the tumor after therapy, were minimal. This had led researchers to ask what made renal carcinoma so resistant to the poisons that worked well against other cancers, including those arising in the neighboring ureter or bladder. Why was kidney cancer so intractable?

The weight of evidence suggested that the malignant cell which multiplies to form kidney cancer has an overactive pump at its surface. This pump, called the P glycoprotein, is a normal component of the cells of the kidney. It works to expel unwanted substances which regularly cross the kidney cell membrane and enter the inner cytoplasm. One could appreciate that cells whose job was to filter unwanted and toxic wastes from our blood to form the excreted urine would be equipped with active pumps that prevented the retention of noxious molecules.

But now this protective armor given our kidney by nature was being worn by a traitor who had made it even thicker and more resilient. When the toxic molecules known as chemotherapy were sent by oncologists to assault the tumor, they were easily repelled by the cancer cells, quickly pumped back into the bloodstream by the P glycoprotein. No one had yet devised a strategy to penetrate the armor, to deactivate the cancer's overzealous pump without destroying the normal one. This maddening disregard on the part of kidney cancer of virtually all chemotherapeutic agents had led it to be labeled, in oncological jargon, as MDR, for multi-drug resistant.

Kirk and I finished reviewing his medical history—how he returned from Palm Beach to see his internist in Tarrytown, New York, who thought the ache in his flank was a pulled muscle from too much golf. But a week later Kirk developed a fever and his urine became tea-colored, prompting the internist to further investigate his complaint.

The tea color proved to be from small amounts of blood in his urine, and he was sent to a urologist to identify the source of bleeding. The urologist did not find anything abnormal on physical examination, but informed Kirk that any blood in the urine required an explanation. A cystoscopy was performed first, a procedure involving the insertion of an instrument like a telescope through the urethra of the penis into the bladder. This had revealed nothing abnormal. So a dye study of the kidneys, called an IVP, and then a CAT scan of his abdomen were done to look for a site of bleeding within the kidney proper.

The urologist had broken the news with a long preamble, explaining that kidney cancer was insidious and hard to detect because, as in Kirk's case, it often grew up and into the abdomen, so that it couldn't be easily palpated on physical exam. There was a mass, some twelve centimeters in maximum diameter, extending from the upper pole of the right kidney to the base of the liver, with tentacles of cancer that had invaded and extended along the channels of the major veins, including the vena cava. One tentacle of cancer had tracked so far upward that it had passed the diaphragm and entered into the venous circulation of the chest. If unchecked, it would soon invade the right atrium of the heart.

Kirk had been operated on during the second week of October at Yale–New Haven Hospital. The primary tumor and adjoining kidney had been successfully excised from his abdomen, as well as the malignant tentacles invading the veins. But numerous deposits of cancer had to be left behind, in his liver, intestines, and pelvic bones. They were too extensive to yield to the surgeon's scalpel.

"I had hoped it would be a replay of *The Exorcist*," Kirk painfully quipped. "Remember how the priest took the demon child out, a bloody, ugly creature? I thought the surgeon would do the same. Maybe I'd have been better off with a priest than a doctor. Never thought I'd need the clergy. But that's what everyone is recommending now."

"Are you affiliated with a church?" I always try to learn the scope of religious feeling, the ties of the patient and his family to faith. God, whether positive, negative, or null, is an essential factor in the equation of dying.

"Episcopalian. I celebrate Christmas. The food. The music. Decorating the tree. Giving gifts. That's fun. But the religion—I can't put much stock in a church founded because Henry the Eighth wanted a younger wife."

My response was a skeptical look.

"Let me put it in my own terms. I'm not a long-term investor. I like quick returns. I don't believe in working for dividends paid only in heaven."

I indicated it was time to move to the examining room. Kirk paused and looked down pensively, averting his eyes.

"I need my wife, Cathy, to help undress me. I can't manage the belt and the pants anymore. Can your secretary call her from the waiting room?"

Cathy, a large-boned woman with brunette hair in a pageboy cut, rich blue eyes, and a flowing flower-print dress, readily removed Kirk's blue blazer and pine green club tie—Dartmouth colors, she informed me. But the buttons on his starched white Oxford shirt stubbornly resisted her trembling fingers, his ballooned cancer-filled abdomen locking them in the taut slits of the buttonholes.

"I was inexperienced when I married Kirk," Cathy nervously laughed. "I guess I never really learned how to undress men."

Kirk failed to laugh with her, and a heavy silence fell over the room. Cathy finished negotiating the removal of Kirk's last article of clothing, a pair of blue cotton boxer shorts, briefly exposing his fluid-filled genitals before I covered him with a hospital gown. I tied the neck string of the gown loosely so I could maneuver my stethoscope to listen to his lungs and heart without exposing him unnecessarily.

"I'm a bag of water. Even my balls are bathed in this sewage from the cancer."

Cathy turned away, waving good-bye with a forced smile on her face as she left the room. Kirk did not acknowledge her exit.

"The hospital didn't stock Brooks Brothers this season," I joked.

"No, this gown is not my style at all," he glumly responded.

There is no avoiding the feelings of shame and humiliation caused by the forced dependency of disease. These emotions are raw at moments like this, exposed before another person, even a physician. I recalled when I was a patient, after the catastrophic spinal surgery, unable to move my legs, lying half naked in an ill-fitting gown. I had pictured myself as a freakish overgrown infant, an object of pity that needed to be carried and washed and clothed by others' hands.

I wanted to signal to Kirk that I understood him not as a pathetic and deformed "patient" but as a person with worth and substance.

"Tell me more about Galveston," I said as I adjusted the head of my stethoscope and prepared to listen to his lungs.

"You invest?"

"Not like you. Nothing high-powered. Fidelity mutual funds. But I'm interested in venture capital."

"Why?"

"Because it has similarities to scientific research. You believe you can see the future. And to realize your vision you take calculated risks. You try to capitalize on unique ideas by mobilizing technology, people, resources. And you need to be rigorously critical with yourself—facing all problems and setbacks head on because there is no room for delusion."

Kirk nodded sagely. He elaborated on the deal, how he was the first one in after he realized that oil demand would increase sharply, partly because Iraq was still shut out of the market, partly because there was continued expansion in the economy. And now, only five months later, everyone wanted in, especially the Japanese. Which meant it was time to get out. He was counting on a tidy twofold return.

"But there's a difference between what I do and what you do," Kirk continued. "I don't give a tinker's damn about the product. In your world, it's the product that matters—new knowledge that can lead to curing a disease. For me, the product means nothing. It can be oil or platinum or software or widgets. It's all a shell game played for big money, and once I win enough, I wave good-bye."

I continued my physical examination as he explained what drove him in his work: the delicious pleasure of seeing where to go before the crowd does; the challenge of making fast decisions; the fun of everyone trying to outsmart everyone else. I palpated almond-sized rock-hard lumps behind his left ear, certainly deposits of his kidney cancer growing outward from the mastoid bone. His breath sounds were harsh and wheezy throughout his chest from the masses of cancer. His abdomen was bulging as if he were in his last month of pregnancy, filled with malignant ascites, a mixed brew of protein-rich fluid that had weeped from his liver, spleen, and lymph nodes and nourished schools of swimming cancer cells. By pressing down over his liver, I could outline the stony metastatic nodules growing out from its surface. There were several tender areas in his pelvis corresponding to the tumors seen on the CAT scan. His legs were elephantine, columns of retained fluid that flared outward at the ankles as gravity settled the edema under the weight of his upper body.

It was easy to understand why Kirk had been turned away at so many medical centers. I had to agree with the prognosis he had been given: his remaining life span was likely no more than a few weeks. He would soon die of oxygen deprivation as the tumor replaced his lungs, or lapse into coma from liver or kidney failure as the cancer strangled these organs. As I examined him, I could feel death rapidly extinguishing the last embers of his life: the coolness of his flesh, the sunken, jaundiced eyes, the mottled color of his skin and lips.

But Kirk was not prepared to die. He had pleaded to be given the chance to fight. And I was his "last hope." But was there really any hope to be offered?

I backtracked in my mind and looked for any opening, any opportunity to devise a therapy that might help him, even in some small way. Although chemotherapy was rarely effective because of MDR, one drug, vinblastine, had been reported to work in some cases. Vinblastine is a poison from the periwinkle plant that disrupts the cell during its mitosis, or process of division. I put its chance of working in Kirk at about 1 in 100 at best. And if it partly shrank the cancer, the benefit would probably be transient, while the side effects of vinblastine could be lasting: lowering of blood counts, with predisposition to infection, and paralysis of intestinal movement, causing painful expansion of the bowel from the pressure of its retained contents. This intestinal paralysis is called an ileus, and with Kirk's abdomen riddled with cancer and bathed in the ascites, an ileus would be a particularly excruciating side effect.

Because men develop kidney cancer three to five times as frequently as women, it is postulated that male hormones promote its growth and female hormones limit it. The female hormone progesterone has been reported to shrink kidney cancer is some cases. But the chances of a meaningful effect on extensive disease like Kirk's were even smaller than those I estimated for vinblastine. The major side effect of progesterone is hyperventilation. With his lungs filled with metastases, hyperventilation would be poorly tolerated: it might even precipitate respiratory collapse as his chest muscles became fatigued from the hormone-induced drive to breathe faster.

I was especially knowledgeable about the dismal status of classical therapies for metastatic kidney cancer because, five years earlier, I had been asked to evaluate a new approach to the disease, in my role as chairman of the advisory committee to the FDA on biological therapies. Biological therapies sought to stimulate the innate immune system to combat infection or cancer by using naturally occurring proteins present in all of us. The idea was to improve upon nature by using nature's tools of repair in more focused and directed ways. It was a field that attracted serious scientists as well as alternative healers: the hope that what was "natural" would be what was most effective and least toxic.

In some cases, that proved to be true. A protein called G-CSF was discovered to be the physiological regulator of neutrophil production. Neutrophils are white cells produced in our bone marrow that exit and circulate throughout the body and protect against bacteria. When they encounter an invading microbe, they engulf and destroy it. Patients with low numbers of neutrophils, like those suffering the side effects of chemotherapy on their bone marrow, are vulnerable to life-threatening bacterial infections. Through genetic engineering, the protein for G-CSF was made in large quantities and tested in cancer patients with low neutrophil counts after toxic chemotherapy. G-CSF had dramatic clinical effects, boosting the production of neutrophils and markedly reducing the incidence of infection. Our advisory committee unanimously recommended approval of G-CSF, and it was now a widely used, lifesaving biological therapy for cancer patients in the United States.

But other efforts at biological therapy are less fruitful, particularly those designed to trigger the immune system to purge the body of cancer. Here, the aim is to exploit the body's system of immune surveillance. We have cadres of so-called killer T cells always on patrol, ready to destroy cancer cells should they be detected. In people with immune deficiency, like those with AIDS, the loss of immune surveillance results in the rapid appearance of aggressive cancers like lymphoma and Kaposi's sarcoma. In people without obvious immune deficiency, like Kirk, it is unclear why the killer cells fail in their search-and-destroy mission.

A naturally occurring protein called interleukin-2 had been discovered to activate killer T cells. Pioneering work at the National Cancer Institute in Bethesda indicated that treatment with interleukin-2 could result in regression of some cases of kidney cancer. That finding prompted widespread testing of interleukin-2, and ultimately an application to the FDA requesting its approval in this disease.

It was my advisory committee that was convened by the FDA to act as independent assessors of the benefits and risks of interleukin-2 treatment for kidney cancer. It proved to be a heated and trying debate. All of us on the advisory committee were acutely aware of the absence of good therapy for this particular malignancy. But interleukin-2, though a natural product, proved to have severe side effects when given in the large doses apparently needed to stimulate killer T cells. Spiking fevers, whole body rash, and severe cardiac and pulmonary toxicities, with leakage of fluid from the circulation and precipitous falls in blood pressure, causing shock, occurred in most treated patients. And the tumor responses, although occasionally dramatic, were generally of short duration. Moreover, regressions of the cancer were usually seen in people with limited metastatic deposits, not with the extensive disease and organ failure manifested in patients like Kirk. Only a small subset of kidney cancer patients was likely to benefit from the treatment, and with the high cost of toxicities. The initial optimism waned that interleukin-2 would prove to be a novel, natural, and potent way to trigger the body to use its own defenses to expel the cancer.

Our advisory committee finally decided to approve interleukin-2 in the United States, but recommended its use in that small subset of patients without extensive disease, and with the caveats of careful monitoring. We felt it important to provide access to the protein for those who might benefit, even if the chances were small, because there were no other real options. By recommending its limited use, we intended to spare the larger population of kidney cancer patients the protein's toxic effects and unlikely benefits.

"Make me a guinea pig."

Did Kirk really understand what that meant? Could he soberly assess the considerable risks and minimal benefits? How rational can our decisions be when we are desperate and feel unprepared to die?

Clinical experimentation was the powerful engine of progress in modern medicine. It was necessary to successfully translate basic research discoveries from the laboratory into bedside treatments. So-called informed consent was the underpinning of ethical clinical experimentation. The free consent of an understanding patient was required before trying unproven therapies. Considerable effort had been put into the process of obtaining such consent, to assure that the clinical experiment was ethically and scientifically valid. After the horrors of the Nazi experiments on human beings, governments mandated that there be reviews of all human experimental protocols by oversight groups composed of scientists, lawyers, patient advocates, clergy, and clinicians. The overriding question asked by these groups was whether the possible benefits to the research subject outweighed the anticipated risks.

But Kirk didn't fit into any ethically and scientifically reviewed research protocol at my Harvard hospital or the prestigious cancer centers he had already visited. He was too sick, too advanced in his disease, a so-called outlier in the crude terminology of clinical trials, who would not likely benefit and would very likely suffer side effects. His failure to qualify as an appropriate research subject had been the reason others had turned him away.

I looked at Kirk's jaundiced, bloated form before me, trying to read something beyond the obvious, beyond what the laboratory tests and CAT scans and physical exam already had written. And I saw still etched in his eyes a burning will to live, a deep determination not to give in, despite what he must have realized long ago— that his situation was terminal, that there was no known effective treatment. I didn't know yet why he wanted to live so much. It was too early in our relationship for me to probe. But I felt the energy that remained within his failing body, the force he had tried to convey when he shook my hand, the intensity in his voice when he detailed the Galveston deal, even the powerful resentment at Cathy's efforts to undo his clothes.

And I looked hard into myself, making sure that what I might do would be for him, not for me. That I wouldn't offer to do something to be the hero, a deputized cowboy who rides into town after all the sheriffs had fled, and in a dramatic flourish unloads his guns in a wild blaze of fire that never hits its target.

What was needed to justify treating Kirk? That there was a real chance of helping him. But what kind of odds constituted "a real chance"? Was 1 in 50 enough? What if Kirk's chances were 1 in 100 or 1 in 1,000? Where was the endpoint in this calculus?

The story in Genesis of Abraham arguing with God unfolded in my mind. It was not an exact analogy to the situation I faced, but the conclusion was relevant. Abraham learns that God is planning to destroy Sodom and Gomorrah, and the patriarch fears that the innocent may be lost alongside the wicked. Abraham asks God how many righteous people needed to be found in the wicked cities to spare them from destruction. A hundred, or fifty, or twenty, or even ten? Abraham drives a hard bargain, and establishes the principle that even one human life cannot be disregarded and must be saved. Not disregarded by God and, by inference, certainly not by man.

I *was* his "last hope." And his chances were not zero. But I had to be sure that he understood as well as a frightened and desperate person, facing death, could understand, what treatment meant. For this, I called Cathy back, and we convened in my office. This time I didn't sit removed from them, behind my desk, but at the apex of a triangle formed by our three chairs.

"Kirk, I'm not a magician or a wizard."

I saw his face drop with the anticipation that what would follow would be another rejection, an exile into hopelessness and certain death. Cathy reached to hold his hand, but he withdrew from her attempt at comfort.

"I wish I were. I wish I could be the alchemist who makes gold from lead, who could transform your cancer cells back to normal. But I'm not. No one is. We, together, have to weigh what is known and what is unknown and come to the best decision, for you.

"I happen to know a lot about your particular disease and its treatments. I chaired the FDA committee that reviewed the world's data on treatment of metastatic kidney cancer. And a wizard's smoke and mirrors couldn't hide the conclusion that there is no effective therapy for most people."

I paused to confirm that he and Cathy understood what I was saying.

"The treatments that are given rarely work in cases like yours, because your disease is so extensive and your organ function severely impaired. The treatments can have terrible side effects. They can increase your pain without benefiting you. They might even shorten

your life. Bluntly said, the treatments might kill you without helping you."

Cathy winced at this statement. Kirk did not react.

"And if you are treated, then it's outside any scientifically and ethically reviewed and approved protocol. We will of course follow
the principles of such protocols, but you take unknown risks and
have to realize we're flying by the seat of our pants without much
precedent."

"May I interrupt?" Kirk politely interjected.

"Of course."

"Jerry, I'm a damn successful venture capitalist. And I know what
a lousy investment I am. The time on my mortgage is almost up. I
have no inventory left. And this fucking cancer is taking my market
share, meaning my life."

Cathy's eyes filled with tears. I reached over for a box of tissues
on my desk and handed them to her. Kirk gave her time to compose
herself and then went on.

"But I'm willing to fight, to my last breath, and to try and make
it. If you will help me, I'll undergo anything. The worst side effects.
They can't be worse to me than"—Kirk paused—"than being dead.

"I am tough as nails. In business and most other matters. My
whole life I haven't really depended on anyone but myself. Cathy
can tell you. I'm a pain in the ass. Filled with piss and vinegar. I'll
hear you out, Jerry, if it makes you feel better. I'll nod when you tell
me all the risks. But my mind is made up to go for it. What the hell?
What other options do I have? None really. Consult with William?"

"William? Who's William?" I quickly went through my mental
Rolodex under "William" and couldn't associate the name with a
specialist in this field. William Peters, a researcher at Duke in Dur-
ham working on marrow transplantation for breast cancer? William
McDevitt, a laboratory immunologist at Stanford?

"William is an Englishman in his seventies in Jupiter, Florida.
Where my mother and her rich widow cronies live. He's a faith
healer, a charlatan. He's also a gigolo. First he sprinkles herbal pow-
ders on the widows, then he screws them. That cures their aches and
pains. Mother is insisting William come to heal me. She wants to fly
him to New York if you turn me down. Are you going to force me
to see William?" Kirk smiled a wry boyish smile.

I smiled too, and realized, at that incongruous moment, that Kirk was capable of making rational choices, that it was his right to fight, despite the odds. Alongside death there was life in Kirk, frail, besieged, and waning, but life nonetheless.

I ADMITTED KIRK directly to the hospital from the office. He was too sick to return home to New York, and if we were going to treat him, we needed to start immediately.

The battle was now engaged, and I could feel flow between us the electric exhilaration that overcomes soldiers who decide to charge forward together into the unknown. We pumped each other up with the medical equivalents of war cries. We would fight with all the weapons in our armamentarium, with a strategy to maximize their meager benefits and minimize their considerable risks. The interleukin-2 would be given for five days, the schedule approved by the FDA, but in lower doses, doses we hoped would not send him into shock but still be enough to activate his killer T cells. And with the first dose of interleukin-2, we would give a single dose of vinblastine. Again, because of his condition, we calculated a modification in the dose to avoid side effects. If these first two treatments went well, he would begin daily progesterone.

Kirk had wanted it that way. "Throw the kitchen sink at it," he declared. It was his gamble. I had made sure he knew the odds, and now it was my role to avoid losing it all on one roll of the dice.

Later that night I decided to return to his hospital room. My euphoria had begun to wane. I had gone to dinner at a café in Brookline with my wife, Pam, on one of our infrequent "dates." We tried to set aside an evening of private time in the middle of the week to talk and catch up with each other without the distractions of work or home, but I found it hard to dissociate from the events of the day and concentrate on our conversation. Pam, reading this, had me explain my distance. I confessed I was feeling unsettled about the course chosen with Kirk, worried that I had been swept up in the emotion of the moment. Perhaps I had endorsed unrealistic hopes, despite what Kirk said about understanding the odds and the likelihood of side effects. I feared we might have chosen a path leading only to pain.

So I returned to check that everything I had ordered for the treatment had been set into motion, and to speak with Kirk once more about our decision. Cathy had already left for New York to bring back things he wanted for the hospital stay. I assumed Kirk would have finished dinner and be preparing to sleep after such an exhausting day. But when I looked into his room I saw all the lights on, the TV playing, and Kirk sitting upright in bed, wide-eyed.

"Ready for tomorrow?" I asked.

"Absolutely, partner."

I suggested he go to sleep after we talked. I knew it was hard to rest in the hospital, so I had prescribed a sleeping pill if he needed one. Should I ring the nurse to leave it at his bedside?

Kirk vigorously shook his head no. I saw his hand begin to tremble, and reached for it, noting its cool, clammy texture despite the blankets that were pulled around him and the warmth of the room.

We sat together without speaking. I surmised from experiences with other patients why he resisted sleep.

"Are you thinking you could die tonight?"

Kirk pursed his lips tightly, containing his emotion. I gripped his hand more tightly, as if to impart to him some of the energy and security that came from my health.

I explained to Kirk that this was a frequent fear when we face our mortality. We think back to the recurring nightmares we've had throughout our lives, where we vividly see ourselves falling or drowning or suffocating. Only now we imagine that we will enter a dream that is no longer a dream, that the terrifying vision of our impending death will not awaken us.

"You won't die tonight, Kirk," I said confidently.

"So you're a prophet, not a wizard. Shall I call you Saint Jerome? I like that name. Saint Jerome."

I smiled uncomfortably.

"I'm hardly a saint. And certainly no prophet. But you are medically stable enough to take a sleeping pill if you need one. And you're in a hospital, being closely monitored. We won't let you slip away."

"I didn't expect to be so afraid, Jerry." Kirk paused, reaching for his thoughts. "I'm not sure why. I rarely feel afraid. Maybe it's because I know this is my last chance and that I'll probably die, and after death . . . it's just nothingness."

I absorbed his words and tightened my grip on his hand. I now understood why he had insisted on treatment, and realized it would be wrong to readdress that decision tonight.

"So then it would be the same as before we were born," I softly replied. "Is that terrifying, to be unborn? That's what my father used to say to comfort me as a child when I asked him about death." ·

"See if you still find that enough comfort when you're the one in this bed. Nothingness. No time. No place. No form. I don't ask for heaven. I'd take hell. Just to *be*."

I THOUGHT AGAIN about those words the next morning as an amber autumn sun filtered through Kirk's window and warmed the room. Tricia McGann, a vivacious curly-haired chemotherapy nurse, was reviewing with Kirk and Cathy the details of interleukin-2, vinblastine, and progesterone: the schedule we had devised for their combined use and their expected side effects.

"I'm ready to be deep-fried," Kirk answered when I asked once again for a clear statement that would constitute his informed consent, with Tricia as a witness. I created an ad hoc document and inserted it in his medical chart, written in the style of an informed consent that would ordinarily accompany a formal clinical research protocol.

I allowed myself to imagine being in that bed, as Kirk had asked me to the night before. It was a dangerous series of thoughts, one that could be permitted for only a moment and that I would not share with him. Kirk needed me not as a patient facing death, but as a physician fighting for life, focused on every detail of his complex clinical condition, working to exert maximum control over the wild diversity that is biology and clinical medicine: idiosyncratic reactions to usually innocuous medications; vague and apparently trivial symptoms that actually indicate a serious development, aberrant laboratory values that may be ignored as artifact but are early signs of organ dysfunction. The unknowns of biology and medicine existed at every moment for every patient. But here, in Kirk's case, they were present in the extreme. We would be mixing three drugs together that had never been mixed together, not in this way, at these doses, on this schedule, and certainly never in this individual, an individual in whom the metabolism and circulation of the drugs would be unpredictably altered by a failing liver, a rising serum calcium, a single functioning kidney, and a slowed circulation.

But while he was in Tricia's hands, it was safe to detach myself from the issues of his disease and its impending treatment and return to the scene of the night before. I thought again how much I had experienced of death, from the moment I witnessed my father die before my eyes to now, each day in my work. I thought about how we all develop our own inner pictures of death and an afterlife, and the stories and words we hear as children, which form our first image. As we pass through life, we redraw these images, hoping that at the end we will be prepared for what awaits.

My childhood concept of death, as I had indicated to Kirk, came from conversations with my father. He had subscribed to the most ancient Jewish concept, that there was no heaven or hell, no state of conscious existence similar to the one we enjoy in this life. What awaited us on the other side of life was vague and indescribable, a sense that in some way we are reunited with the divine energy of God that permeates the universe, but in a form that we cannot imagine or grasp. My father's focus was on memory—that existence is perpetuated in the hearts and minds of the people who remember those who are gone. That was the only notion of immortality he could conceive. "I will live on in my children," he would say.

When I was in college, I was dissatisfied with this answer, and pushed harder to have him explain what it meant. I asked: And when we, his children and his children's children die? And direct memory of him is lost? Is all residue of existence then gone? Or is memory passed in some way like genetic material, diluted at each generation by one half but never entirely lost, still exerting its imprint on words and actions, even in a person who has no conscious experience of the dead?

My father only shrugged silently in response to my metaphor, as if to say, where does such speculation leave you? There was no way to respond beyond a shrug because no one has ever returned to tell us.

After he died, it was impossible for me to imagine my father as disintegrated into nothingness. Perhaps that was why I rarely visited his grave. It was too painful and stark an image in my mind, that his body, the warm expansive body that had snuggled me in bed as a child when I feared the shadows of the night, held me in the deep water when I learned to swim, embraced me with surprising strength when I succeeded, and embraced me with even greater strength when I failed, that that body was now matter, inanimate matter, dispersed in the soil as atoms of carbon and nitrogen, hydrogen and sulfur. And nothing more.

His presence was felt by me every day, sometimes at unexpected moments, triggered by an event that stirred my memory, but more often deliberately invoked. I conjured his presence and created a dialogue in my mind, providing answers to my questions framed in his words and voice. As time passed and the particulars of my life became more removed from those that I had shared with him, I strained to articulate what he would say, how he would say it, why he would say it. I knew it to be a fantasy, a form of psychological comfort for a loss that would never be overcome, that should never be overcome, for who willingly lets go of such deep and unconditional love?

But then I began to wonder whether there was a dimension where he actually still existed, and whether the thoughts and feelings I had conjured up were only a delusion, a psychological balm, a convenient mechanism to draw upon the wisdom and insight he had shared with me. Could these ideas and senses possibly come from another place, the place where human science and rationality find their limits, the place where speculation ends?

I hoped I would not lie terrified in bed, like Kirk. I hoped my intimate relationship with death, beginning with the death of my father, through the deaths of so many of the patients I cared for, would somehow lessen the fear, allow me to face the unknown with the sense that others I had known had passed before me, and all I now knew would go after.

The unknown then might be understood not as a terror but as a comfort, because it held within it the possibility that I would be reunited with those I loved who were gone, in some form and in some dimension, and that I might be linked, like my father, through memory with those I would leave behind.

At some future time I might share some of these thoughts and feelings with Kirk. I had with other patients, when we became closer. I felt they received comfort and strength in knowing that I too had fears and uncertainties.

But this moment was not such a moment, because we had stubbornly "decided" not to surrender to the inevitable. I needed to help Kirk concentrate his energies on the battle that loomed and bolster him to resist the toxic blows of his treatment, particularly the interleukin-2.

"Ready to fight, Kirk?"

"Absolutely. I'll surprise you. There'll be a tenfold return on your investment."

"I like that kind of payout. Much better than my Fidelity funds."

When I cared for patients, a metaphor sometimes emerged that drew on a unique element in their work or family or cultural heritage. Throughout the course of our relationship, when we assessed an option or embarked upon it, when it succeeded or it failed, when we entered remission and returned to living or when we acknowledged that our therapy had not succeeded, that the end was near, at each critical point we invoked our metaphor. It became our intimate form of communication, drawing us closer, like children who invent a secret language, or siblings with special words and phrases that have resonance to them and no one else.

Kirk and I had created our metaphor after only two days, and I saw at this moment it was a good one for his condition. He would gain courage and strength from returning to the images that had spelled success in his life. He again could be the triumphant contrarian, betting against the market's prevailing wisdom, and fight to show the world that the commodity of his life had a future.

AS EXPECTED, Kirk developed a high fever and severe shaking chills from the interleukin-2. On the third day of treatment his blood pressure dropped precipitously, and we had to infuse fluids to support his circulation. He developed a blistering rash as well, and needed steroids to calm his angry skin. On the fourth day his wheezing worsened. The chest X ray showed seepage of fluid from the circulation into his lungs, called pulmonary edema. I feared we would need to insert a breathing tube and place him on a respirator to support his oxygenation, but luckily we did not need that invasive measure, managing instead to provide oxygen through a face mask and relieve the spasms in his airways with adrenaline-like drugs and high doses of diuretics.

I had been very careful about his dose of vinblastine, because that drug is excreted from the body through the bile, and with his jaundice and liver dysfunction it risked accumulating to very toxic levels in his system. Despite the modified dose, his blood counts fell from the vinblastine, and we had to administer the white cell booster G-CSF, which gradually returned his neutrophil count to safe levels.

On the fourth day he had copious bleeding from his colon. It was likely a vessel had been eroded by a growing deposit of kidney cancer penetrating the bowel. He needed to be transfused with six units of red blood cells before his anemia was reversed. Shortly thereafter, Kirk developed an ileus, the ballooning of paralyzed intestine from the vinblastine, and we were forced to pass a long tube through his nose down his esophagus and into his bowel to decompress his painfully swollen abdomen.

Through all this he did not complain. Cathy sat at his bedside, occasionally trying to distract him with idle chatter, more often in silence, reading a novel or working on her needlepoint. I visited him several times a day, both for emotional support and to keep close track of his tenuous medical state.

Although Kirk maintained his stoicism with the doctors and nurses, he was increasingly demanding of Cathy. She responded to his every request, applying cool compresses to his flushed head, softly massaging his painful swollen feet, adjusting the gatch of his bed so he could more easily watch the news on TV. But it was as if nothing she did was right. She sustained a high degree of civility in front of me and the medical staff, but a sharpness grew in her tone with Kirk.

"You want another compress, dear? Or not? Is the pillowcase soaked—I can ring the nurse to change it."

"The pillowcases are in the closet, Cath," Kirk replied. "Don't bother the nurse. You find one and change it. She's got better things to do."

"You were never so considerate of workers before, dear."

Every day Cathy had a fresh dress on, a flowered print or a pastel-colored one, and some new piece of jewelry, a string of pearls that enhanced her long neck, emerald earrings that offset her azure eyes. She looked as if she was dressing to be attractive and noticed on a date, or make the right impression at an expensive dinner with important clients, and her fastidious and elegant appearance sharply contrasted with the unkempt state of Kirk in his cotton hospital gown.

Kirk and Cathy had two children, Roanna and Paul—the former a docent at a museum in Philadelphia, the other working at a small marketing firm in Chicago, run by a Dartmouth classmate of Kirk's. I offered to speak with them by phone, but Cathy said it wasn't necessary. In private I emphasized to Cathy again that Kirk could die at any time, from the side effects of the treatment or the rapidly advancing cancer, and that there might not be another opportunity for their children to visit. Cathy stated she knew that, as did the children, but dropping everything would disrupt their schedules and probably only upset Kirk, making him think they were summoned for a final deathwatch.

Kirk slowly recovered from the toxicities of the interleukin-2 and vinblastine, and was discharged from the hospital. He began the daily progesterone. He was even more debilitated than before he had begun the treatment. We decided it was prudent to stay close by for regular monitoring, so Kirk and Cathy moved in with Kirk's cousin Grant in Cambridge.

I felt great relief that he had not died during the therapy and could be discharged from the hospital. I still believed that it had been right to have treated him, but held little expectation he would survive much longer or be in any condition to undergo a second course of therapy.

I examined Kirk the week after discharge from hospital, some fourteen days from his first dose of interleukin-2. I thought he looked less jaundiced, but indoor fluorescent lighting often distorts its true intensity. His liver seemed smaller. Its rock-hard nodular edges were softer, more compliant to the palpation of my fingers. And his edema was definitely reduced. His abdomen was less distended, and now I could encompass the circumference of his ankles in my open hands. Kirk confirmed that he hadn't taken any diuretics to reduce his edema since his discharge from hospital.

I felt a growing excitement that the treatment might be working, that this massive aggressive monster of a cancer was yielding, retreating just a few inches, in its onslaught.

"Let's get a chest X ray and a full panel of blood work today," I said to my secretary, Youngsun, as I finished my exam.

"I thought you were going to wait until next Friday for the tests," Kirk interjected.

"I sense a drift in the market," I replied. He sharpened his gaze and waited for me to elaborate. "You know, Kirk, I follow your lead. I'm a momentum player. If there's going to be a change, why not find out earlier than later? We'll better leverage our options that way, don't you think?"

Kirk tried to contain his growing smile, like a poker player opening his cards and seeing the first two are aces, wondering how much luck he had.

"Sure, we should play it at max leverage. No other way to play with odds like this. But I thought, Jerry, we did it all on the first tranche, that there was nothing left in the kitty."

"Do you think I can't find some new capital? We don't need to stick to the exact plan if there's some news to make a fast move. So let's increase the doses of interleukin-2 and vinblastine, and give them both ahead of schedule."

"That's what you meant before by upping the leverage. I'm game. Let's go for it all."

An hour later Kirk and Cathy stood by me as I mounted his new chest X-ray film on the viewbox next to the one taken fourteen days earlier. The opaque circles that filled the black space of Kirk's lungs still hung like moons frozen in orbit, but they had become smaller. No question about it. I took a ruler and pen, marked each metastasis, and measured its perpendicular dimensions. Most were reduced by more than half. I also pointed out to Kirk and Cathy that the mountain of cancer-filled fluid above his diaphragm was almost gone, just a trace lip remaining that curved up in a weak snarl. The objective evidence was indisputable.

"It's melting away!" I exclaimed. I surprised myself and Kirk and Cathy by drawing them into a three-way hug, almost knocking an unsteady Kirk off his feet with the sudden and forceful pull.

"WASPs aren't used to so much emotion," Kirk quipped after he wiped his tearstained cheeks with the sleeve of his shirt. "Well, Saint Jerome, there you are. A miracle before our eyes."

It felt like a miracle. The tumor had seemed invincible, massive and aggressive, but fell like Goliath before our hastily made slingshot. How could I explain this stunning outcome?

Kirk's immune system might be exquisitely sensitive to the interleukin-2, his killer T cells activated to the extreme of biological potency. The cancer might have an unexpectedly feeble P-glycoprotein pump, and have become stuffed full of vinblastine, unable to expel the toxic agent. Or the surface proteins that trap progesterone might be robustly displayed on the kidney cancer cells, rendering the cells unusually susceptible to inhibition by this hormone. Studying his T cells and his tumor in the laboratory might shed light on these possi-

bilities or give entirely new insights into kidney cancer and its therapy. Medical science delighted in understanding the exceptions to
the rule and, from that new knowledge, broadening the scope of
its effective treatments. Kirk's case could serve as more than an
anecdote.

While appreciating the range of scientific possibilities, part of my
mind searched for an explanation. Why Kirkland Bains, at this moment, in this place? That this "miracle" was simply the physical con-
vergence of cells and chemicals and proteins seemed an incomplete
answer. I closed my eyes in our shared moment of joy and awe and
strained to see a different dimension, one not described by chemistry
and biology and physics, that had intersected with science and returned Kirk to life. I thought I glimpsed its shadow, but couldn't be
sure.

KIRK UNDERWENT three more courses of interleukin-2 and vinblastine while continuing the progesterone. He gradually regained
his healthy form, as though he had been morphed by a funhouse
mirror and had now stepped out of the bad joke back into his true
self. The protuberant abdomen filled with malignant ascites returned
to its normal flat contour, the accumulated edema in his legs disappeared, and the stonelike nodularities of his liver melted into the
smooth and compliant edge of a healthy organ. We repeated his X
rays and CAT scans. The dozen metastatic deposits studding his
lungs were entirely gone. The ragged lacunae where the cancer had
been eating into his pelvis were being filled with healthy calcified
bone. He had entered a complete remission, with no evidence of
residual disease.

Kirk's case became the talk of the hospital. The interns presented
him in their monthly clinical case conference as a "fascinoma" to the
chairman of the Department of Medicine. A fascinoma is medical
slang for a fascinating case that lies outside the usual boundaries of
medical experience, because of its rarity, course, or outcome.

After the case presentation, I received choruses of praise from my
colleagues and the medical team. Although I rejoiced in this result, I
took no real credit for it, because what had occurred was not the
product of wisdom. It was more like playing a slot machine with one
silver dollar left in your pocket, figuring that you were going to lose

but you had lost so much already that you might as well play it down to the last. I deserved no praise for being lucky. If I could go back to the laboratory and determine why this wildly aggressive cancer in this particular man had melted away, and then use that knowledge to create new treatment strategies that helped others, then congratulations would be in order.

As Kirk and Cathy prepared to move back to New York after two months of recuperation with Grant in Cambridge, we sat in my office again reviewing the schedule of return outpatient visits syncopated with weekly checkups with his internist at home.

"Ready to return to real life?" I lightly asked.

Cathy responded with a forced smile, the kind produced for parties you really didn't want to attend.

"I guess so," Kirk offered without much conviction.

"It's natural to feel unsettled at this juncture," I reassured them. "You've been umbilically tied to me and the hospital for months, and now you worry the cord is being cut. It's not really being cut, just stretched a bit, from Boston to New York. Each day it will become easier. You'll gain confidence that you're stable and no catastrophe will occur out of the blue."

Averting his eyes, Kirk looked glumly away. I continued to reassure him.

"You're still shell-shocked, Kirk. You've been entirely focused on one thing, the war with your cancer, and living in the trenches of the hospital and the outpatient clinic. Everything else—your work, your social life, your recreation—was suspended. And, frankly, no one thought you would so quickly and so completely eradicate the cancer. It's normal to feel unsettled. But now you'll return home and see that you can resume your prior life."

Kirk didn't answer. Cathy smiled stiffly again, and then abruptly rose from her chair.

"Let's get going, Kirk. Jerry is a busy man. If we leave now, we can beat the rush-hour traffic."

I spoke with them every day for the first week, and then spaced out the calls to every other day during the following week. We would try to speak just before lunch, because as expected, Kirk was still exhausted from the hospitalization, and couldn't make it much past noon without a long nap. Cathy and Kirk were always both on the phone. We would first go through a checklist of symptoms, and once satisfied that nothing new or worrisome had occurred, discuss how much exercise Kirk had been able to tolerate that morning. He was making good progress, taking daily walks, negotiating the three flights of stairs in their home, and sitting forty-five minutes to an hour at the breakfast table. When Kirk expressed frustration at how little he could do compared with his former schedule, I re-emphasized that this would be a long recuperation. He had absorbed many body blows, first from the cancer and then from the therapy.

"He won't read the newspapers," Cathy interjected as we were closing the call at the end of his second week home. "Kirk used to devour them. We take three: *The New York Times*, *The Wall Street Journal*, and *Investor's Daily*. Now I bundle them unread for recycling."

I asked Kirk if he couldn't concentrate on the papers because he was inattentive or slow of thought, possible signs of depression.

"Not at all," he replied.

I probed further, knowing depression was common after severe illness. Was he awakening early in the morning, anxious and unable to return to sleep? Were his bowels irregular or his appetite poor?

"No, none of that, Jerry. I don't think I'm depressed. It's just that the information in the papers doesn't seem important anymore."

I wasn't sure I understood what he meant, but I was pressed for time. With his physical condition improving and no obvious signs of a psychological state that needed immediate attention, I wished them a good weekend and confirmed our appointment in Boston for the next week.

I saw Kirk every two weeks for the next three months. His physical functioning returned more quickly than I expected. He was able to travel to Manhattan a few times for business meetings to close deals, was playing nine holes of golf on weekends, and was planning his first trip away over Easter, to visit his mother in Jupiter, Florida.

All seemed in order, an uncomplicated recovery. But I did note that in our conversation his tone was less assertive, that the "piss and vinegar" that had been so prominent seemed diluted by bland and disconnected phrases.

I tried to rekindle his spirit using our investment metaphor, prompting him to update me on the outcome of the Galveston deal.

"Oh, those two Japs backed out. Maybe they caught on to my golf trick. But no worry. I'll sit and wait for other duffers to come by," he said halfheartedly.

A month after Easter I saw Kirk at a scheduled appointment. After talking about the fine weather they had enjoyed in Jupiter, he said, almost in passing, that he had a persistent pain in his back.

"I played a set of tennis the last day I was there, on a hard court, and twisted going for a down-the-line return. I thought it would pass with a warm compress and a few shots of bourbon. But it hasn't."

I noticed then that his face was drawn and his tan not as rich as would be expected after several weeks in Florida.

On physical exam I could not hear breath sounds at the base of his right lung. On his inner left thigh I felt a hard nodule, the size of a quarter, that was fixed to the underlying muscle. When I pressed on his lower spine he winced. After having him lie supine, I extended his right leg and lifted it in the air. This maneuver triggered an electric pain radiating down into his toes.

Even before the blood tests and X rays were done, I knew the cancer had returned. I sensed Kirk did as well.

"The back pain came on three weeks ago? Why didn't you call me from Florida?"

"And ruin the vacation for Cathy and the kids? And scare the shit out of my mother? It won't matter, waiting to see you and being told it's back."

"It likely is," I cautiously replied, not having direct confirmation by tests or biopsy, but unable to think of an alternative explanation, particularly for the nodule in the soft tissue of his thigh. "But we need to be sure by X ray. And it does matter. If it's pressing on the nerves in your spine, you could lose strength in your legs."

"Legs working, legs not working, it doesn't much matter if you're dead."

I looked at Kirk in shock. His attitude was 180 degrees from what it had been at the onset of his disease. Had we both struggled so hard just to reach this state of despair?

I explained to Kirk that it did matter if his spinal cord became compressed, even if we couldn't ultimately defeat the cancer. To spend the time that was left paralyzed and incontinent was a miserable end. Remember, I argued, the biology of your kidney cancer is capricious. Its quirky character might again play out in our favor. It had an Achilles' heel that we should try to hit again. It's premature to surrender without a fight.

Kirk listened, but I could see the blankness in his eyes, the distance that he was building between himself and hope. After a long moment of contemplation, he begrudgingly agreed to proceed.

"O.K., Jerry, run the tests. Do what you have to do. I'll humor you."

I didn't have time to explore the roots of his resignation further. I needed quickly to arrange an MRI scan to assess his spinal cord and brain. There is no waiting in the face of a possible spinal cord compression. Every hour is critical, since the paralysis and incontinence can be permanent. I was also concerned about his brain. I wondered if his apathy was caused by a metastasis to the frontal lobe, which can blunt the sharpness of one's personality like a surgical lobotomy.

I alerted the staff in radiation therapy that my patient might need emergency treatment. Should the MRI show metastases to the cord, we would have to deliver high-dose radiation to burn the tumor and release its strangling grip on his nerves.

That evening I visited Kirk in his hospital room, 706, the same he had occupied during his treatments. He was lying on his side, in a fetal position, legs drawn to his chest so as to avoid stretching the inflamed nerves from his spine by extending his legs.

He had already received his first radiation treatment. Cathy had just left to spend the night in Cambridge with Grant and his family. I had talked with her by phone briefly, and she seemed to understand that we had reached the limits of hope. I explained that while there were no brain metastases, the cancer had grown through his vertebrae and begun to wrap itself around his spinal cord. Radiation would hopefully prevent paralysis and incontinence, but there was no chemotherapy or biological treatment that was likely permanently to arrest the cancer in the central nervous system. I asked if she wanted to be present when I gave Kirk the news.

"You tell him alone. Kirk is more candid about this with you than me."

I sat by the bedside, my eyes level with his, and for a long time we were silent, absorbing the indistinct sounds that filtered through the room from the hospital corridor. I felt we were speaking telepathically, acknowledging to each other that we knew that we had tried and tried hard but now the end had come. We were silently saying good-bye.

"I'm sorry the magic didn't work longer," I finally offered to Kirk.

"It did more than anyone expected, Jerry. But you shouldn't feel sorry. There was no reason to live anyway."

His harsh repudiation of the remission hit me like a sharp blow to the head. What had happened to the Kirk Bains who was so desperate to live he tried to persuade every consulting oncologist to treat him? Uncertain how to respond, I searched for elements of pleasure and substance that I thought he had enjoyed during his remission.

"You closed a few more deals. Cathy and the children and your mother had you for four pretty healthy months. You avoided William."

Kirk didn't smile at my weak attempt at humor.

"You read newspapers?" Kirk abruptly asked. I recalled Cathy's comment that Kirk used to devour them, but had stopped reading when he had returned home. I didn't know where Kirk was headed, but knew I had to follow.

"I read three early every morning. *The New York Times, The Wall Street Journal,* and *The Boston Globe,*" I said.

"And what do you look for in them?"

I thought for a while, and explained how I had a set order, first reading the *Journal,* then the *Times,* and finally the *Globe.* In each, I skimmed articles on domestic and foreign affairs and read more carefully those on technology and medicine. After the news, I looked at the book and film reviews and the editorial page.

"I don't read newspapers anymore. I don't know how to. Or why I should." Kirk paused and his voice lowered. "Newspapers were a gold mine for me. They're filled with what to you looks like disconnected bits of information. A blizzard in the Midwest, the immigration debate in California, the problems of West Germany absorbing East Germany. For you, Jerry, those articles are about the lives or fortunes of individuals and nations. For me, they mean nothing beyond information for deals and commodity trading. I never really cared about the world's events or its people. Not deep down inside."

Kirk stared coldly into my eyes, and I could feel the truth of his words.

"And when I went into remission, I couldn't read the papers because my deals and trades seemed pointless. Pointless because I was a short-term investor. Like I told you, Jerry, I had no patience for the long term. I had no interest in creating something, not a product in business or a partnership with a person. And now I have no equity. No dividends coming in. Nothing to show in my portfolio."

Kirk grimaced in pain.

"How do you like my great epiphany? No voice of God or holy star, but a newspaper left unread in its wrapper."

I tried to comfort him by saying he was being too harsh with himself, and that people often find it difficult to readjust after the shock of severe illness.

"Don't try to soften it, Jerry. And don't write me off as depressed, because I'm not."

I asked about Cathy and the kids. Hadn't he enjoyed the time with them?

"They'll be fine without me."

I was at a loss for words because I feared he might be right. I had been amused by his biting wit and sarcasm, but beneath those quips I couldn't see what he truly believed in. It seemed our shared metaphor would painfully conclude with Oscar Wilde's famous remark, that a cynic knows the price of everything but the value of nothing.

"Jerry, you realize I'm right. The remission meant nothing because it was too late to relive my life. I once asked for hell. Maybe God made this miracle to have me know what it will feel like."

I felt the crushing weight of Kirk's burden choke my heart. There is no more awful death than to die with regret, feeling that you had lived a wasted life, death delivering this shattering final sentence on your empty soul.

For a brief moment I was gripped by the fear that I might one day feel this way. I felt my life was richer than Kirk's, my love and appreciation for my family, my friends, my work giving it substance and meaning. But there was much still to be in my life, children to grow, relationships to evolve, work to mature. The constant in life is that it changes. And I had witnessed countless times how it could change in terrible and unexpected ways. So much that had been created and enjoyed could be destroyed or lost.

The metaphor I shared with Kirk sculpted my thoughts. The investments we made in life could not be made without risks, in family and career and relationships. We needed to learn how to hedge those risks, to diversify our portfolio and, most important, to build long-term equity that could resist an unanticipated and uncontrollable crash such as Kirk had suffered.

But how could I help Kirk at this stage? What more could I say? I thought again about my father's belief in memory as our one trump card against death, and realized that Kirk could still redefine himself in an important way with words even if there was no time for deeds.

"Have you thought about telling Cathy and the children what you've told me?" I gently suggested.

Kirk recoiled in shock.

"Why? So they can hear what they already know? That I was a self-absorbed uncaring shit? That's really going to be a comforting deathbed interchange."

"Kirk, you can't relive your life. There is no time. But Cathy and Roanna and Paul can learn from you. And when you're gone, the memory of your words may help guide them."

KIRKLAND BAINS DIED in a hospice in Tarrytown, New York, on May 8, 1995. A private funeral service at the Episcopal church in Hastings-on-Hudson was planned. Cathy called and explained it was to be strictly family. She simply thanked me for everything I had done, and said I had been very important to Kirk. She and the children would travel to Florida and, with Kirk's mother, inter his ashes there. She said she had been at his bedside through the night, and sounded drained. Cathy didn't volunteer and I didn't probe further into what was said before Kirk's passing.

After Cathy's call, I put aside the paperwork on my desk and took a moment to offer a prayer, as I always do when a patient of mine dies. I prayed that, before his passing, Kirk's soul had found some comfort, and that if there is a beyond, it would be at peace. I then composed in my mind a eulogy, addressed, as eulogies are, to the living. The words I chose were not those of a holy text, but from Kierkegaard: "It is perfectly true, as philosophers say, that life must be understood backwards. But they forget the other proposition, that it must be lived forwards."

Dan

DAN BERGER ARRIVED on his first day at my laboratory and promptly set up his assigned desk in the office that housed the research fellows. But instead of the usual arrangement of sober technical reference books and accompanying pens, calculators, and notepaper, there appeared a miniature café: two aromatic gold-foil bags of dark French roast coffee beans, a sleek black grinder, one sturdy glass and chrome coffee press, and, on a thick faux mosaic placemat, two yellow ceramic saucers and matching mugs sporting a blue fleur-de-lis design.

"I make the lab a second home," Dan explained to the curious scientists who came by through the course of the day to meet the new research fellow. "Come by for a cup of coffee when you get a chance."

I heard about the desk and came by to view it. I found Dan drinking coffee and chatting with Roberta Ferriani, my lab supervisor, who was orienting him on his first day.

"Jerry, I hope you don't mind. I had the same arrangement as a graduate student at McGill. It helps me relax and think creatively. It makes the workday more fun."

I had no objection. And I was not surprised when his desk became the focal point for relaxed interaction among the researchers.

Short and wiry, with sandy-brown hair and a boyish smile, Dan appealed to me from the moment we met at his interview for a fellowship in our department in cancer medicine and blood diseases.

Dan was a Canadian, born and bred in Montreal. He had graduated from McGill at the age of twenty-six with both M.D. and Ph.D. degrees, and had served his internship at the affiliated Royal Victoria Hospital. His doctoral thesis was on hemophilia, an inherited bleeding disorder that primarily affects males. A normal clot is formed by a succession of clotting proteins that build on each other like bricks laid on a wall. In the case of hemophilia, a critical clotting protein called "factor VIII" is defective. The clot crumbles upon even trivial stress. Dan had studied the genetic mutations that cause the factor VIII protein to fall apart.

"I want to completely devote myself to the field of blood diseases," Dan affirmed when I spoke with him at the fellowship interview. I often heard applicants say such things in the hope of securing this much-sought-after position, but the way Dan's voice quivered made me think he meant it.

He had volunteered while a student in McGill's hemophilia clinic. Some of the adult patients still showed the ravages of the disease, struggling on crutches with arms and legs deformed by repeated hemorrhages into their joints. The younger hemophiliacs were largely spared such complications with the advent of factor VIII concentrates. A method had been developed to concentrate the vital clotting protein from the blood of literally thousands of different blood donors. These concentrates were regularly self-infused by the patients to try to maintain adequate levels of normal factor VIII in their blood. Many hemophiliacs now were able to lead more active lives, less prone to massive bleeding upon the most trivial trauma.

"The kids in the clinic are the most remarkable," Dan averred. "How they don't allow themselves to be stopped by their disease. Some are competitive swimmers, others tennis players. We teach them how to time their infusions before each competition. But when they want to get on the ice and play hockey, we have to draw the line." He smiled with pride. "Too much a blood sport for our guys."

Fellows in training are apprenticed to senior physicians, sharing their clinical responsibilities until they master the specialty and become competent to care for patients independently. Dan was assigned to work with two faculty mentors, me and James Levine. Jim's clinic was largely made up of patients with bleeding disorders, and Dan's assignment there was a logical extension of his earlier interests. My patient population was more heterogeneous, and included many people with AIDS.

I was impressed by how quickly Dan acquired the knowledge to make diagnostic and therapeutic decisions in the care of my AIDS patients, and even more impressed by the warmth and concern he expressed for them as people. After addressing the specific clinical questions relevant to the case, Dan would engage the patient about his interests, what he did before he became ill, who in his life was present to give pragmatic and emotional support, what personal issues and conflicts needed resolution.

It was assumed Dan would proceed along the classic academic medical track, eventually becoming a faculty member at a medical school and establishing an independent research program of his own. Despite my hope that Dan would pursue his future with us, he informed me that he would return to Montreal.

I understood his reasons. His parents were aging. They were Hungarian Jews like my mother's family, who had survived Auschwitz and come to this continent to start a new life. Dan was their only child. Dan, his wife, Rina, and their two young daughters, Becky, three, and Emma, four, were very close to them.

After his year of clinical training, Dan chose to work on AIDS rather than continue his prior studies on hemophilia. He joined the team in my lab working to genetically alter blood cells and make them resistant to HIV.

"Sounds like creating a force field for *Star Wars*," he quipped when I first outlined the project.

It was a futuristic approach, but one that grew out of the concept of AIDS as an acquired genetic disease. The biology of AIDS is fundamentally a case of genetic kidnapping and brainwashing. HIV works by sneaking into the T cells of the immune system and taking them hostage. The abduction results from the virus integrating its own genes, like a fifth column, into the normal DNA in the patient's cells. Once the viral genes are in the nucleus, the command center of the cell, they brainwash the cell into thinking its aim in life is to serve the needs of the virus. The T cells are subverted from acting as central defenders in the ranks of the immune system into factories that produce millions of new viruses. After HIV exhausts the resources of the T cell in making new viruses, it kills its host. The immune system without T cells is so weak that normally innocuous microbes cause life-threatening infections. In addition, cancers like Kaposi's sarcoma and lymphoma arise.

If T cells could be pre-armed with artificial genes that made them impervious to HIV, the virus could not propagate in the body. We both knew this effort to develop gene therapy would be a long and arduous haul, but Dan said he was eager for the challenge.

He would have breakfast with his daughters before they went to nursery school, arrive in the lab midmorning, and work until ten or eleven at night. I often found him in on Sundays, setting up his lab bench for the coming week's experiments, or at his desk reading recent scientific articles while nursing his hallmark mug of coffee.

Not that Dan was alone in this kind of driven schedule. Most of the research fellows worked six or seven days a week. The process of laboratory research requires it. The commonly held idea that progress is made in quantum leaps, that at one moment the solution appears like an epiphany, and the classical "Eureka!" is proclaimed, is far from the reality. Each experiment is designed in meticulous detail, down to the size and type of plastic pipettes and conical test tubes to be employed.

The reality of research is that, despite the planning, your experiment often fails. Or the controls that are done in parallel to verify the integrity of the reagents and the logic of the procedures suggest that your initial design was flawed. So you start over, changing one detail in the experimental method, one concentration of a certain chemical, one length of time in incubating the mix. And it generally fails again.

Stubbornly you search for the problem. Thinking you had identified the pitfall, you repeat the experiment. Then it might yield partial data, not definitive enough to proceed to the next step in the project, but enough to better perform the procedure. So the experiment is repeated yet again, incorporating the single lesson learned from the last try into a revised design.

It is this succession of toddler's steps, small, uncertain, occasionally listing to the side or falling back, that ultimately connects into a march that arrives at discovery.

I assigned Dan to work in my lab with Phong Phen. Phong was a cell biologist, and her role was to isolate the T cells to be altered by Dan's blocking genes. She was expert in manipulating HIV, and was teaching Dan how to work safely with live virus.

Phong was a very special person to me, a woman I admired not only for her scientific skills but for her strength of character. I had hired Phong through a nonprofit refugee agency that had canvassed Harvard Medical School for job opportunities for its clients. When she arrived, she spoke haltingly through nearly closed lips. Her case worker at the agency recounted that Phong had been a technician in a Red Cross laboratory in Phnom Penh. The Khmer Rouge had brutally entered the facility, summarily executing the administrative director and the two physicians who supervised the blood bank. Phong had tried to grab hold of one guerrilla's rifle, and had been smashed in the mouth with its butt. She had lost all her front teeth, and although fitted with a bridge upon her arrival in the United States, had a permanent speech impediment.

Why she hadn't been killed for interfering with the executions Phong never understood. She was classified by the Khmer Rouge as a "technocrat" and sent, along with her husband and three-year-old son, to be "re-educated" in a labor camp deep in the northern jungle.

Phong's husband disappeared one day during a work detail dredging a nearby swamp. The guards and terrorized fellow prisoners never told her what had happened. Phong suspected he had committed suicide, worn down by the starvation and beatings. He had surrendered to despair, believing he and his family would perish in the camp.

Phong soon realized that she and her child, as well as the hundreds of others being "re-educated," would never leave the camp alive. Phong had seen bulldozers arrive on lorries, and had heard the guards joking about "building new homes" for the prisoners. She and her son would be killed and thrown into a mass grave.

Phong decided to escape. She waited a few days until there was a moonless night. She traded her hidden gold wedding ring to the camp cook, saying she needed a kilo of boiled rice and a flask of water for her dysentery. Phong then carefully stuffed a rag into her toddler's mouth so he could breath through his nose but make no sound. She crawled first under the razor wire at the perimeter of the camp, dragging her silent son beside her, and continued crawling deep into the surrounding brush before stopping to look behind. There was no movement from the sleeping camp, no sign her escape had been detected. The guards in the towers usually got drunk and dozed at night, thinking anyone mad enough to venture into the merciless jungle would eventually meet the same fate as receiving a bullet from their guns.

It took her two months to arrive at the Thai border. Phong never told me what had happened during her march through the jungle. When I asked her in quiet moments, after reviewing the results of her day's experiments, more about her experiences under the Khmer Rouge, Phong would respond with a soft smile, the teeth of her well-made bridge just perceptibly false:

"Dr. Groopma', tha' was a long time ago. There were people I knew in Cambodia who live' through wors' than me. I think abou' the future, not the pas'."

"How do you see the future, Phong?"

"It's fine, Dr. Groopma'. It's fine. My son, he's a smar', good boy. Teachers like him. And I love my work. I am a very lucky person."

WINTER ARRIVED EARLY in New England in 1993. By the first week of October there was already morning frost on the ground as a chilling wind from Canada lowered the nighttime temperatures to the 20s. The trees quickly surrendered their exuberant foliage and the grass turned brittle and brown. Boston became draped in the somber gray light of the northern latitudes, transforming the pedestrians that coursed her narrow streets into indistinct shadows bundled against the blowing north wind.

Dan had returned that week from ten days in Montreal that spanned Rosh Hashanah, the Jewish New Year, and Yom Kippur, the day of fasting and contemplation. He looked drawn and haggard. His usual bright complexion had been replaced by a sallow pallor. Although he started back in the lab with his rigorous schedule, there was lethargy in his step. I noted also that his smile was often absent. He had a blank, faraway look to his deep-set brown eyes. I asked him whether everything was O.K. in Montreal. Had some problem come up at home? He looked hesitantly at me before answering.

"No, no problems—in Montreal or Boston."

I nodded skeptically. Dan went on:

"Hey, I heard a good joke last week from my dad. Nelson Mandela, Yitzhak Rabin, and Patrick Buchanan are at a global conference in Miami Beach. While they are walking along the oceanfront, a bottle washes up on shore and a genie pops out."

Dan's face brightened with a growing grin as he built the story.

"The genie says he holds a total of three wishes. Each of the men on the beach will be granted one wish. Mandela goes first. His wish is that all the world's black people be reunited in a free South Africa. The wish is granted."

Dan looked at me to confirm my attention.

"Then Rabin asks that all the Jews dispersed over the four corners of the earth return to live in Israel. His wish is granted.

"The genie then turns to Buchanan and says, 'You get the third wish.'

"Buchanan says to the genie: 'Let me get this straight. All the blacks go back to Africa? And all the Jews leave for Israel? Then I'll just have a Diet Coke!' "

We laughed together, but Dan's laughter quickly turned into a prolonged spasm of harsh coughing.

"Damn this cough. I must have picked up something in Montreal."

Over the ensuing weeks, my concern about Dan increased. He didn't seem the same. During the weekly lab meeting where we analyzed the data from recent experiments, he wasn't as sharp as before. His presentation at our monthly review of recently published scientific articles was, for the first time, poorly prepared. He wasn't regularly in the lab on weekends, explaining that he needed to take care of some things at home.

One afternoon in November, shortly before Thanksgiving, I stopped by Dan's desk and saw that his café setup was gone.

"I've lost my taste for coffee," Dan stated. "Maybe I overdosed on caffeine."

"Overdosed? Why not just take a break and drink decaf?"

"I guess you just tire of these things over time," he sighed.

I wasn't convinced.

I had often compared Dan in my mind to a sprightly Canadian beaver. He would dart from bench to bench collecting chemicals, test tubes, pipettes, and other laboratory items, which would be rapidly assembled into an ordered pile for his planned experiment. He was an amateur photographer and liked to wander around the lab with his Nikon camera, searching for an opportune scene to capture. The wall in front of his desk was a nest of these photos of researchers in the lab, some soberly engaged in serious work, others sophomoric, posing with crossed eyes and silly grimaces.

I told Phong once that Dan reminded me of this animal. She informed me that Dan was born in the year of the monkey, according to the Asian calendar. Monkeys, I learned, were conceived of as consistently clever, occasionally irreverent, and very facile. But Dan was no longer energetic or animated. He had become listless and slow, like an aged and failing man.

I asked Phong if she knew of anything that might make Dan depressed or distracted. Were Rina and the kids O.K.? Was there a problem in Montreal with his parents or his planned return that was weighing on his mind? Or was he burning out, like a shooting star consumed by his own intensity?

Phong looked at me with a blank face. I assumed that she didn't know.

The first Sunday in December was brisk and clear. I came into the lab after a long swim, feeling energized and intent on spending the afternoon catching up on technical reading. After a few hours, I located an article on different methods for measuring production of HIV by T cells. It was certain to be of interest to Dan and I wanted to discuss it with him if he was in. Entering the fellows' room I noticed an open lab notebook on his desk, with an outline of work to be completed that day. Dan was likely working in the BL3 facility with Phong. I decided to visit them in BL3 and see how far along they were in their experiment.

BL3 stands for biosafety level 3, the secure facility that is designed for work with dangerous infectious agents like HIV. To enter BL3, you first have to pass through an air lock. The inner facility has a special ventilation system so that its air is under negative pressure. This is done so that in the event of an accident, where HIV or other dangerous agents might become airborne, the lab workers can exit the facility without releasing a cloud of infectious material. Instead, the exterior air comes rushing in to contain any dangerous particles that may have spewed into the inner atmosphere.

Once in the air lock, you dress in a sterile gown, cover your shoes with sterile paper booties, double-glove with special nonporous latex gloves, and don shatterproof goggles. With these protective measures in place against contaminated material contacting your regular clothes or body surfaces, you are ready to enter the actual BL3 lab. Ours is a large L-shaped room with a low tiled ceiling punctuated by long rows of fluorescent lights. Within the ceiling is hidden the powerful ventilation system that exerts the negative pressure relative to the outside atmosphere.

The researchers sit on low chairs facing specially constructed glass and metal chambers. These chambers, six feet wide and five feet high, are called "laminar flow hoods." It is within these chambers that the virus is manipulated. The researcher inserts his gloved hands and gowned arms through a wall of air that is emanating from a grating at the base of the laminar flow hood. This wall of air courses from the grating in a perfect parabolic arc. The arc of flowing air moves any dangerous particles from the lower part of the chamber to a specialized filter at the apex. This upper filter traps these contaminated materials before passing the air to another decontamination system within the ceiling.

Despite these elaborate precautions, one works with the assumption that everything in BL3 should be treated as if it had become contaminated with virus. Thus nothing leaves the room, except the researchers, without being decontaminated at fierce temperatures. This is accomplished by steam sterilization in a cavernous autoclave, two feet in diameter and three feet in depth, that is built into the wall of BL3. It resembles a huge cannon. The autoclave is loaded with the material used within the facility, as well as the gloves, gowns, and other protective gear. After several hours at high heat and pressures, the autoclave releases its spent charge through its exit portal. The now safely sterilized contents are emptied at the outside wall of the air lock.

Entering the muted fluorescent light of BL3, I quickly spied Dan. He was sitting in front of the laminar flow hood next to Phong. His motionless arms rested on the metal grating of the lower border of the chamber. Phong was in the middle of pipetting a solution into a large petri dish. I waited silently until she had finished the task so as not to distract her.

"Dan," I softly said.

"Oh, hi, Jerry." His voice was a bit hoarse.

Dan withdrew his arms from the hood and turned his chair to face me. "What are you doing in BL3 on a Sunday?"

"Looking for you. I have an article I thought you'd find interesting."

"Oh, thanks," he sighed. "I may as well go out and look at it. I'm not getting much accomplished in here today. Phong, could you finish the experiment for me?"

Phong silently nodded her assent.

We exited into the air lock together, and there ritually reversed the order of dressing, as required in leaving the facility. After the gloves, gowns, booties, and eye gear were sealed in a nonporous plastic bag and placed in the autoclave, we washed and returned to the outside world.

Dan walked with me down the long corridor of the lab toward my office. He stopped to gaze into the instrument room.

"What a place," he softly stated.

This Sunday the instrument room was empty of people, filled with motionless machines. I shared Dan's reverence. Each instrument had a unique purpose and temperament, and received the respect and care one gave to precious works of art.

Dan walked in and I followed. He made his way slowly to the far corner of the room. There, in a segregated space, he stood for a long moment, as if paying homage to the automated gene sequencer—the king among the instruments. The gene sequencer was recently born out of Cal Tech, and there was only a handful among the scores of research laboratories on the Harvard Medical School campus. Each sequencer cost $120,000 and required a dedicated scientist and about $20,000 per month in disposable supplies to operate.

The gene sequencer had tripled the pace of our gene therapy project. Before the creation of this instrument, determining the DNA sequence of a gene was a painstaking procedure. First the gene had to be cut into smaller and smaller pieces until it was fully dissociated into its component units, called "bases." There are only four bases that make up all of DNA: adenine (A), thymidine (T), guanine (G), and cytosine (C). These chemical units are grouped as triplets in the DNA, such as ATG or GGG. A gene is composed of hundreds to thousands of these triplets. The cell has the capacity to read this series of coded triplets as a blueprint for its entire structure and all its functions.

After the researcher has broken down the gene into thousands of these individual chemical units, he has to piece them together again. It is like reassembling a giant jigsaw puzzle. It often took eight to twelve months to correctly figure out the puzzle, or sequence, of a gene. And it had to be done in the precise order, because there is no punctuation in the code. If one base is skipped, or placed in the wrong part of the puzzle, the entire sequence reads as gibberish.

A trained scientist operating the automated sequencer could fit together the two to four thousand pieces of the gene puzzle in two or three months of intensive work. This is how it works. First, large fragments of the gene are inserted into the machine. Then four laser beams are focused on the exposed DNA. Each beam interacts differently with each base in the gene fragment. This unique interaction causes changes in the beams' wavelengths that the machine's computer interprets using a sophisticated program. After the DNA fragment is scanned by the lasers, a printout emerges. It displays a series of four different-colored peaks, strung together like the jewels of an extraordinary necklace: a ruby, a diamond, a sapphire, an emerald. Each colored peak represents a different DNA base—A, T, G, or C. Analysis of the order of these colored peaks yields the sequence of the gene.

The automated sequencer has allowed us both to rapidly analyze the genes of different strains of HIV and to verify the desired composition of the blocking genes designed to paralyze the virus. In a scientific world where genes are understood as the foundation of all normal body functions, and their derangement as the basis for most diseases, it is easy to understand why this elegant and powerful new creation is the recently crowned king.

"I do love the lab," Dan stated heavily as we left the instrument room and proceeded down the hall. "I'm not religious like you, Jerry. But lately I find myself quietly offering thanks to have my life as it is, to work in the world we do."

I nodded silently, wondering why Dan was pondering such issues now.

"It sounds corny, but medicine allows you to live a *moral* life. You know how they always ask you at your medical school interview: 'Why do you want to be a doctor?' Most people say they want to help mankind. Or they're excited about human biology *and* want to help mankind. Some of course say this and really just want to help themselves, or make their parents happy. You might say that every profession provides the opportunity to help mankind. But other professions are not as *consistent* as medicine in doing this, and not always as clearly moral."

Dan looked at me intently, asking with his eyes if I understood what he meant. I arched my eyebrows in some uncertainty.

"I mean, a lawyer upholds the law, which is supposedly moral. But he may defend a client who is guilty, or work in a corporation where his job is basically to figure out how to legally stretch the rules and enrich the company. Or a businessman. He contributes morally by creating employment for people. But he knows that business is war, there are winners and losers, and he has to fight the competition every day of his life."

I stood silently, still not sure where Dan was headed.

"Medicine offers the possibility, the choice of a *fundamentally* moral profession. You work as a team with your colleagues. You have the same goals as your patient: to cure the disease, to return him to health. You don't have to compromise kindness or caring for the sake of success."

I was still silent, not wanting to interrupt the flow of his thoughts.

"I feel thankful because we, as physicians, live so much human experience. We learn as much about ourselves as we do about our patients when we care for them. Especially caring for people with cancer or AIDS. We learn every day that we are mortal." He paused briefly and added, "But of course, I already knew that."

Dan laughed nervously, and then fell deeply silent.

We entered my office. Dan picked up the photo on my desk of my wife and three children. As he studied it, he started speaking without looking up from the picture.

"Jerry, I actually went to synagogue on Yom Kippur. The first time in years."

He picked up his head, displaying a tense smile.

"I even sat through most of the service. It's awfully long, you know."

"Believe me, I know."

"So you're familiar with the metaphor that on the New Year, Rosh Hashanah, our names are inscribed in the Book of Life. And on Yom Kippur, our fate is sealed?"

"Sure."

Dan, whom I knew as an agnostic, surprised me by quoting from the jarring liturgy:

> *"On Rosh Hashanah it is written,*
> *And on Yom Kippur it is sealed:*
> *How many will pass,*
> *And how many will be created;*
> *Who shall live,*
> *And who shall die;*
> *Who early,*
> *And who late;*
> *Who by fire,*
> *And who by water;*
> *Who by sword;*
> *Who by famine;*
> *Who by plague—"*

Dan stopped in midsentence, and looked at me with a solemn expression. He said in almost a whisper, "Jerry, my fate is sealed. I have AIDS."

I felt like I'd been hit in the face, unexpectedly and with great force. My balance and senses were briefly lost. As I slowly recovered feeling, I sensed my heart expanding in my chest, my eyes blurred with tears.

I stood up and moved unsteadily toward Dan. I opened my arms and embraced him, holding him for a long time, as if the energy of my embrace might be infused into him and give him one more bit of strength to fight off death.

We sat together late that Sunday, watching from my office window as the somber silver twilight gave way to a star-filled black night. I listened as Dan recounted what he called the "other story of my life," the one that did not appear on his medical school transcripts and letters of recommendation.

He was a hemophiliac. Hours after his birth at Montreal Jewish Hospital, the pediatrician noticed that the umbilical cord was still oozing blood. The doctors questioned his parents, who did not recall any family members with bleeding problems. A specialist in pediatric hematology was called, and half a day after Dan's arrival into the world the diagnosis was confirmed. He had severe hemophilia, with levels of factor VIII that were less than 2 percent of normal.

Dan really didn't know how his parents took the news, but he thought he could extrapolate from his knowledge of their character. I knew that character as well, since my mother's family also had survived Auschwitz. They acted at all times with the goal of survival before their eyes. Everything was quickly calculated in their minds, and translated into an almost abnormal pragmatism. No action or emotion was wasted. So Dan imagined them forcing themselves to appear calm as they absorbed the shock of the news, choking off their inner waves of pain and fear before these could break into a flood of panic or confusion. Because no risk was allowed that would lessen the chance of surviving, Dan knew that his parents had sought the very best specialists to care for him.

Dan had grown up, as I had, with the Holocaust powerfully influencing his perceptions and reactions to the outside world. He knew from an early age that there were evil and deadly forces in life, sometimes apparent and sometimes covert, and that you always had to be prepared for them.

Death was a real and constant companion in his life. He was informed as a young boy that he was named after his father's brother, Daniel Hershel Berger, who had a deformed foot and was selected by Josef Mengele for the gas chambers within minutes of the Berger family arrival at Auschwitz. Daniel often fantasized as a child that his hemophilia was another curse of nature, like his dead uncle's club foot, that marked him for an early death.

As he grew older, he secretly stole to the library and read about hemophilia. He quickly learned that every action was fraught with great risk, that an unintentional fall from his bike or a cut from a sharp edge could result in bleeding so severe as to be fatal.

While his friends seemed to live carefree lives, with death no more than a caricature with a black cowl and a scythe, Dan knew differently. He understood from his parents' stories that life was uncertain and dangerous, that death was real and took many different forms, none of them comical, and could choose at any time to extend its merciless hand.

What was so remarkable to Dan was that his parents, despite the suffering and horror they endured, despite the countless times they had stared death in its terrifying face, despite their only child coming into the world with a potentially fatal genetic disease, still enjoyed life. He believed they had never surrendered to despair. How they accomplished this was slowly learned by Dan, and formed the basis for his own capacity to cope, first with hemophilia and now with AIDS.

His parents had told Dan at an early age that he was different from other children, but that those differences could be overcome. They would not be made into serious limitations. He was encouraged to compete in nontraumatic sports, like swimming and tennis. His condition was never accepted as an excuse for misbehaving or laziness. It was almost like propaganda—time and again they asserted that he, not his condition, was in control of his life. And they said that if you control your life, you can fill it with pleasures to lessen its hardships.

This was sometimes hard for Dan to understand or believe. But he gradually became convinced that it was possible to overcome the curse that had been visited on him. He was not *certain* it could be overcome—it was hardly guaranteed, despite all the encouraging words from his doctors in the hemophilia clinic at McGill, despite the air of confidence that his parents assumed when he asked them if he would ever have a normal life like his friends.

"Normal life?" his father said, answering his question with yet another question. "What is a normal life? Is there such a thing? You *make* life normal, even when it is not."

Dan did not understand the references inherent in his father's words until later in his teenage years. They were key to his parents' survival in Auschwitz.

Why had they survived when all of the other members of the family had perished, Dan often asked himself. Dan thought he had discovered the traits that explained their survival. Many Hungarian Jews had clung to illusions about the intentions of the Nazis from the time that racial laws were passed to the establishment of ghettos to the deportations to the camps. Dan's parents seemed able to see what was planned for them. They realized early on where events were leading—to their extermination. This anticipation of the worst-case scenario gave them time to prepare themselves psychologically and pragmatically to survive.

By being psychologically prepared for the worst, they better absorbed the shocks of each devastating step along the road to Auschwitz. They were able to make decisions and take actions which helped them to endure. They believed nothing the Germans told them and trusted no rumor or information other than what they knew to be true themselves. This was a difficult and contrarian mentality to sustain, since most of their community found comfort in believing the manipulative lies of the Nazis. Several of their friends became angry with them for puncturing the bubbles of delusion that were so prevalent, yet they were firm in their views.

His parents were always pragmatic. They prepared themselves for the uncertain by hiding small pieces of jewelry that might be useful to barter for food or use as a bribe in a threatening situation. They carefully rationed the food they were given, first in the ghetto and then in the camp, since it was never known whether food would be distributed on any given day. They tried to guess which tasks and skills would be useful and thus selected for by the Germans. His father had been a schoolteacher in Hungary, but when the Nazis made teaching forbidden in the ghetto, he realized that he should never identify himself as such. So when carpenters were called for by the Nazis, he said he was a carpenter, and when stonemasons were needed, he said he had skills in stonecutting. But when the Nazis asked for translators who knew Russian and German, his father did not step forward, thinking that although he would be working inside a warm office and might find some rest from the brutal manual labor, the risk was too great—he might be privy to secrets, so that when the translation was complete, he would be executed to eliminate any witnesses.

These elements of a stark confrontation with reality, preparation for the worst, and the measured taking of risks all seemed to have contributed to his parents' survival. But the lesson that Dan learned above all, that informed his heart and mind when he considered his own situation, was that there was no absolute formula for survival.

Many others in the ghettos and camps had taken the same approaches as his parents and had perished. So one had to accept the element of uncertainty, of chance, of caprice—one had to understand that despite all one's preparations and actions, there were critical situations in life that were beyond prediction, that could not be fully controlled.

At first this realization had overwhelmed Dan with fear and anxiety. And then a paradox had become apparent to him. As hard as it is to accept uncertainty, accepting it lessens its contribution to your outcome. Learning not to be overwhelmed by the fear and anxiety that are triggered by uncertainty, learning not to panic, is perhaps the most important element in increasing your chances of surviving. If you give in to these emotions, you lose the capacity to act, to take intelligent risks that help you survive.

Dan understood how this approach to life's cruel uncertainties had been communicated to him by his parents not only in their stories of survival under the Nazis but also by how they had dealt with his hemophilia. First, they had learned everything they could about the disease, so as to know the enemy that was threatening their child. Then, after his treatment was begun with the director of the hemophilia clinic at McGill in Montreal, his parents insisted that Dan be followed as well by specialists at the hemophilia center at McMaster University in Hamilton, Ontario. Each therapeutic decision was weighed by his parents following the recommendations of at least two expert physicians. They also were willing to take certain therapeutic risks. When factor VIII concentrates first were prepared, the hemophilia clinics asked for volunteers to participate in experimental trials of this new therapy. His parents took a week to decide. They analyzed it in terms they were familiar with—choices that are made in the effort to survive. They knew that few children with severe hemophilia lived beyond their teen years before the advent of these concentrates. Despite the most careful attention to activities, the capricious and trivial risks of daily life almost always ended in precipitating a fatal hemorrhage. His parents had viewed the factor VIII concentrate like a set of false Aryan papers in the ghetto: they might prove to be useless, or even increase the risk of harm if found to be false, but the possibility that they would provide an exit from an otherwise certain death was too great an opportunity to forgo.

Dan had contracted AIDS from the contaminated factor VIII concentrates that had initially saved his life. This cruel truth made me wonder whether he felt angry at his parents or his doctors for their decision to give him this therapy in lieu of the uncontaminated, but less effective, plasma product called "cryoprecipitate." Dan said at first he had felt profound anger, although clearly no one knew at the time that a strange and fatal virus existed and could travel from the blood of infected donors along with the factor VIII protein. It occurred as a risk of the unknown, a fact of life that revealed once again the uncertainty that we all face but few acknowledge. As Dan matured to accept the reality of life's uncertainty, he found that his anger dissipated.

Dan was becoming fatigued. We had talked for more than two hours. He had spoken calmly and deliberately, as if all this information were carefully organized in his mind, ready to be called up like a file in a computer. He had prepared himself to present these details and insights to me like a scientific seminar. I was disturbed by his emotional detachment, because my heart was breaking as I listened to his story. Perhaps Dan had adopted the public behavior of his parents, maintaining a tight grip over his inner emotions to keep fear and panic at bay. Perhaps he had lived with it all so long that he had truly overcome its devastating force and could demonstrate his emotional victory through calm.

Dan looked at his watch and realized it was time to go home for Sunday dinner with Rina and the kids, but wanted to recount one more of his father's lessons before we parted. It came from the harsh winter of 1945 in Auschwitz, and the narrow course that his father had navigated to endure it. His father explained to Dan that there were two kinds of death he had seen that winter in the camp: "When a person surrendered to despair, he would die. And if he didn't surrender to despair, but survived as an angry, vicious animal, stealing crusts of bread and bowls of soup from others, then he died inside as a human being." Dan's father said that just as there were two types of death, there were two types of life. That was what Dan had meant when he said he was trying to live a moral life as a caring doctor, and why it was so important to him. Dan's choice to become a physician, to work first on hemophilia and now on AIDS, was not only a moral act, but also an act of resistance against despair. It was a decision that was self-serving, but that was the basis of resistance. Dan wanted to do everything possible to live. He was focusing his considerable talents to change the expected outcome of the illness, for himself and for others.

As I walked Dan to the door, we embraced again. This time tears fell from both our eyes, and I felt relieved to see Dan cry.

I sat for a long time alone in my office, absorbing the impact of what I had learned. Imagine what it was like for Dan to care for AIDS patients, daily to watch life be drained from young people like himself. And then to work in the BL3 facility, seeing in a culture dish how the virus mercilessly destroyed T cells, as it was doing that very moment within his body. Yet Dan had chosen to place himself in the jaws of the lion, to face his deadly enemy squarely and without flinching. Was he constantly testing himself, and with the passing of each test, gaining strength from one more victory over fear? Was that his method?

It was still hard for me to assimilate and believe what Dan had revealed. It seemed surreal. I was his mentor. I had for three years watched him serve his fellowship, in the clinic and now the lab, and he worked like a normal fellow. Was it normal to be doing what he did, constantly to subject himself to such terror? His father's answer to such a question would be with another question, the typically Jewish response that indicated that no human answer was absolute: What is normal? Dan chose to make his life normal. This choice was an assertion of his courage and dignity. Dignity, for a person with an incurable illness, as for a prisoner in Auschwitz, was created by the capacity to remain a person with a will, to make choices, even when life offers such brutally limited options.

His parents. Holocaust survivors. It was unbearable to think of how much pain they felt with their only child likely marked for death. Rina and the kids. Those beautiful towheaded girls, growing up without their father's boundless love.

I had seen myself in Dan. His background was so similar to mine, his tastes, sense of humor, passions. We could communicate at times without speaking, just with a knowing glance or a shrug of the shoulders. We shared the same roots, we were cut from the same cloth, mine a generation earlier, and that fabric bound us together in an almost mystical embrace of heart and mind. I felt sick with grief.

But Dan, Rina, and the children seemed happy and energetic, a typical young family. They did the things that Pam and I did with our kids—excursions to the Boston Children's Museum, Sunday brunches with friends, explorations of Toys "R" Us, coordinating scheduled drop-offs and pickups at day care and school. They lived an ordinary life under extraordinary circumstances.

I searched my memory for the connection between the ordinary and the extraordinary, how there was an alchemy that transmuted the mundane into the sacred. It came to mind. Again, it was a story from the Holocaust, the story told by Primo Levi, the Jewish Italian chemist, who used the transmutability of the elements as a metaphor to explain the radical change in the substance of his life when enslaved by the Nazis. He wrote that it was the performing of ordinary things that had sustained his sanity, his dignity, his humanity in hell's inferno. The Nazis systematically dehumanized their victims, asserting they were subhuman, without freedom or choice, and not deserving of life. Levi recounted how, when he was close to despair and considering giving in to death, he was instructed by a comrade in the camp to wash his face every day. This ordinary and simple act restored dignity and structure to his person, because he exercised his will to do it, and it was a conscious choice. Levi also found that sustaining the life of the mind in the senseless world of the concentration camp gave him strength. With another friend, he regularly recited verses from Dante, as he had before his enslavement. He had chosen to introduce beauty in the form of poetry in a place where beauty was not meant to exist.

Levi believed the greatest form of resistance was to continue to act in the ordinary, normal ways that had marked one's life before the deportation. It demonstrated a sense of control, an exercise of will, and signaled the potential to triumph over the forces that sought to destroy you. With the restoration of dignity came a renewed capacity to hope.

Primo Levi, like Elie Wiesel, asserted that life in the camps was unlike any other situation, and great care was to be taken in drawing analogies. But both also understood that there were important insights about man and his behavior in the face of destructive evil that were to be learned from that unique time.

DAN SPENT THE Christmas and New Year's break in Montreal, seeing his parents and checking in with his treating physicians at McGill. He returned improved, with more of his former mien and energy. I deliberately did not press him to speak with me about his disease, thinking it was more appropriate for him to take the initiative and control the dialogue. One afternoon in early January he approached me and said he wanted to explain what had happened medically over the past year in more detail.

He had suffered a light case of pneumocystis pneumonia between Rosh Hashanah and Yom Kippur. It had been his first opportunistic infection. His T cell number had fallen over the past decade from a normal level of 600 to a severely depressed count of 40. He had al-

ready exhausted anti-HIV therapy with ddI, ddC, d4T, and nevirap-
ine. In early December, he began treatment with AZT and an experimental drug, 3TC. He was anxious to try any experimental
therapy that made sense, and 3TC was the most appealing. The experimental combination seemed to be working well. He had noted a
significant increase in appetite and energy and had gained weight.

He originally had received Bactrim as a preventive antibiotic
against pneumocystis, but had become allergic to this medication.
His physician in Montreal appropriately switched to dapsone, a different sulfa drug. Probably because of his very low immune function, dapsone had failed to ward off the pneumonia. The pneumocystis pneumonia was treated with high doses of pentamidine, an
effective but highly noxious antibiotic that caused a nauseating
metallic taste. This was why coffee had become so repugnant. He
subsequently was desensitized to Bactrim by taking it in a series of
increasing doses, and was now tolerating this superior medication
against pneumocystis without any allergic problems. Dan felt he had
turned the corner after a difficult autumn.

I offered him a leave of absence if that would be helpful. Dan said
that was the last thing in the world he wanted. He lived for his family and his work. Not working, in the laboratory or the clinic, would
make things worse. He had been offered many fellowships and had
intentionally taken ours because of our program in HIV. The three
years with us treating patients and training in the lab had actually
given him great hope and comfort.

Dan knew I must wonder how he coped with seeing AIDS in all
its misery every day as a treating physician. Of course there were
moments when he was terrified. Occasionally, while examining a
patient racked by an infection or a cancer, a ghastly mirror appeared
in his mind's eye. In this mirror he saw his own face merge with his
patient's. He fantasized about his death, which route it would take,
whether by infection or by cancer, like the liturgy in the Yom Kippur service.

But he still was not convinced he would die soon, or at all, from
AIDS. Important therapeutic advances had been made over the past
decade. He was optimistic that the gene therapy project we and others were working on could add decades to his life. He hoped that he
would see his children grow up. He hoped he would continue to be
productive in his work. Until it was clear that nothing could be

done to sustain him in such a functioning state, he would work and fight to live.

Imagine being his parents, Dan said, during the Holocaust. How many times had he calculated their chances of living when they were deported with all the other Hungarian Jews to Auschwitz in 1944? Fifty thousand people a week were being killed at the camp. He saw things the same way with his prognosis. The odds were heavily against him. It was unlikely he would survive. But he knew that his chances were not zero. He would continue to struggle to live regardless of the odds, as his parents had.

Dan then thanked me, in a curiously formal but sincere manner, for the lab's commitment to HIV research. He knew there were many other medical issues less fraught with politics and social stigma that one might want to pursue. As my heart tightened with pain and admiration for him, I told Dan that I would do everything and anything to help him. I would participate as actively in his case as he wanted, but would not cross the line between our work relationship and our care relationship if he wanted my clinical assistance.

Dan nodded his appreciation. He said he was very aggressive about his own therapy, and would not hesitate to ask my advice about his treatment regimen or the risks and benefits of an experimental therapy.

I asked him why he had not told me before of his condition.

Dan said that he had adopted a consistent and, he believed, fair approach to disclosing his illnesses, first hemophilia and now AIDS. It was based on the principle of "need to know." Those people who were essential to his medical care and emotional framework were told. Thus his parents and physicians in Canada knew his diagnosis, and of course, his wife, Rina. The children were simply told that their father was sometimes sick. If he got worse, more would be explained to them.

If his condition were widely known, Dan was concerned he would be limited in what he could undertake, either out of ignorant discrimination or misdirected sympathy. Would he have had the latitude to do everything he had already done? Would his suggestions at lab meetings, his critique of experimental design and results, have carried the same weight if in the back of everyone's mind these opinions were colored by the shadow of his disease? Would his patients have trusted his advice if they worried it was tempered by his personal involvement in the disease rather than the objective perspective he believed he had sustained? He would be unable to continue his normal life, and that would mean capitulating to the disease.

Despite all this, finally telling me had provided a deep sense of relief. He had done so because it had become obvious to me that something was wrong. He felt duplicitous in not informing me, but it made pragmatic sense to sustain the secret. His first responsibility was to himself, to keep his life as ordinary, as normal as possible. And because of that, Dan asked that I keep the information strictly confidential.

I agreed to his request. We decided he would continue working in the lab as long as he could. If he flagged in his efforts, he would transfer his research project to others until we recruited a replacement. No one else needed to know, unless Dan wanted them to.

As our conversation drew to a close, Dan added almost in passing: "Jerry, you're not the first to know in the lab."

I was a bit taken aback. Who would learn before me, his mentor, his friend, his *landsman,* and the chief of the lab?

"Phong has known for a while. We've become very close. You know what she's been through. She has that understanding and quiet strength which remind me of my parents. I made her promise to keep it a secret, so don't be annoyed with her for not telling you."

Now I understood her blank silence months before.

"Don't worry. Phong was right to respect your confidence."

THE SPRING OF 1994 arrived early, as if to make up for the premature onset of the preceding winter. The warm moist air and the first buds of New England's resplendent flowers lifted everyone's spirits. The lab was abuzz with the refound energy that accompanies earth's season of life. It was soon June, and time for welcoming the new trainees and sending off the graduates of the fellowship.

Dan was returning to McGill, planning on setting up a laboratory there in HIV. We would continue to collaborate scientifically. He had had some positive results in preventing HIV from killing the genetically altered T cells, but more work needed to be done. When a small amount of virus was incubated with the altered cells, they appeared resistant, but when larger amounts of virus were added, the artificial gene was overwhelmed and the cells died. We would have to synthesize other blocking genes, and then repeat the experiments with the large inoculum of virus. We would keep on trying until we had created a truly potent therapy.

Dan continued to do well medically. He was excited about a new treatment protocol with protease inhibitors. These were a novel family of drugs that prevented HIV from assembling itself within the cell. They were designed by computer and worked differently from AZT and all the other drugs Dan had received before. He was determined to receive these new agents and was negotiating with his physicians in Montreal about whether he could add the protease drug to his AZT and 3TC combination and deliver a triple blow to the virus.

It came time to say good-bye. Dan brought Rina and the kids to the lab. They scampered around his desk as he packed up his books, coffee press, and mugs. He had brought in his camera, and after Dan photographed the lab, Roberta, and Phong, he asked for a picture to be taken of us all together, like family. We were a comical group, my six-foot-five frame towering over Dan's short wiry figure, Phong helping Rina restrain the squirming Becky and Emma. As Roberta prepared to snap the picture, I put my arm tightly around Dan and pressed him closely to me. I fought back tears, thinking how remarkable a person he was. I thought of how I was meant to be Dan's mentor, his teacher, instructing him in the diagnosis and treatment of cancer and blood diseases, training him in the laboratory in molecular biology and cellular virology. Dan proved to be my teacher. He taught me how we can draw strength and courage from choosing to celebrate the ordinary pleasures of life in the shadow of death. He taught me that accepting life's uncertainty can paradoxically overcome fear and enhance survival. That knowledge has helped me direct my patients with cancer and AIDS to discover the ordinary acts and choices in their lives that may fortify them in their battle against their disease.

The photograph of Dan and his family with Phong and me stands framed on my desk. I often gaze at it, and daydream. His spirit, like the light from a distant star, continues to illuminate my life, long after its source was extinguished.

Cindy

I SEARCHED for Cindy Cohen in the crowded waiting room of the HIV clinic one Tuesday morning in October 1995. I was far behind schedule, running late because I had seen a new patient early in the day who had required nearly two hours to sort out a host of complex medical problems.

I finally located her in the far corner of the waiting room. On my way to her, I passed the Miltons. Jack, his mother, Betsy, and sister Sarah were planted as usual next to the Belmont Springs water cooler. Jack Milton was blind from a cytomegalovirus infection that had destroyed his retinas. He had to drink two liters of fluid a day to excrete foscarnet, an effective but toxic drug against this destructive virus, from his system. His mother, Betsy, sat observantly at his side, carefully filling the conical paper cup and passing it to her son. I nodded hello to Betsy Milton and greeted Jack by squeezing his thin forearm as I quickly went by.

Mark Hynes was seated next to Mrs. Milton. He was wearing a red flowered bandanna over his broad hairless cranium. Mark tried to smile in greeting but only achieved a taut, pained grimace. Mark had the AIDS-related cancer Kaposi's sarcoma, which had distorted his once finely drawn features into a coarse relief map of crimson mountains and craters. His swollen cheeks would not rise in response to his command to smile. Mark had recently received Taxol, a very potent drug extracted from the bark of the rare Pacific yew tree. Taxol had been developed to treat advanced ovarian and breast cancer and was found in our studies to be very effective in combating Kaposi's sarcoma. I was hopeful it would significantly shrink Mark's tumors and restore his facial features and functioning.

I finally reached Cindy deep in the corner of the waiting room. Her head was bowed and her face buried in *The New York Times*. Only her rich black hair was visible. She sensed my presence and quickly raised her head. It was a full-moon face from the steppes of Russia: deep almond brown eyes set above broad white cheeks. I smiled and indicated with a nod of my head that she was next to be seen. Cindy folded the pages of the *Times* expertly along their broad crease, collected her *Cosmopolitan*, *The New Yorker*, and *Allure* from the seat next to her, and briskly stood up.

We walked quickly from the waiting room to the combination office/examining room at the other end of the corridor. I apologized for running late, and we exchanged the usual pleasantries about the trip up from New York and the uncertainties of traffic from Logan Airport to the Harvard Medical area.

Cindy neatly laid her pile of reading material on my desk, gracefully turned her full form to me, and waited. It took me a moment to realize that I had forgotten to give her the ritual hug that began each office visit. I moved my arm around Cindy's back and gave her a brotherly embrace.

"That's better, Jerry. I needed your hug after sitting in that awful waiting room."

I first had met Cindy Cohen three years before, shortly after her thirty-third birthday. She had telephoned for an appointment after seeing an article in the *Times* about AIDS research at Harvard. Struggling to maintain a level register in her voice, she explained that her problem was urgent and asked to be seen as soon as possible.

A week later we met at the HIV clinic. At that first visit, Cindy recounted in detail a story known only to her general practitioner, Dr. Jules Weksler, in Huntington, Long Island.

A few weeks before her thirty-third birthday she had broken up with Doug Geller, her boyfriend of long standing. Before Doug, she had dated here and there, but she was "not that social a girl." She had found it hard to meet the right kind of men. She would never go to a bar or a club, and most of the guys introduced through her mother's friends Cindy found "uninteresting" or "immature."

Cindy was a senior accountant at a large commercial bank in Manhattan. She commuted each day on the Long Island Rail Road, catching the 6:24 out of Huntington and arriving at her desk before eight. Doug Geller was also an accountant, working for the same bank but in a branch office in Brooklyn. They had met at a corporate retreat.

Doug was the first man that Cindy had ever slept with, and also the first man Cindy felt she truly loved. He was considerate, funny, a serious worker, kept up with the latest movies, as Cindy did, and was not unattractive.

Cindy had seen marriage as the natural outcome of their relationship. After three years of courtship, Cindy pressed this point of view one Sunday night in a restaurant overlooking Long Island Sound. Doug listened carefully while shifting a piece of grilled halibut from one side of his plate to the other. After politely waiting for her to finish her rehearsed presentation, Doug explained that although he thought he loved her too, he just wasn't ready yet to make a lifelong commitment.

"He felt we should wait a bit longer, a year or two at least, before readdressing the question," Cindy recounted.

"I told Doug, right then and there, that I didn't have two years to let things unfold. I mean, thirty-three years old, a good job as a senior accountant, working in the city, it was time—time to define the future, to start a family, to settle into a *life*. So we just sat there, not saying a word through dessert. Finally I let him off the hook and said, 'Doug, let's take a breather.'

"I thought I could handle it, just pick up and go on, but I went into a funk, a real blue period," Cindy explained.

After Cindy had spent several weeks feeling low, her mother, Lena, suggested that Cindy take a break from work and go away somewhere fun for a long weekend. It would get her mind off Doug. Lena had read about the winter weekend package at Club Med Martinique in *Travel and Leisure*. To Cindy, it seemed colorful, exotic, and a million miles from Doug and New York.

Cindy recalled how at first she felt out of place at the Caribbean resort: her pale complexion made whiter by number 21 sunblock (she had read an article on the increasing incidence of skin cancer in the Tuesday science section of the *Times*), her one-piece chalk-blue swimsuit, her simple braided gold necklace, all contrasting with the bronzed, bejeweled bodies displayed in bikinis and G-strings and thongs. Some European women at the club were even bare-chested, and paraded along the beachfront without a hint of self-consciousness. Cindy had found it all very exciting.

"I felt completely transported, like I was in that Brando movie where they are shipwrecked in Tahiti. I wanted to be transformed into a native," she explained in a dreamy voice.

After a day spent wandering shyly alone through the club, Cindy became bolder and hooked up with a trio of women from Dallas. They seemed to be triplets, all bleached blondes with finely tapered noses, long slender fingers that ended in red press-on nails, and admirably trim figures for women in their midforties with children. They were neighbors and told Cindy they observed a tradition of one "freedom weekend" a year—freedom from their husbands and kids, from their car pools, cooking, housecleaning, and churchgoing. They would mostly drink, but sometimes, as they said, "find some guys—if we're lucky!" They were off to do some snorkeling with Frederic, a diver from Nice who spent each winter working at Club Med Martinique. The leader of the trio, Peggy, invited Cindy to come along.

Cindy gladly accepted the invitation. She loved to swim, and had never been in such soothing waters. The beaches on Long Island were crowded and the waves rough. You couldn't really risk a leisurely swim far from shore for fear that a current might pull you out, or at least that was what her mother had warned. Cindy felt reassured that Frederic would know the currents and find the safest coves for snorkeling.

Cindy described Frederic as of medium height, about five-foot-nine or ten, and very muscular with a neatly groomed mustache and closely cropped brown hair that was lightened at its ends by the sun or perhaps by bleach, Cindy wasn't sure. He seemed to be a very gentle and patient person, helping each woman in turn fit her mask tightly over her face and position the snorkel correctly.

Cindy had never snorkeled before. Frederic showed her how to grip the mouthpiece with just the right amount of tension, his thick, callused fingertips gliding smoothly over her lips. He had a diamond stud in his right ear that intermittently reflected the sun in sharp flashes that made Cindy think of electric sparks. He wore what Cindy described as a "tight nylon jockstrap" instead of a regular bathing suit. Frederic, Cindy remarked, was not a "knock you dead" handsome man, not like one of those Calvin Klein models who lay sprawled on the beach advertising cologne or underwear in the Sunday *Times Magazine*. But Cindy found that his imperfections, the harelip that she discovered hidden under the mustache, the few pock marks on his upper cheeks from teenage acne, made him more attractive.

Frederic shared a thatched cabin at the club with Peter, a young, slender Austrian who wore an identical diamond stud in his right ear. Peter was in his early twenties, dressed in a flowered sarong and sandals, and worked winters as a cook at the club. Cindy couldn't remember whether the native men in the Brando movie wore dresses like Peter.

The next morning was breezy, with a thick tropical wind coming from the west that Frederic explained was perfect for Windsurfing. Since Cindy's Dallas friends still hadn't emerged from their cabin, Frederic invited her to learn solo how to manage the wind and guide the small shell. She told me how surprised she was by the feeling of speed and power that came with gliding on the choppy bay. Frederic suggested they try reaching a cove about two kilometers from the club beach. Taking up the challenge, Cindy succeeded in arriving at the shore without falling over. She felt proud of herself, and noted that in three short days her skin, despite the sunblock, had lost its pallor and taken on a vibrant hue.

As they rested on the secluded beach, Frederic moved confidently to Cindy, gently smoothed her wet sandy hair off her face, and kissed her. Cindy closed her eyes, as she always did when she kissed, and imagined again she was a native in Tahiti, and this time Frederic was Marlon Brando. They made love on the beach.

This seemed to Cindy to be just the kind of "freedom weekend" she needed after Doug's rejection. During her four days at the club, she and Frederic stole away three more times to make love. Cindy felt that she was desirable again, that when she returned to New York she would be ready to meet new men and look for love.

During the last night of the winter weekend package, the Dallas trio drank heavily. Cindy, who had never really been drunk in her life, joined them. She first felt giddy, and then started reviewing her situation in life: the rupture with Doug, the lack of other prospects at work, the unchanging routine of crunching numbers at the bank. She soon fell deeply asleep, feeling morose.

Cindy awoke with the urge to urinate. It was the middle of the night and she realized she was on the floor of the trio's room. Walking outside in the balmy Caribbean night, she used the illumination of a full moon to find the mulch path back to her own private cabin. As she passed Frederic and Peter's shared cabin, she heard muffled grunting noises. Cindy stopped and peered through the screened window. She could just make out the form of a slender woman, or perhaps *not* a woman, lying under Frederic's thrusting pelvis. She saw stuttering sparks of reflected moonlight fall from the diamond stud in Frederic's ear.

Cindy turned quickly away. It was none of her business. She didn't truly know him. He had helped her escape for a while from her problems, and had shown her how to let herself go. For that she thought she would be forever grateful. It really didn't matter what Frederic did. In a few short hours she would be on her way home, and Frederic would be gone from the rest of her life. It was up to her to rebuild her future.

Returning to New York on a bleak Tuesday evening in February, Cindy felt refreshed. Her mother remarked that the weekend had been a "cure" for her blues. The other girls in the bank's accounting office commented on the renewed energy in Cindy's voice. She dared not share the details of her wild escapade with even her closest friends, who, she thought, probably wouldn't have believed her anyway. But that was not important in Cindy's mind. What mattered was that the trip marked a turning point in her life. It had proved to her that she could venture out on her own, overcome her caution, relax her inhibitions, and pursue a fantasy.

About a week after returning from Martinique, Cindy developed what she thought was a "bad flu." She had a fever of 103 degrees and a viselike headache, the light bothered her eyes, her neck was stiff, and her muscles ached down to the bones. She noticed that the glands in her neck were very swollen. She contacted her supervisor at work and said she was sick and wouldn't be in. She then called her mother. Lena wanted her to see the family doctor, Dr. Weksler, if the fever didn't go away in twenty-four hours.

Three days later she still had a temperature of 102 degrees and the glands were more tender. Dr. Weksler saw her briefly, commenting that her father would have been proud to see his daughter as the woman she had become. Dr. Weksler had been a close friend of her father's, and had become almost a surrogate parent to Cindy after his sudden death. Dr. Weksler was tall and rotund, with hardly a speck of hair left on his broad pate, and when Cindy was a little girl she imagined he was Humpty Dumpty.

Dr. Weksler's office was located downstairs in a split-level house, and Cindy had spent many afternoons on the floor above as a young girl doing her homework until Lena finished work at a local department store. After her homework was finished Cindy would watch television and hope there was a break between patients when Dr. Weksler would come upstairs and chat with Cindy or share a snack with her. If Lena worked very late, Cindy would stay for dinner.

During the summers, Dr. Weksler, who had no children and whose wife had died in an accident years before Cindy was born, would take Lena and Cindy with him on weekends to his bungalow in the Catskills. They would stay up late into the warm night, watching for shooting stars and talking about the news on the evening telecast. As Cindy grew into her teens, she would go to Dr. Weksler for advice when she had a problem and Lena seemed at a loss.

Dr. Weksler confirmed that Cindy had all the symptoms of what people called "the flu," even though it was unusual so late in the winter and the lymph glands didn't usually swell to such a degree. It was more likely that rather than being true influenza, it was just a "bad virus," he thought. Dr. Weksler suggested they also check for strep throat and test for mononucleosis—the "kissing disease," he called it with a wink.

Cindy returned to Dr. Weksler ten days later. Her fevers and headache had gone, and the muscle aches were diminishing, but the glands in her neck were still swollen. They bothered her. She felt them when she turned on her pillow at night, as if she had swallowed hard-boiled eggs that had gotten stuck on both sides of her neck.

Since Martinique, Cindy had tried to change her "look." She had cut her hair, started wearing a bolder red lipstick, and bought a few flashy blouses. She told Dr. Weksler that the glands made her look like a chipmunk just at the time she should be meeting new fellows.

Her skin had changed too. It wasn't really acne, but there were rough, red areas that caused one close girlfriend to ask if Cindy wanted the name of her dermatologist. Dr. Weksler said it was eczema.

Over the next two months, Cindy saw Dr. Weksler four more times. She was quietly worried she had Hodgkin's disease. She had first read about it in *Love Story*. Cindy had seen the movie as soon as it was released, and cried from the time Ali McGraw withered away until the end of the credits.

Cindy made Dr. Weksler promise that Lena would not be informed of her visits to him. She explained that she was thirty-three and, after the trip to Martinique, had decided to take complete charge of her own life. Her mother would only worry and drive Cindy crazy, calling several times a day for updates on her symptoms. Dr. Weksler agreed to respect Cindy's wishes and not tell Lena. He did more blood tests, another throat culture, and a chest X ray, and repeated her physical examination. All he found was enlarged lymph nodes in her neck, groin, and armpits.

At the end of two months, they seemed no closer to a diagnosis than at the outset. Dr. Weksler said he was ready to send Cindy to a surgeon to biopsy the enlarged lymph nodes but wanted her written permission to do one special test before proceeding with that invasive procedure. He explained that even though they were like family, he needed her to sign a consent form to test her for HIV, the virus that causes AIDS.

"An AIDS test? Are you really thinking I have AIDS?"

Cindy told me how she strained to maintain her composure. Deep inside, she had felt for a while that something was seriously wrong. Her body was just not the same. It was not only the persistence of the swollen lymph glands and the eczema but also her total lack of energy. Even on weekends, she felt so fatigued by evening that she couldn't stay awake through a rented movie.

Cindy's most detailed knowledge of AIDS came from a profile she had read in the *Times* of Ali Gertz, a "nice Jewish girl from New York, just like me," who eventually died of AIDS. Ali Gertz contended that she hadn't used drugs. She had gotten infected through regular sex with a man. Probably a man she really didn't know, Cindy surmised. A man like Frederic.

Cindy agreed to take the blood test but demanded from Dr.

Weksler his solemn promise that if she was infected with the AIDS virus, he would not tell her mother without her permission. Cindy felt she alone had to be in control of information that would change her life.

Jules Weksler nodded his assent. Cindy then broke down and cried for a long time in his familiar arms.

After Cindy finished recounting her story, the first question she asked me was if Dr. Weksler might be wrong, if the blood tests really proved, "one hundred percent," that she had been infected with HIV. Her question did not surprise me. Nearly every patient with a catastrophic disease clings to the belief that the diagnosis could be a mistake. Cindy had come to me as a court of last resort, desperately hoping that I would change the verdict given in New York.

Looking deep into her almond brown eyes, I told Cindy in a calm and level voice, hiding the pain I felt as I said the words that would irreversibly change her life, that there was no question about her diagnosis: she was infected with HIV, the AIDS virus.

Cindy shuddered, but maintained her composure.

I watched her closely as I went on to explain the meaning of the tests Dr. Weksler had done on her blood. After contracting HIV, we develop specific antibodies against the virus. These antibodies are only found in infected people and are detected by the ELISA and Western blot tests she had undergone. I affirmed again that there was no doubt about their accuracy.

I went on to explain that the "flu" she had had was a classic presentation of what is called *acute* HIV infection. The virus enters a person through an orifice during sex, or enters directly into the blood during IV drug use or from a contaminated transfusion. It then races through the body via the bloodstream, delighted to have found a new residence with so many susceptible T cells and macrophages to attack. The headache, stiff neck, and sensitivity to light, or photophobia, come from HIV passing from the circulation into the central nervous system, causing a viral meningitis.

Her rapidly enlarging lymph nodes were due to the virus invading those structures. Our lymph nodes normally serve as base camps for cells of the immune system, including T cells, macrophages, and antibody-producing B cells. The entry of the viral invader into the lymph nodes triggers a counterattack by battalions of such immune defender cells. These determined conscripts charge into the nodes, causing them to swell. Although our immune defenders succeed in slowing the production of virus, and limit its spread within the body, they cannot eradicate the pathogen entirely from the battlefield. Over time the virus changes and escapes from the containment of the immune system. As it gains the upper hand, it progressively destroys our body's defenses.

I informed Cindy that once a person has been infected, he or she is infected forever, because the virus takes up permanent residence inside the cells of the immune system. And because the person is permanently infected, he or she is potentially infectious to others. Forever.

I had said these painful words so many times to so many patients over the past decade that they came out in stylized sentences and paragraphs, like the prepared text of an informational pamphlet. But I had not become immune to their impact. As I said them, I saw Cindy's face tighten and her eyes close. I knew that rush after rush of terrifying thoughts were flooding her mind, of suffering, debility, isolation, and death.

I had performed the awful but necessary task of destroying her final bulwark of false hope and releasing this torrent of fear and anguish. I never knew at this painful moment whether my patient would find the strength to resist these emotions or would be overwhelmed by them, surrendering to despair.

OUR RELATIONSHIP DEVELOPED more quickly than I expected. Cindy shared intimacies at each appointment beyond the details of her weekend at Club Med. I learned more about her family, her workplace, her interests and talents.

Her ease in talking to me came in part from the relief of sharing her painful secret with someone other than Dr. Weksler. It also stemmed from our similar backgrounds. I had grown up in New York, in Queens, in a neighborhood like hers. There was little need for editorial explanations or interpretations in our conversation. Cindy knew that I "got it" when she described in bittersweet terms Lena's overprotective mothering, the manners of her fellow commuters, the stunted maturity of men like Doug. We also talked about the films she saw, the failure of the Clintons to create a new health care system, the content of the articles in the Tuesday science section of the *Times* that she read on the plane coming up for her appointment. I enjoyed her sharp insights and dry sense of humor. We had become friends, not just doctor and patient.

But whenever we talked, I sensed that there were things she wasn't telling me, that locked deep in her heart were her real secrets, her real dreams, and that the disease had made their impossibility too painful to discuss.

That Tuesday in October, the day I was running late and trying to catch up, Cindy finally opened her heart to me. Not immediately, and not on the dry ground of our usual discussion of family and work, but in the midst of an unexpected deluge of fear and despair.

"I *hate* sitting in that waiting room," she began.

I nodded silently, taken by surprise by the sudden anger in her voice. In my mind I saw the distorted smile of Mark Hynes, the cups of water passed to Jack Milton.

"I just sit there, look at the sickest patients, and imagine myself five years down the road. I'm not ignorant, Jerry. I know what this disease is. It's a slow death sentence."

She waited for my response, breathing hard, her face tightening as if to hold back the torrent inside her mind. It was the first time in three years she had brought up the issue of death.

"Cindy, I've dealt with this disease for fifteen years. I've seen literally thousands of people with HIV get sick and die. And I will see many, many more people die. That's certain. But it's not certain that HIV is a death sentence, not now, not in 1995. Cynthia Marlene Cohen does not have to die from HIV."

I paused to let my words be absorbed. Her face relaxed briefly, and then reassumed its taut grimace.

"I don't believe everyone with the virus is going to get sick and die from AIDS," I continued. "You're recently infected, you haven't had any major complications, your immune system is at a normal level on your medication. These drugs have improved the duration and the quality of life for patients at your stage of the illness. I can see a time when HIV becomes a chronic controlled condition, like diabetes, rather than a progressive downhill disease. Taking anti–HIV drugs will be like a diabetic taking insulin. When will this happen? I can't say exactly *when*, but I believe it *will*. I don't agree with you. HIV does *not* have to be a death sentence, not for people like you."

Cindy's face became impassive and her rich brown eyes distant.

She moved her gaze to her medical chart opened on my desk, and after a long pause, focused again on our conversation.

"You're always so full of optimism—telling me how healthy I am, giving me news about progress in research, pointing out positive articles in the *Times*, making me feel hopeful. I know you honestly believe that you may save my life. You're not just saying these things to make me feel better. And I *do* feel better after we talk, at least for a while.

"But sitting in that waiting room I see what AIDS is. I see the present, not some future dream. I see myself becoming like *them,* and it's hard to live every day with that image before your eyes."

There was no avoiding the horror of the disease. In a way, I wanted my patients to admit its horror, to confront it, because after facing their worst nightmare there was nothing more to fear or imagine. They then could look away and find other images in their lives to replace those of suffering and death: images of love and productivity and fulfillment that were conceivable despite their disease.

It is almost impossible to find such images alone, blinded by the darkness of isolation and pain. One needs another person—a friend, a lover, a family member, or a professional, in therapy, or in a support group, to draw aside the blackness of despair and show you what remains in your life beyond your disease.

I explained this to Cindy, and suggested that her mother, with Dr. Weksler, could help her cope better.

She rejected this suggestion out of hand. She had decided not to tell Lena until she got sick. Lena just couldn't handle it. She would pester Cindy about her symptoms and become hysterical at the slightest change, even if it proved meaningless. Dr. Weksler was there for her, always, but since her diagnosis he seemed to purposely avoid discussing her condition. Cindy thought it was too frightening for him. She was not just his patient, but virtually his daughter. He was like a parent who needed help and support himself.

I had once before given her the name of a therapist whom she might consult and a support group downtown. I suggested these possibilities again.

"I don't know. I really don't know," Cindy said with a sigh. "There are days when I think, yes, I'll call the therapist on Sixty-eighth Street you suggested. And then I think, no, until I'm outwardly sick I don't want to have this disease change my life more than it already has. What can he really do? What can he really change? No. This whole situation has made me realize I *am* strong. I can handle my fears on my own. I don't need to tell anyone other than you and Dr. Weksler."

Cindy took a tissue from the box on the Formica and chrome clinic office desk and dabbed the tears from the corners of her eyes. Her mascara tattooed the thin fibrous tissue. She carefully folded the tissue and went on.

"Of course that's what I think most days. But then there are moments when I feel so alone, so afraid. I go to work, talk with my mother, see a movie with a girlfriend. But behind me is this huge leering monster, a horrible thing with fangs and sharp claws. It's always stalking me. And I'm the only one who knows it's there. It's invisible to everyone—to everyone but me."

Cindy started to sob, deep, wet sobs like a child shaken by a nightmare. Her sobs rapidly accelerated into true hyperventilation.

"Cindy, slow down." I wrapped my fingers around her tensed fist.

She gradually gained control of her breathing, exhaling slowly and rhythmically.

"I'm sorry. I'm really sorry. I usually don't lose it like that anymore. I used to in the beginning, just after I was diagnosed. I guess sitting out there today so long waiting for you—that poor blind guy sipping cup after cup of water, and that other fellow you said hello to who can hardly open his eyes, from his cancer—it's like AIDS makes us into the monster that stalks us."

I sat silently, thinking of the depth of suffering wrought by this plague. There were times I also felt overwhelmed by the extent of the pain, the cruelty of its infections and cancers. The disease was doubly cruel because it was so public—as if the virus wanted its victims to be on display.

I too had imagined AIDS as the monster in Cindy's nightmare. Every day it flaunted its prey. Every day I saw how it drained the energy from my patients by choking their lungs and eating away at their muscles. Every day I saw how it distorted their features, removed their hair, blunted their senses. The monster's taste for human flesh was insatiable. While we desperately struggled to combat it in our laboratories and clinics, it mocked us by continuing to devour men, women, children.

I hated AIDS. I hated it with an intensity that sometimes shocked me. But I had learned to use my hatred. When I felt I might be overwhelmed by the suffering of people like Jack Milton and Mark Hynes, my anger helped hold me up, turning me outward to fight when I felt like collapsing inside.

Was AIDS really unstoppable? Wasn't HIV just a puny parasite, nothing more than eleven genes in a feeble protein shell? We had deciphered its entire genetic code. We had crystallized parts of its protein framework and charted its topography. We had, within a decade of its discovery, learned how to poison many of its enzymes and thereby slow its killing of our blood cells. We had put our scientific hooks deeply into it, we were scaling its defenses, finding its soft vulnerable parts, which we would eventually crush. Yes, hatred was vital in defeating AIDS. Despair had no place in a battle to the death with this merciless predator.

"As I was saying—" Cindy paused to compress the wet tissues in her hand into a small ball and drop them into the wastebasket next to the desk. "As I was saying, what am I supposed to do? You said a support group? Where? Downtown at GMHC, the *Gay Men's Health Crisis*? I'm not a *gay man*. All those support groups and help organizations, those Hollywood celebrities wearing red ribbons and hugging each other at the Academy Awards—they're not thinking of Cynthia Marlene Cohen of Huntington, Long Island. I don't fit into what they call the 'community.'"

I decided not to interrupt as Cindy talked on.

"Even if I went to a support group, what would I do? Sit in a circle with a bunch of gay guys who I have nothing in common with—nothing except this virus. And talk about what? I mean, I don't mind them—it's not that I have anything *against* gays. But I have nothing *for* them, either. I can't open up my feelings to them.

"They don't act real to me. They're like imitations of girls, with effeminate gestures, talking about clothes and 'cute guys.' I hear the chatter in the waiting room: 'I saw this incredibly beautiful guy at so-and-so's beach house last weekend.' Or: 'Can you believe how so-and-so wears those tight, tight Levi's that pinch his ass? If I had an ass as fat as his, I wouldn't *dare* wear those jeans.'"

Cindy laughed, despite her tears.

"They sound like silly high school girls. I mean, I know women who like to hang around gay men. I have a girlfriend like that at the office. She explained it to me. The gay guys call them 'fag hags.' I think most of them are afraid of regular men. They feel safe since they know that with a gay man there is no risk—no real romance, no sex. Well, *I'm* not a fag hag. Why spend an evening a week holding hands with them in a circle? They can't give me the support I need."

If the usual AIDS support groups didn't make sense, I suggested, what about a support group especially for women?

Cindy responded impatiently.

"Jerry, really—you know the statistics. They're drug addicts or pregnant teenagers from the ghetto. How many Cindy Cohens are there with HIV?"

I knew the statistics but I told Cindy she might be surprised to find she shared things with women so different from her. Patients had common fears, common needs. Being so isolated and carrying this alone increased her pain and suffering. I felt strongly she needed to share her burden with someone other than me and Dr. Weksler. If not in a formal setting, perhaps a trusted friend?

"There is no *girl*friend who can be trusted with this bombshell. And how can I have a *boy*friend with my condition?"

It was clear that Cindy was not receptive to any solution or attempt to create a solution. She seemed intent on keeping her world strictly divided, with a wide gulf between what lay outside and what was hidden inside. And even if inside was a lonely and painful place, it was still hers, familiar and controlled. To change the landscape required energy and courage that Cindy might not have. Perhaps all her energy and courage were used to simply get through the day, to wake up, go to work, talk with friends, handle Lena, and not constantly think of death.

I dropped the subject and asked Cindy to go to the examining table and get into a gown.

Cindy's physical condition was unchanged. Except for the enlarged lymph nodes in her neck, groin, and armpits, there was no sign of HIV. Her T cells had dropped six months ago below the normal lower limit of 500 to 340. She had complained of significant fatigue at the time and her HIV-associated eczema returned. After repeating the T-cell count to assure its accuracy, we began a new experimental triple combination of moderate doses of the older drugs AZT and 3TC with the recently developed protease inhibitors.

These new inhibitors had been designed by computer to block the protease enzyme, a scissor the virus carries to cut its proteins into the correct forms to make an infectious virus. If the cutting is interfered with, the virus decomposes.

Cindy had tolerated the experimental combination without any side effects. Her T-cell count had rapidly risen to the normal level of 580. Her fatigue and her eczema disappeared.

Cindy quickly dressed and returned to the chair facing my desk. As she sat down, she carefully folded her navy blue jacket over her white-stockinged knees and clasped her hands together, like an attentive pupil in grade school.

"Still no problems with the three drugs? No headache or muscle aches? No diarrhea, nausea, or stomachache? If you have side effects from these drugs, there are several alternatives that are equally potent."

"No, no problems like that. And I've taken the medicine as prescribed, precisely on schedule."

I nodded my head and smiled, signaling that everything was in order. We would check her T-cell number again along with a test called the "viral load." This was a recently developed measure of the amount of HIV in the bloodstream, and gave an accurate assessment of how well the antiviral treatment was working. When the results were in hand, we would discuss whether to continue her current regimen or modify it. Overall, she was doing extremely well.

I said I was pleased that she had improved on the combination treatment, ending the appointment on a positive note after a hard beginning. I closed her chart and moved my chair back a bit from the desk as a sign that the visit was over.

"Jerry, I want to talk about one more thing. Something important we haven't discussed yet."

I noticed that Cindy had not gotten up from her chair and was sitting with her hands still tightly clasped.

"Of course." I moved my chair back to the desk.

"Do you think I'll ever be able to have children?"

Cindy lowered her eyes and began anxiously to study her fingers, head bowed, avoiding my gaze, as if she really didn't want to hear the answer she already knew.

In Cindy's question, I felt the pain of a life's dream denied. It was so intense that I sat speechless for several moments. Ineptly, I responded as a professional rather than the friend she needed.

Did she mean having intercourse and carrying a child to term? I asked. Or being artificially inseminated? Or was she considering in vitro fertilization? Or the scenario of in vitro fertilization and implantation in a surrogate mother?

Cindy squinted, as if to focus her vision in surprisingly bright sunlight.

"I'm not sure, Jerry. I was asking about having my own child, like a regular mother." She paused thoughtfully. "But I'd like to hear all the options—if there really are any."

I silently regretted my clinical response, and tried to get back on track, but something held me back, the training as a doctor to remain detached from the raw pain of a patient.

I answered by saying that there really were no safe options, no options that justified the risk of transmitting the virus to a child. The chance of transmitting HIV to a newborn via the birth process was about 25 to 35 percent. Recent studies showed that this risk was lowered by half if the mother took AZT, to about 10 or 15 percent. Still, I could not condone taking *any* risk intentionally.

The only course at present was not to have children.

Cindy grimaced in pain.

"But haven't women patients of yours decided to become pregnant? Or become pregnant by accident, and then decided to have the baby? What did you do then?"

The ultimate decision at that stage was, of course, the mother's. But I recommended terminating the pregnancy early in gestation because of the chance of bearing an infected child. And Cindy needed to realize that even if the child was born *un*infected, there was the issue of the mother eventually becoming sick, too sick to care for the child, and dying. In the case of an unwed mother, like Cindy, this left an orphan who might not be easily placed in a loving environment for a host of reasons.

But what if the woman *insisted* on having the child? Cindy asked again.

I was worried by the pressure in her voice. Was that what she was considering? I wondered aloud.

"I really don't know exactly what I'm *considering*. I do know what I'm *feeling*. I feel this clock ticking in me. I'm nearly forty. Since I regained my energy on the medicine, I feel *alive* again. And I want to feel life *inside* me."

To be a mother, to bring life into the world. To love that life, to nurture it, to make it everything in the present and to anticipate its future. Cindy's life would never be whole.

"And the risks of those alternative ways you mentioned to have a child?" Cindy asked.

"I'm sorry I brought them up, because they're not really options yet. It's all very, very remote. Researchers are evaluating in vitro insemination and implanting the egg in a surrogate mother. But this is only in experimental animal models—in mice and monkeys infected with viruses similar to HIV. The aim is to see if the egg from the infected mother can be harvested, washed free of virus, inseminated in a test tube, and implanted in a surrogate mother without passing the virus to the surrogate and later to the offspring. But this is still strictly research. We don't have any real data yet. And the infected mother would still not carry her own child."

Cindy turned her head so that her eyes seemed focused on something beside me.

Should I explain something more clearly? I asked.

Her attention returned.

"No, you were clear. I actually did some background reading about how the virus is passed from mother to child before I came up. I anticipated your answers. It was just that I was thinking how different men are from women. You sounded so factual, so *clinical*."

I paused, unsure how to respond. She had sensed my professional distance, and mistakenly attributed it to my maleness. But it was not my being a man that accounted for my demeanor. I knew that a female physician would have responded as I had. It was the protective mechanism we learn in medical training to keep our emotions at bay in order to function effectively, to make sound decisions, take appropriate action, offer sober advice. Perhaps my love of my own children and my fondness for Cindy also made her case particularly disturbing, and I had withdrawn my heart from the discussion to protect it.

There were times when professional distance worked against you, when you did more for patients by opening your heart and absorbing their pain than by maintaining your dispassion. But I had been so focused on persuading her not to do anything risky, like getting pregnant, that I had cut myself off from her. I wondered whether my clinical detachment might weaken the impact of my advice.

We sat silently together for a long time, each lost in thought. I remembered other women with HIV whom I had cared for, and was convinced again that I had been right in giving Cindy such an absolute and negative answer. I recalled Kathy Tigree, whose ex-husband had used IV drugs and died early in the epidemic. She was left alone and infected. She emerged from his death a determined person who thought only of the future. She finished community college, went on to advanced training in computer programming, and fell in love with another programmer, Kevin. He told me he loved Kathy so much he would gladly die with her. I tried every argument, every approach to dissuade them from their plans. They made love regularly without a condom, and Kathy eventually became pregnant. On AZT, she delivered a thankfully healthy uninfected son. Kevin also escaped infection, and raised the boy after Kathy died. He called me after her funeral in Maine, on a dreary January morning. He told me that as she lay dying in their bed at home from disseminated mycobacterium avium, an opportunistic infection related to tuberculosis, Kathy had affirmed that she had lived a "happy and charmed life." This joy and magic had come from bearing her child, Kevin's love made flesh.

Kathy had ignored not only my advice but also the counsel of a pediatrician who cared for pediatric AIDS patients, a psychiatrist, and her social worker. She believed she had gambled and won. And what would Kathy have said if her son had been born with AIDS, and she had spent the last months of her life watching him wither and die? Would she still have felt lucky?

I thought of Barbara Malvern, who had become infected from using IV drugs. Barbara was a seventeen-year-old unwed mother of one uninfected four-year-old boy. She had become pregnant again. While in her second month, Barbara was hospitalized with pneumocystis pneumonia. She recovered and was placed on AZT for her HIV infection, and preventive antibiotics against recurrent pneumonia. She also received Diflucan for a bad case of esophageal candida, an opportunistic fungus common in immune-deficient people. The effects of all these drugs on the fetus so early in gestation posed a serious concern in addition to the issue of HIV transmission. But Barbara wanted the baby: "He's my child" was her response to the physicians and social workers involved in her case. Her mother, Gloria, a clerical worker for the Department of Motor Vehicles, tried vainly to "get some sense into her," telling me that "her whole life, Barbara hasn't listened to anyone."

Barbara Malvern gave birth to a premature HIV-infected baby

girl, Chantell. Barbara explained that she chose the name because she was so excited by having a daughter after a son that she wanted to sing.

Chantell spent the first several weeks of her life in the neonatal intensive care unit. She survived her multiple medical problems, including cytomegalovirus. At one year, she was a dull, sluggish infant. The pediatrician was certain she had suffered mental retardation and other developmental abnormalities from HIV, her mother's medications, and the prenatal cytomegalovirus infection. Chantell received AZT and the usual prophylactic antibiotics against opportunistic infections but died of bacterial pneumonia at sixteen months. Barbara was suffering from anorexia and severe weight loss, so-called "HIV wasting," and died shortly after Chantell. Gloria reluctantly placed her uninfected grandson in a foster home in Roxbury, lacking the funds to care for him herself. I had not heard from Gloria since, although I had left several messages on her answering machine at home. Perhaps even expressions of concern and sympathy were too painful to receive.

I returned from my reverie and noticed that Cindy's eyes had become heavy with tears.

"Jerry, now you know all my life I've wanted a child. And after today's appointment I know I can't. And whatever suffering, whatever awful infections and cancers attack me, the pain will be nothing compared to that realization. I *am* sentenced to death, because my life's desire will never come true."

I QUICKLY PUT Cindy's words aside. I had long before, during my medical training, learned to create rooms in my mind in which such disturbing thoughts could be shut away so as to not distract me from the myriad issues that required attention and action. But three months later, at her next scheduled appointment, Cindy's words came back with full force.

It was a Tuesday morning in January of 1996. We were having yet another snowstorm, the fourth of the season, and the city was absorbing the rhythmic blows of a pounding nor'easter that had swept up the coast from the Carolinas the night before. Most of my patients had canceled their appointments, and I had an unusually light schedule. I used the time to phone the patients who were unable to come in, check on their symptoms and medications, catch up on paperwork. I was considering whether I should leave my car in the hospital garage and take the trolley home after seeing the few patients who would make it in, when the front desk buzzed to let me know Cindy was in the waiting room. I had expected her to cancel and reschedule for another Tuesday.

Cindy was unusually cool when I greeted her. I noticed that she was seated in the center of the room, not hidden in the corner with her newspaper. She was talking to Edward, a professor of physics. They had been laughing about something; but as I approached, their conversation quickly died down. Edward and Cindy arranged themselves stiffly in their seats in mock horror, as if they were students who had disturbed the decorum of the classroom and I was coming to discipline my errant pupils.

I didn't forget to give Cindy our customary quick hug of greeting after we entered the exam room. She explained matter-of-factly that she had taken the train up and that it had been surprisingly leisurely to cruise through silent snow-covered New England towns that looked like postcards.

She was composed and precise in her answers to the usual battery of questions. No, she had not noted any fevers, sweats, or changes in appetite or energy since we last spoke. No, there were no signs of side effects from the medicine. Everything was status quo.

Cindy's physical condition was also stable. Her lymph nodes had not changed in size, and there was no evidence of activity of the virus such as reappearance of her eczema. Her T-cell numbers tested at the last visit were still well in the normal range. The viral load measurement gave an exciting result: it was below the level of detection, indicating that her experimental triple combination had eliminated virtually all HIV in her bloodstream.

I explained to Cindy that she was not alone in having her immune system restored to a normal level and the virus disappear from her blood. It did not mean she was cured—virus was likely lurking in her lymph nodes, being produced at extremely low levels and contained by the three drugs from spilling into her circulation. Moreover, we did not yet know how long the benefit of the triple combination would last or whether side effects might occur with long-term use of the drugs. The virus was a wily opponent. In the past it had mutated to escape from our therapies, so we had to be alert to any changes in these laboratory tests or in her clinical status.

Despite this caution, we should celebrate the triumph. It was an advance that had never been seen with any of our former therapies in my fifteen years of treating people with AIDS. It supported what I had been predicting these past three years, that research would ultimately change the nature of this illness, that there was real hope.

I felt a sense of embarrassed relief that the visit would end on a very positive note, without the emotional turmoil of the preceding one. Cindy's first words after her examination proved me wrong.

"I'm going to adopt a baby."

I tried to hide my reaction, which was one of shock, and sat dumbfounded.

"You don't like it, do you, Jerry?"

She waited for a reply. I was still mute, and shifted uncomfortably in my seat. Cindy shrugged and went on.

"I can understand why. You're thinking, 'Is she crazy? What kind of mother can she be if she gets sick? Who will take care of the baby if she gets AIDS and dies?' "

I nodded, agreeing that these thoughts were coursing through my mind.

"But I've thought it all through. I have a plan. And I'm going ahead. In a few months, Dr. Weksler and I will fly to Slovakia to an orphanage and come home with a new baby boy. Here's his picture."

Cindy reached into her jacket pocket and withdrew a small snapshot of a newborn, with dark black hair like hers and a soft olive complexion. He was beautiful.

"I've told Lena I have HIV and I'm going to adopt. I told her no more questions. She will just have to accept what I am going to do and be a loving grandmother."

Cindy paused as her eyes became moist.

"I'm going to name him Max, after my father."

All I could think to say was that I had named my first son after my father as well, that it had meant a great deal to me to know that his name was now carried by my child. I reached for Cindy's hands and asked her to explain her plan in greater detail.

She looked uncertainly at me, and slowly her face relaxed. Assured of my sincerity, she eagerly took up the conversation.

Cindy explained that she had left our last appointment devastated. She returned to New York feeling so distraught that she had not gone to work for the rest of the week. She had stayed home and cried most of the time. She wanted to be a mother, and could not foresee a life without children. If her condition meant that she could not have children of her own, now or in the near future, then she had to find another option. After her week of crying at home, she had thought of the one option that I had failed to present, the option that made sense to her. She would adopt a child.

She had thought through all the scenarios, and had come in for today's appointment not knowing if I would agree with her decision. But she was determined to go ahead, regardless of my opinion.

She guessed that she would live at least five to ten years more. That was a conservative estimate based on everything I had told her about these newest anti-HIV medications. Adding other experimental drugs to the triple combination might give her more time, optimistically another five years. So she would be a mother until her child was at least five or ten years old, perhaps even fifteen.

She decided it was only justified, given her expected life span, to adopt a newborn who otherwise would enter a life of neglect and suffering. The orphanage in Slovakia was a state-run facility, poorly staffed and anxious to have its unwanted children adopted by affluent people outside the country who could provide a proper home. None of the basic elements—food, shelter, clothing, education, or love—were assured for abandoned children in the orphanage.

There was no requirement about HIV testing. You didn't have to be married. The only medical question asked was whether the parent or parents were currently healthy, and hadn't I told Cindy that her immune system had been restored to normal levels and she had no clinical effects of her virus?

I started to interject, but she cut me off with a wave of her hand.

It *was* an entirely moral decision. She wasn't forced to lie about anything. And it was moral for a more important reason. She would be a good mother. How many children had mothers who were alcoholic, or drug addicts, or physically and emotionally abusive? Weren't those mothers far worse for a child than someone like her? And hadn't I made the analogy to diabetes? Would everyone raise their eyebrows and object if a woman with diabetes got pregnant or, if unable to have her own child, went ahead and adopted?

Cindy paused and, hearing nothing from me, pressed on.

There were risks, but what in life didn't have risks? What was the worst thing that could happen? That she got sick and died? O.K., that was the worst scenario. Parents got killed in car accidents and plane crashes. They developed diseases like breast cancer and leukemia. They got shot in New York and Boston every day. In these cases, there was rarely a good backup plan. Who lives thinking they're going to die?

Cindy said she was at an advantage in this way. She knew she might die and her child would lose his mother. So she had arranged with Dr. Weksler and Lena to be the guardians of the child should she die. Neither was that old, both being in their early sixties, and still in good health. Jules Weksler had never had a child of his own, and if the worst came to pass, would help raise hers. It was not a perfect solution, but it was one that had a chance of working.

Cindy admitted that she was charting new territory, trying to structure things in ways that had no real precedent. But that was the only way to move ahead. She was no longer the passive, frightened girl who was terrified of dark shadows in her room. She still feared AIDS and all its misery, but she believed there would be less suffering if she had love in her life, the pure love of a mother returned by her child.

She would love her son with a special depth and intensity, because she knew that every day was a gift to them both, that her time in life was very finite, that even if I performed my medical magic, the odds were that finally she would get sick and die. But before then, a child, whose life in rural Slovakia would otherwise have been one of misery, would find himself in Huntington, Long Island, with a dedicated working mother who would cherish him as her own flesh and blood.

I sat in silence for a long time, watching the fire in Cindy's eyes slowly subside. She had made her case passionately. I still felt the power of the arguments she had marshaled.

But I continued to wonder about the child. Who could say that life in the orphanage in Slovakia was worse or better than growing up to see your mother wither and die from AIDS? Might her son one day feel angry and cheated that his mother had adopted him to fulfill her need of love and then abandoned him in death? What if Jules Weksler fell ill or accidentally died, and Cindy was too sick to work, what then? Could Lena alone support them all as an aging grandmother? Would Cindy still feel she had made the right decision when she became sick and realized she would be making her son an orphan again?

I could have gone on and on, pondering the risks and imperfections of her decision. But I knew it was of no significance. Cindy could not live without love, the love of a mother for her child, the love I had felt from my mother and the love my wife gave to our children. It was a love that one day might be lost, but that is always the risk we take in loving.

I would do everything I could to keep Cindy healthy and alive. I made that commitment to all my patients, but I felt the extra responsibility now of sustaining a life upon which a new life would depend. I would help Cindy live her dream, a dream that could not be deferred. Only time would tell if her decision was the right one, not only for her but for her son. Her first son, Max.

Matt

The world endures for the sake of the breath
of schoolchildren.

TALMUD TRACTATE SHABBAT 119B

DURING MY FELLOWSHIP TRAINING in blood diseases and cancer medicine I spent a year working at the Boston Children's Hospital. I made many friends among the staff there and, although I ultimately pursued adult medicine rather than pediatrics, always felt a close tie to the institution. It was no surprise then when, in the summer of 1989, my friend and colleague Dr. Marvin Samuels, a specialist in childhood leukemia at the hospital, called me for help on his patient Matthew Jenkins.

"It's the first case like this we've encountered, and you have expertise in both his problems," Marv explained.

I readily agreed to care for Matt in conjunction with Marv. Later that day, I walked the two blocks to the Children's Hospital, read the voluminous medical record, and then sat into the evening with Matt's father, Billy Jenkins, and listened to the story of his son.

On a sultry August afternoon in 1984, Matt fell hard on the rough concrete of the St. Sebastian's schoolyard after missing a poorly aimed football. His knee just wouldn't stop bleeding. A friend removed Matt's Larry Bird T-shirt and tied it tightly over the scrape, but the blood quickly soaked through the cloth and filled his right sock and sneaker. The eight-year-old hobbled home with the help of his friends, leaving behind a trail of irregular red sneaker prints.

Matt opened the door and collapsed on the rug in the foyer. Billy rushed in from the kitchen and quickly assessed the situation. A tall wiry laborer who daily carried heavy packages of baked goods, he deftly lifted his bleeding son and laid him in the back of his delivery van. Honking his way through red lights down Harvard Street to Longwood Avenue, Billy reached the emergency room of Boston's Children's Hospital from his home in Brighton in less than fifteen minutes.

Matt arrived pale and faint. His pulse was thready and his blood pressure so low it was difficult for the intern to measure. An intravenous line was quickly inserted into a flaccid vein in his arm and saline infused. Soon a bag of red blood cells was hanging like a bloated sausage from a steel pole at Matt's bedside.

As the blood dripped into Matt, his body arched in a tense convulsion and he vomited. Billy Jenkins had to hold his ground next to his son as a team of doctors and nurses pulled at Matt's limbs, injected medicines into the intravenous line, positioned the boy's chin, and pushed a thin plastic cylinder down his airway.

Billy told me that he could not erase this scene from his memory. It often appeared in his sleep. It would be played either quickly or slowly, like a rented video: fast forward; play; slow rewind; fast forward again. He would pass through this scene and then freeze on a later single frame: the intern's soft fleshy hand clutching a small white slip of paper with a column of hieroglyphics from the hospital's hematology laboratory:

WBC 102,600
HCT 20
PLT 5,000
MORPH: BLASTS

"WBC" stands for white blood cells. The normal range in our bloodstream is 4,500 to 11,000, so that Matt's count of 102,600 was dramatically elevated. "HCT" indicates hematocrit, the measure of red blood cells. Matt's hematocrit of 20 signified a severe anemia, normal being 40 to 48. "PLT" is an abbreviation for platelets. A normal platelet count ranges from 150,000 to 400,000; severe bleeding often occurs with a count as low as Matt's. And "MORPH" refers to the morphology or appearance of the patient's cells. The blasts seen in Matt's blood signify primitive blood cells not normally present in our circulation.

Parents of children like Matt are quickly forced to learn this new language of blood tests and disease. When versed in its vocabulary and grammar, they become translators—in Billy's case as a widower, interpreting the medical jargon alone for his brother, Andrew; his elderly mother, Mary; and his boyhood friend, Father Daley.

Matt was given twenty units of platelets before the bleeding stopped. He required eight units of red blood cells to restore his hematocrit to normal.

After Matt was clinically stable, he was transferred to the intensive care unit. He was placed on a respirator, which assured adequate delivery of oxygen, and was administered Dilantin, a medication to prevent further seizures. The saline and blood products returned his blood pressure to the normal range. His care was assumed by Marv Samuels.

A short, soft-spoken man with a thick pepper-and-salt beard, Marv appears much older than his forty-five years. That first day, it was Marv who communicated the diagnosis to Billy Jenkins, standing with his family and Father Daley in the jaundice yellow twilight of the ICU waiting room.

"Mr. Jenkins, your son has leukemia."

I have stood countless times, as Marv Samuels did that day, looking into the faces of a family and telling them that their loved one has cancer. You steel yourself for the moment. You lock tightly within your heart the pain that comes with your knowledge of the reality of the disease, its devastation of body and spirit. You block from your mind's eye the projected images of months of torturous chemotherapy that lie ahead. You calm your face and maintain a firm voice, so that while you tell the family the truth, that the disease is aggressive and its treatment toxic, you simultaneously assert another truth, that there is a chance, a real chance, that the cancer can be defeated and the loved one saved.

With this compassionate but determined show of force, you prevent the family and the patient from being overwhelmed by the ferocious surprise attack of the illness. Yes, you emphasize again that a cure is never assured. But once this is said, you move decidedly from despair to hope. You have to show that the battle already has been engaged, that you are the general of the army, that there is a strategy in place, that powerful weapons are in hand, and that no mercy will be shown the enemy. And as you mobilize your resources, of medical science and clinical experience, to fight to save this person, you look hard into the eyes of the family and search for the core of their strength. You need to find this, to nurture it, because it will be sorely tested in the months to come. You need to understand this inner strength, where it comes from, how deep and resilient it is. Once you find and comprehend it, you try to take it in your hand and fuse it with your own, because together this creates the unified force required to sustain the patient through the hell that awaits and to carry him back to normal life.

As Marv Samuels finished describing the nature of Matt's leukemia and the treatment that lay ahead, Billy struggled to draw on the wellspring of his strength: his faith. But, like most parents at this moment, all he sensed was shock and disbelief. He turned to his mother, Mary. She grasped Billy's thick-callused hands in hers, and whispered, "Christ in His mercy loves Matty. He is a good boy, the best boy. The Almighty will save him."

"Matt's a trouper, he is. Just like his old man. With God's help he'll make it," Billy's older brother, Andrew, offered.

Father Daley asked that they all pray.

As Father Daley spoke, Billy dropped slowly to his knees. The events in the emergency room played in his mind again. He pressed his hands together in a powerful upward arc and begged God to make Matt better.

"LEUKEMIA" IS A TERM derived from the Greek, meaning "white blood." The word was introduced into medicine in 1847 by Rudolf Virchow, the noted German pathologist. Virchow observed enormous numbers of white cells in the blood of a dying patient. His report stated that the origin of the acute "leukemia" was unclear. One hundred and fifty years later, the precise cause of this cancer of the white blood cells is still unknown.

Leukemia arises following mutation of the genetic program of a *single* white blood cell. How do such mutations arise? Radiation and chemical toxins can cause widespread damage to DNA and predispose to leukemic mutations in some cases. Certain inherited genetic abnormalities, such as Down's syndrome, increase the likelihood of leukemia as well. But in Matt's case, as in the majority of children with acute leukemia, no environmental or inherited factor could be identified.

Regardless of the setting, the behavior of the leukemic cell is that of a pernicious sociopath. The mutation in the genetic blueprint radically changes the temperament of a normally courteous white cell. The transformed primitive white cell, called a "leukemic blast," becomes grandiose and aggressive. It grows without restraint in the bone marrow, inconsiderate of the needs of its fellow blood cells. The marrow is soon congested with the bullying leukemic blasts. The normal blood cells are crowded out and fail to develop.

But the leukemic white cells are not satisfied with simply overrunning the bone marrow and elbowing out their normal brethren. They are like a gang of punks on a wilding spree, and race through the bloodstream, invading and damaging vital organs like the liver and brain.

Despite our incomplete understanding of why the genetic mutations occur and exactly how they result in leukemia, the disease in children is now often cured by combination chemotherapy. The conquest of childhood leukemia stands as one of the cardinal achievements of modern oncology. It is the paradigm of how years of painstaking laboratory research can ultimately be translated into a clinical therapy that changes a uniformly fatal disease into one that can be cured. This triumph provides me with hope and inspiration when I daily face so many still incurable afflictions.

THE DAY OF MATT'S FALL in the St. Sebastian playground, Randy Johnston had returned to work after a week on the Cape. I came to meet Randy many years later and heard his story as I conducted his medical interview in my office. That summer of 1984, Randy had just turned twenty-one and was studying accounting at Bentley College in Waltham. He supported himself by driving a taxi in Boston. Tall and athletic, he had a thick mane of black hair that tumbled boyishly over his wire-frame glasses. He lived with his boyfriend, Jay, an insurance underwriter for a large Connecticut firm that had its branch office just a few blocks from their apartment in Boston's Back Bay. Jay was only the second man that Randy had ever been with, and he felt this relationship was likely to be lifelong.

Randy, although regularly propositioned, had no taste for the fast-track scene in the gay bars and baths. The idea of having sex with someone he didn't know turned him off. He wanted affection with his love, and that feeling didn't come with anonymity.

On that first day back at work, Randy had dropped off a saleswoman from a medical device company at the Red Cross building in Kenmore Square, and decided to look for a water fountain inside. The radio had said it was 94 degrees at three o'clock. The drink rejuvenated him. As he walked down the corridor to leave, he noticed a sign soliciting blood donations. He decided that he should donate. He was young and healthy, he thought, and his blood would help some patient in need.

Randy sat before the talkative blond Red Cross technician who gave him a small number 2 pencil and asked him to read carefully the list of questions and then check off his answers in the small boxes under YES and NO. No, he had never had hepatitis. No, he had not been sick recently. No, he had never had syphilis or any other sexually transmitted disease. No, he had never been told he was anemic. No, he was not from Haiti. No, he was not a *promiscuous* homosexual man with *multiple* partners. Jay was his second lover, and Randy was teased by his friends for being so sexually conservative.

After the blood was donated, apple juice and graham crackers were offered by the same smiling blond technician who had taken his interview form. She sat close to Randy and chatted with great animation, her knees occasionally brushing against his. She asked Randy where he lived, what he liked to do for fun. Randy answered in a politely cool voice, not offering any more than was asked and not returning her questions with queries of his own. He was used to this misdirected interest from women. After a second glass of apple juice, she pressed two more graham crackers in Randy's hand for the road, and reluctantly returned to her post.

Randy's blood passed the screen of tests at the Red Cross for hepatitis and syphilis. The red blood cells were separated from the platelets. Each component was sent to the Children's Hospital. The blood bank had called earlier that day alerting the Kenmore center to its dangerously low inventory of blood products. A Red Cross van loaded Randy's blood, along with a dozen or so other units collected that afternoon, in a brown cardboard box filled with Styrofoam. The blood bags bounced gently along the short route from the Kenmore center up Brookline Avenue to Longwood Avenue and the Children's Hospital. Randy was O negative, a relatively rare type, as was Matthew Jenkins. It was Randy Johnston's blood that helped restore Matt to life that day in the emergency room.

THE EIGHTEEN MONTHS OF MATT'S TREATMENT passed very slowly for Billy Jenkins. Matt was in and out of the hospital. He didn't have the usual type of childhood leukemia, called "lymphoblastic," which is most readily cured. Matt had the more aggressive and resistant myeloblastic kind.

Matt received a tightly choreographed succession of toxic drugs, each with a different mechanism of action against the leukemia but each with deleterious effects on his normal tissues. Adriamycin: the cranberry-colored infusion that, while shattering the DNA of the leukemic cells, removed all Matt's hair and weakened his growing heart. Ara-C: deceptively clear and transparent but responsible for ulcerating Matt's mouth and damaging his cerebellum, the balance center in the brain, while interfering with the reproduction of the blasts. 6-TG: yet another toxic weapon against the blasts' reproductive machinery that also inflamed Matt's liver. The blast count, which was initially greater than 100,000, gradually fell with each round of this chemotherapy.

In addition to his antileukemic drugs, Matt received multiple antibiotics to combat infections, nausea medicines to control the vomiting induced by the chemotherapy, and nutritional supplements for his weight loss. These supportive therapies had been systematically developed over the past decade. They were essential to minimize the complications of the disease and the chemotherapy, and significantly increased Matt's chances of survival.

Matt was known to the medical staff as a reserved, stoical boy. As he underwent the leukemia treatment, he took to wearing a bright green Celtics cap over the moonscape of his bald head. A few thin strands of his dark brown hair had heroically resisted the toxic assault of the chemotherapy. Matt would consent to take his hat off only to be examined, telling the staff he wore it because he liked to be on a winning team.

In helping patients cope with the suffering of such intensive toxic treatment, the staff try to identify those things that amuse and distract the person over the long weeks in the hospital. In Matt's case, along with the numerous comics, video games, and puzzles, the nurses and his family assembled a team of miniature plastic Red Sox figures, which were kept on the table next to his bed. During the worst of it, lying on his side for hours with dry heaves from the chemotherapy, his contracted stomach long since empty of the saltines and apple juice he had tried vainly to keep down, he would look at the plastic figures and weakly move them around an imaginary baseball diamond. The nurses would try to engage Matt by prompting him to report the statistics from his imaginary games—how many RBIs, errors, home runs.

Billy told me he felt as if he lived those months in the hospital as well. Mostly he sat quietly at Matt's side. Sometimes he read aloud from the *Herald*, reporting to Matt on the progress of the 1984 seasons of the Red Sox and the Celtics. Wade Boggs was on his way to setting a new record for the Sox for most hits in one season. The Celtics were hot, and it looked like Larry Bird might be the NBA's MVP two years in a row. Billy took this as a good omen for Matt.

Father Daley came regularly and was like a second parent to Matt. He was well known at the hospital and joked with the nurses and ward clerks, many of whom were also from Brighton. Father Daley informed Matt of the scores from late games of the previous night, and together they debated the strengths and weaknesses of the competing teams.

Dr. Samuels would arrive each afternoon in Matt's room on rounds with a team of interns, residents, medical students, and pharmacists. It is a ritual of every senior physician. It allows you to hear the clinical status from the assembled team while probing the emotional state of the patient and his family. It is a show of force, a concrete display of the commitment of a large, expert, and dedicated group to the care of a single ill person. For patients with leukemia like Matt, the senior physician often begins rounds by asking the intern on the case to state the leukemic blast count in the blood as an index of the efficacy of the ongoing treatment. Billy told me how he anxiously awaited this daily countdown, how each morning before rounds he would pray it had fallen to zero.

It required three intensive courses of chemotherapy before the leukemic blast count in the bloodstream was zero. Billy wondered aloud if God had heard his prayers.

Dr. Samuels explained that before they were certain the leukemia had been eradicated, Matt needed to undergo another bone marrow exam to make sure the blasts were not lurking there. Billy recounted to me how, before the marrow biopsy, Matt prepared himself for the pain by bitterly describing it to his father.

"They make me lay on my stomach and then they shoot Novocain right into my butt. Then the intern pushes a gigantic needle into my back. I can feel that needle crash into my bone and it makes pain shoot down my legs. Then the doctor pulls on the syringe attached to the needle to suck out the marrow, and it hurts so bad I think I'm going to pass out. It's awful and I have to stay still and I can't do anything about it."

Marv Samuels told me how, two days after the bone marrow exam, he came into Matt's room with a quick step, almost out of breath, raised his right hand and triumphantly demanded: "Matt, give me a high five!"

He told Matt he felt like a Celtic who had just nailed a three-pointer and it was nothing but net with two seconds left on the shot clock to win the game. It was like that. He explained to Matt and Billy that the marrow had no blasts at all, and the blood cells that were recovering after the battering of the chemotherapy looked normal.

I know how Marv Samuels felt at that moment. It is a moment of unique relief and of exhilaration. The relief comes as the burden of the battle is lifted. You savor a sweet exhaustion from the months of struggle that finally have yielded victory. During those months, you focused with an intensity that was almost superhuman, because your goal was perfection. You were laboring at the border of life, and knew that one inadvertent error could result in your patient being pulled to the other side by the unrelenting hand of his illness. So you tried to control every treatment variable and follow every clinical parameter, you checked and rechecked your strategy and decisions countless times, straining to give every possible advantage to your science to triumph over its adversary, disease. You knew that despite this, there was no guarantee of success, that even the correct therapies and best care were not certain to save the patient. That is the simple truth of medicine: the inexact nature of biological events and their treatments means there is an element of mystery to the process of cure. Until the very last second, you remain vigilant and worried that the life of the patient may be wrenched from your hands.

But it is not just relief that impels your joy. There is magic and intimacy in the moment when death appears defeated. It envelops the patient and his doctor in an almost mystical embrace. A powerful force, the force of reclaimed life, flows between you. At the moment of cure, it is as if all the energy invested in your patient during the arduous months of treatment is returned in an electric current of love and gratitude that potently repletes your fatigued being.

Matt had to go through three more intensive cycles of chemotherapy, and then six months of maintenance treatment. Leukemic cells are devious and like to hide. The prolonged treatment regimen was designed to eliminate every leukemic blast, and was necessary if the cure everyone now expected was to be achieved.

It would take five years of monitoring, blood tests, and physical exams, and occasional bone marrow exams, to be sure it was gone. But with these caveats, Marv Samuels informed the family that the chances were *excellent* that the leukemia would never reappear.

When Matt came home after his last intensive course of chemotherapy, there was a celebration at the Jenkinses' home off Gordon Road. There were cold cuts from the Polish delicatessen on Winship Street, mountains of sliced rye and trays of pastries from Billy's bakery, and a plastic trash can filled with ice in which bottles of beer and soda were buried. The house was jammed with neighbors, Matt's teachers from St. Sebastian, his nurses from Children's, and Dr. Samuels. Father Daley offered a prayer of thanksgiving.

The ensuing year was a hard one for Matt. He had lost a considerable amount of weight and nearly all of his muscle tone. He spent three afternoons a week at physical therapy to accelerate the return of his strength. There were residual toxicities from the high doses of chemotherapy. He had a mild tremor and difficulty coordinating fine movement. His therapist gave him special exercises to teach Matt how to compensate for this. His hair grew back, lighter and silky, like when he was a toddler. His skin regained its pink hue.

Matt returned to his former life profoundly changed in character. He had acquired a unique perspective. Even the most ordinary things in his day took on deep significance: eating breakfast without nausea and the fear of vomiting; ending the morning without a needle being stuck into his arm to take blood tests; sleeping in his own familiar bed rather than the never-comfortable one in the hospital. Their substance and pleasure were felt in ways unknown except to those who thought they might never return. Matt understood that he now was different from his friends. He felt distant from many of the seemingly childish diversions that occupied their attention.

These initial feelings of reclaimed joy waned over time and were replaced by a profound anxiety. Matt's life had been defined and structured by his disease—the visits to the doctor, the schedule of chemotherapy and preventive antibiotics, the forgiving indulgence of his moods by friends and family. There had been a paradoxical comfort in that defined life, even if it had been dictated in the painful terms of illness.

Matt had to learn to function in a world that no longer focused on him exclusively throughout the day. He had to begin to rebuild his inner life upon a new foundation formed by his experience of severe illness. Despite Matt's accelerated maturity, he was anxious, unsure where to find the mortar and tools to reconstruct his life.

Billy understood this, and saw how it caused marked swings in Matt's moods. Matt would be angry at one moment and withdrawn the next. Billy tried to help Matt, but his son kept him at arm's length, feeling he needed to persevere on his own. Matt was coming into his teens, and the psychologist at the leukemia clinic informed Billy that this was a normal and necessary reaction.

Like many patients after a traumatic illness, Matt kept a memento of his life in the hospital. He had framed and mounted in his bedroom a picture of himself taken in the middle of his chemotherapy: Celtics cap jauntily cocked on his bald head, an almost mango hue to his sunken jaundiced eyes, his lips cracked and red from raw ulcers, but a defiant grin challenging the camera. Matt told his father that he used the picture to strengthen himself. When he was feeling low about how far behind he had fallen in his schoolwork, distressed by his weak and unsteady throwing arm, by the trouble his feet seemed to have in staying on the pedals of his bike, he would meditate on this photograph, like a priest before the cross. He would think how he had virtually died and was resurrected. The current frustrations then seemed small to Matt compared with the vomiting and the diarrhea and the bone marrow examinations and the fevers and the hair loss and all the other miseries that had become his regular companions during the months of intensive chemotherapy for his leukemia. Matt gradually came to believe that he had the resources and ability to construct a new life. As his physical functioning improved, his feelings of anger and anxiety slowly subsided. He told

Billy he knew he was fortunate to be alive, and would eventually be as strong and active as his friends.

Despite Matt's feelings of gratitude for his return to health, church and prayer became a point of contention between him and his father. Matt respected his father's wishes and finally compromised. He would have to go to mass only every other Sunday. Matt told Billy that before his illness he had liked church. There had been a beauty and mystery to the mass. He had looked forward to the childish bribe of a chocolate bar in Sunday school if you didn't fidget too much when the nun recounted stories from the scriptures. But that all seemed false and empty to Matt now.

Father Daley responded that God had been good to Matt, that His love had been extended through the hands of the doctors and the nurses. But it just didn't make sense. Matt asked Billy and Father Daley why God had given him the leukemia in the first place. Father Daley said the righteous suffer, and that earns them a place in the kingdom of heaven. But Matt replied that he wasn't righteous, certainly not a saint, just a regular ten-year-old boy in Brighton, Massachusetts. And why did he have to suffer to get into heaven, anyway? Father Daley explained that man did not know the answer to that question, only God. Matt decided that until his unanswered question was addressed, he was unable to believe.

Three years passed. The visits to Dr. Samuels became less frequent. Matt's blood tests were fine. His strength and coordination became almost normal. Despite all the chemotherapy, he had entered puberty and was developing well. Matt talked less about suffering and God. His breath was spent on discussing sports with Billy and Father Daley, and sports and girls with his neighborhood friends.

Matt also found he was interested in learning. He threw himself into his studies at school, and caught up on what had been missed during his illness. His grades were excellent, and the teachers informed Billy that Matt had the intelligence and drive to get into a good college, perhaps even one in the Ivy League. It seemed that life in the Jenkinses' home had regained its order, its purpose, its promise.

THE FRIDAY BEFORE THE FOURTH OF JULY, 1989, Billy decided to quit work early to take Matt to see *Naked Gun*. It was an intensely hot, dry day, and he stopped at the Star Market to pick up

Gatorade for his son. Despite the heat, Matt would spend the day playing in the schoolyard at St. Sebastian's. He had taken to basketball, using his increasing height and his determination as a skilled center under the boards.

Billy Jenkins drove by the schoolyard and saw a game in progress, but Matt wasn't there. It was not like Matt to miss a Friday afternoon basketball game.

Billy entered the house carrying the two jugs of Gatorade. The lights were on in the living room.

"Matt. Matt. You in there?" he yelled toward the closed door of the bedroom.

No answer.

Billy opened the door and saw Matt napping, deeply asleep with his face down on the bed. He roughly massaged Matt's shoulders with his muscular hands.

Matt did not respond. Billy rolled him over, and noticed Matt's jaw slacken and his mouth fall open. His eyes half opened, the lids falling back from the weak pull of gravity. His breathing was slow and deep, his forehead hot, and his face flushed. There was a collection of thick mucus at the corner of his mouth. His limbs were completely limp, and his pajama pants smelled of urine.

Billy told me that he felt he was in another video, fast forward this time.

He picked up his son in his long, powerful arms and ran to the van. Driving at breakneck speed, Billy almost hit a car in the intersection at Coolidge Corner. A police car turned on its siren and chased him down Longwood Avenue. Billy didn't stop until he reached the Children's Hospital.

The cop leaped from his car. Billy ignored him, running to open the back door of the van and then quickly lifting out his flaccid son. Matt's breathing was forced and very deep, like someone snoring.

"My kid. He's sick. He's sick," he yelled to the policeman as the automatic doors of the emergency entrance rapidly opened.

The medical team immediately put in a large intravenous line and infused saline into Matt's body. The intern inserted an endotracheal tube down his throat, and oxygen was pumped into his lungs. A nurse announced that Matt's temperature was 104.5 degrees. Billy took up his vigil in the corner of the room. The intern informed Billy that his son was in a coma and required an urgent spinal tap to determine why.

Billy watched breathlessly from the corner of the room as the intern guided the spinal needle into Matt's back. Soon drops of viscous, cloudy spinal fluid fell slowly from the open head of the needle into a sterile collecting tube below.

"Meningitis," the intern said, not turning his head but still addressing the observation to Billy. "Your son has some form of meningitis."

Billy was too shocked to respond.

All parents who grew up in the 1940s, like Billy, had heard the word "meningitis" in sentences like "The poor kid, he went so fast, it was *meningitis*. They couldn't do anything for him."

Meningitis signifies an infection of the membranous covering of the brain and spinal cord called the "meninges." Although still an infection of grave severity, the advent of antibiotics in the post–World War II era has made childhood meningitis due to bacteria curable in many cases. Meningitis caused by fungi or tuberculosis is much more difficult to cure.

Some children develop meningitis as a random event. In Matt's case, the occurrence of this infection could have heralded a relapse of his leukemia with invasion of the blasts into his central nervous system. Alternatively, the meningitis might have developed because of a lingering defect in his immune defenses. Matt's immune function had been lowered first by his leukemia and then by the toxic chemotherapy necessary to eradicate it.

The specimens of spinal fluid were sent to the hospital laboratory for a battery of tests and cultures. Portions were first studied under the microscope for bacteria, fungus, and tuberculosis organisms and then cultured for these microbes. A special fixative solution was added to another tube of spinal fluid to preserve any floating cells; this sample was sent to the pathologist to be examined for leukemic blasts.

Matt was placed on broad-spectrum antibiotics that penetrated well into the central nervous system to empirically treat a presumed bacterial meningitis until the tests on the spinal fluid revealed the causative microbe. A cooling blanket was placed under his flushed body to reduce his fever. Still comatose, he was transferred to the intensive care unit and placed on a respirator.

Billy Jenkins stood by Matt's bedside and made an effort to control the speeding thoughts and images that rioted in his brain like wild crossfire in a night battle. He later recalled how he recovered from his initial shock and felt a growing wave of fury move up from his belly into his chest and then down his arms. He wanted to smash his fists hard against the white plastered wall, and then smash again and again until the wall was destroyed.

Two hours passed. Billy's thoughts slowed and his muscles began to relax. He felt almost hypnotized, watching Matt's chest expand and contract in response to the push of air coming from the respirator. Matt's eyes were now fully closed, and he seemed peaceful. Billy felt he had to put the anger aside for the moment and focus on practical issues.

Billy called his brother, Andrew, from the nurses' station in the ICU and asked him to contact the rest of the family, except for their mother, Mary. He would call her himself and try to keep her calm by explaining that there were effective antibiotics for meningitis. Andrew should try Father Daley, too, although he might be at dinner and not in the parish rectory. Billy couldn't decide whether or not he wanted to pray with Father Daley right now anyway.

Dr. Samuels described to me the scene in the ICU that evening when he informed Billy of the cause and poor prognosis of Matt's condition. It was a scene I had lived many times, and it never lost its painful and emotionally draining intensity.

Matt had an unusual and often fatal form of meningitis, caused by a fungus called *Cryptococcus neoformans*. It is an organism usually found in pigeon droppings.

"Pigeon shit!" Billy had exclaimed. He told Marv Samuels that Matt didn't have any pigeons for pets. Of course there were pigeons all over Boston. But that would mean that everyone should get it.

Billy was correct in that *Cryptococcus neoformans* is ubiquitous. This fungus normally does not cause disease in healthy people. It is a pathogen when given the opportunity by impaired immune defenses. That is why cryptococcal meningitis is termed an "opportunistic infection."

A powerful antibiotic against the fungus, amphotericin B, was given to Matt, in conjunction with a second agent, 5-FC, that boosted the effect of amphotericin. Nonetheless, to effectively eradicate the aggressive fungus, these antibiotics needed to work in conjunction with Matt's immune system.

The immune system has two major arms. One arm is made up of antibodies, and is called the "humoral immune system." The other is composed of T cells and macrophages that form the "cellular im-mune system." Cryptococcal meningitis occurs as an opportunistic infection when cellular immunity is impaired, when the T cells and macrophages are unable to recognize the fungus as a foreign invader and eliminate it from the body. One of the causes of impaired cellu-lar immunity is HIV infection, Dr. Samuels explained, and Matt needed to be tested for this virus. A parent's written permission was required by law to perform the test. Dr. Samuels had brought the consent form for Billy to sign.

Billy told me he was confused by Dr. Samuels's request. He had thought of AIDS as a disease of "queer guys and addicts." Matt had just gone through puberty. He liked *girls*. And he didn't use drugs. He hated needles after getting stuck so much when he had leukemia. Why would Dr. Samuels bring up the issue of AIDS in a kid like Matt?

Marv Samuels had listened to Billy's reaction without interrupting him and then patiently explained that AIDS is a viral disease. And one way HIV, the AIDS virus, is transmitted is by transfusion of blood from an infected donor. Matt had received a large number of blood products in the last five years. Matt's first transfusion had oc-curred on August 31, 1984. He had received a total of sixty-six units of platelets and nineteen units of packed red blood cells during the ensuing months *before* all blood donations in the United States were tested for HIV. He *could* have contracted HIV during that window of time between the discovery of the virus in 1984 and the develop-ment of a reliable test in 1985.

Billy Jenkins heard Dr. Samuels's words and understood their lit-eral meaning. But more important was what he read in the doctor's eyes. Dr. Samuels thought Matt had AIDS.

Billy recounted to me how all his strength suddenly vanished. He was sinking, being pulled down into a murky darkness by the pow-erful undertow of his paralyzing realization. He had no will to resist.

Then hands were on his elbows, guiding him to a chair. Billy felt himself descend farther, his head bowed to the ground. It was diffi-cult to think. Dr. Samuels was saying things to him, but the words were hollow and hard to comprehend. Billy just wanted to leave his eyes closed and rest in the empty darkness, but was roused by water dripping down his face. Billy Jenkins realized that for the first time in five years he was crying.

The preliminary HIV test on Matthew Jenkins's blood was a so-called ELISA. The HIV proteins are first placed on the bottom of a small plastic well. Then the patient's serum is overlaid on the coated viral proteins. If antibodies against HIV are present in the patient's serum, the antibodies attach to the viral proteins and a chemical reaction occurs, generating a blue color in the well. If no antibodies against HIV are present, then there is no chemical reaction, and the well remains the yellow color of the viral proteins and uninfected serum. The well with Matthew Jenkins's serum turned a deep navy blue.

It was then that Marv Samuels contacted me and asked if I would care for Matt in conjunction with him. It was the first instance of transfusion AIDS in a cancer patient at the Children's Hospital. Given my expertise both in AIDS and in leukemia, Marv felt I was needed as a consultant in this complex and tragic case.

As I entered the ICU to examine Matt, I saw Billy seated at the bedside, stroking his son's pallid hand. Matt lay like a mannequin, his eyes closed with tape to prevent drying and ulcers, his mouth closed around the tube of the respirator. For a moment the constant noise of an intensive care unit, the whoosh of the respirators, the shrill beep of the monitors, the charged voices of the nurses and the doctors, vanished. There was a space of silence filled by the intense bond of love evident between father and son, a bond that I feared would soon be severed as AIDS took Matt from this world.

I stood quietly for several moments before Billy noticed me. I took the time to do what was required of me as a physician, as Marv Samuels had done some five years before. I removed from my mind's eye the image of father and son embraced by death, an image whose pain threatened to shatter my heart.

I introduced myself to Billy by taking his hand into mine, so that for a long moment he was released from Matt and could feel the determined strength of my grip. I told him that I was an expert in both leukemia and AIDS, that I not only cared for patients but directed a large research effort, and that every possible treatment that might help Matt would be undertaken. I, with Marv Samuels, would take responsibility for the care of his son. I told him that I had two sons of my own, and that I understood a father's love as he did. That was the most I could allow myself at that moment without opening up the locked compartment in my soul and releasing its devastating contents.

I explained in a deliberate tone what tests needed to be done, what decisions still needed to be made. Billy strained to focus and understand my words, seemingly unable to assimilate the reality of his son lying in a deep coma, struck down by the insidious hand of AIDS. I repeated what I said but sensed little was really absorbed.

My words and approach differed importantly from those I use when there is a genuine chance of cure. They were honest and determined but more modulated than those Billy had heard in the beginning of the battle against Matt's leukemia. I wanted to communicate to Billy that we were now in a war of attrition. The hope, I informed him, was to regain territory for Matt, to restore some level of functioning. I needed Billy to understand that success would be measured short of the victory of cure. We were trying to negotiate a temporary truce with death. While we were prepared to bargain on hard terms, putting all our scientific expertise and resources into buying precious time, in the end we would be forced to cede. This awful truth had to be painfully but honestly revealed in order for Billy to begin the process of preparing himself to endure the ultimate loss of Matt.

When I finished addressing the clinical plan with Billy, I encouraged him to tell me Matt's story, in detail, knowing that the process of retelling can be one more way that the reality of the situation is accepted.

MY LABORATORY FIRST CONFIRMED the diagnosis of HIV from the ELISA test by performing a second, more definitive test called a "Western blot." Here, the various HIV proteins are separated according to their sizes on a special filter paper. The larger proteins are at the top of the paper and the smaller ones migrate to the bottom. The patient's serum is layered over the filter paper. If antibodies against HIV are present, they will bind to the viral proteins. Again, a developing solution is added, and a ladder of colored bands appears on the filter paper. Each rung in the ladder represents antibody attached to a specific viral protein of a certain size. A tall ladder with thick, colored rungs appeared when we layered Matt's serum over the filter paper. He definitely had AIDS.

To assess Matt's cellular immune status, we measured the number of circulating helper T cells. The helper T cell is a major component of cellular immunity and the primary target of HIV. It is estimated that, on average, about eighty helper T cells are lost per year due to HIV infection. This number comes from several prospective studies of cohorts of HIV-positive gay men in California and New York who volunteered to be monitored regularly. Presuming that Matt had a normal minimum baseline T-cell number of about 600 in 1984, we expected his helper T-cell number to be approximately 200 five years later. But the count was only 20.

Marv Samuels and I discussed Matt's surprisingly low T-cell number. It could have reflected the virulence of the particular HIV strain he received, his own genetics in handling the virus, and/or the devastating impact of contracting HIV at a time when his immune system was being suppressed by the chemotherapy. I thought this last mechanism was the most likely.

My research group previously had studied *adult* cancer patients who, like Matt, were transfused with HIV-contaminated blood during their treatment. The adult immune system seemed particularly sensitive to the destructive effects of HIV in the presence of toxic chemotherapy. It was likely that a child's would be similarly vulnerable. We also learned from these studies of adults that the medications needed to treat HIV, particularly AZT, were poorly tolerated in patients whose bone marrows had previously been exposed to chemotherapy.

We decided, though, that we had no choice, given the gravity of the situation and Matt's severely impaired immune system. We administered not one but two anti-HIV medications, AZT and ddI. We felt we could not rely on a single drug to reduce the amount of virus in his system.

Matt's blood counts fell because of the side effects of the antiviral treatment. We supported his marrow by giving him two newly available blood cell growth factors, erythropoietin and G-CSF. These growth factors boosted the production of his red cells and white cells, respectively. He did not need to be transfused. The development of these growth factors made that intervention unnecessary in 1989.

Despite the intensive antibiotic therapy for cryptococcal meningitis, the anti-HIV medications, and the supportive growth factors, the infection did not abate. Matt's repeat CAT scan revealed that the fungus was invading from the meninges into the brain tissue and forming multiple brain abscesses. His coma deepened. It seemed likely that we would lose him.

After three weeks, the consulting neurologist felt that even if Matt survived, he would have major motor and intellectual deficits. He informed Billy of his opinion. The neurologist further pointed out that Matt's coma was now so deep, he was unresponsive even to painful stimuli, and showed no signs of improvement.

Billy coped by flatly denying what he heard. He insisted to the neurologist that Matt often responded to his father's familiar voice, although what Billy observed was really just random reflex movement. He forcefully asserted to family, friends, and medical staff that Matt's "expert Harvard physicians," Marv Samuels and I, were going to find a way to save his son. Our most advanced medical science would miraculously cure Matt.

We tried to move Billy from this state of denial by candidly informing him of our limited therapeutic options, of Matt's deteriorating medical condition and prognosis. But our daily reports seemed to make little difference. It was painful to persist in trying to break his denial, but we knew that Billy had to begin to prepare himself inside for the loss of Matt. We feared that if he did not, if his denial continued to the end, he would be shattered by the powerful blow death strikes in its finality.

Billy slowly acknowledged that science would not provide a miracle, but he still expected one from his faith. He prayed fervently each morning and each night, saying the rosary, begging the Lord for Matt's life. He asked Father Daley to forward a request to the Cardinal to say special prayers for Matt's recovery. Billy told himself that a merciful God would not punish him by taking his beloved son from this world. He brought a Bible to the hospital and read from Scripture, recounting to Marv Samuels and me Jesus' miraculous healing of the lame, the blind, and the leprous, and the story of Lazarus' return from death to life. Billy affirmed once again that we were God's agents of healing, and that with His guidance, anything was possible.

I didn't know how to respond to him. I believed that God does provide man with the means to create miracles. The means are curiosity and intellect. The miracles are born from scientific research and discovery. The idea that Matt's leukemia could be cured when I was a child his age in the 1950s would have seemed a miracle. Marv Samuels and I could hope that one day we would create a miracle and cure a child of AIDS. But we knew that that child would not be Matt, and couldn't bring Billy to accept that.

So much pain and loss in God's world. I looked down at Matt in coma and, although knowing there was no answer, had to ask why. I did not picture an unknown afterlife to correct the injustices and to reward Matt's suffering in this life. I could not conceive of a beneficent God using disease as a perverse weapon of punishment for Matt's abandonment of his religion. So, like my rabbinic forebears, who seventeen centuries ago wrote the Talmud, and my familial forebears, who one generation ago survived the Holocaust, I stood confused, still stubborn in my faith but harshly questioning it in the midst of senseless suffering. Despite these feelings of bewilderment and doubt, I too prayed in my heart for God to help.

WHILE MATT LAY MOTIONLESS in coma, a team of physicians and epidemiologists quietly worked behind the scenes. In cases of transfusion of AIDS, it is standard practice to trace the source of the contaminated blood and determine if other recipients might have been infected. Among the many donors contacted and then tested for HIV by the Children's Hospital and the Red Cross, only one was found to be positive. He was the donor of Matt's second red cell transfusion. The donor was informed of his HIV status. It was Randy Johnston.

Randy had given blood on four occasions in 1984. Dr. Edward Leaf, the director of the regional Red Cross, proceeded to trace all the recipients of Randy's red blood cells and platelets. As usual, most of the recipients had died within a year of their transfusion from their underlying conditions: cancer, cardiac surgery, trauma, and so on. One surviving recipient, a man operated on for a ruptured aortic aneurysm, was identified. He proved to be HIV positive but asymptomatic.

I had a close scientific collaboration with Ed Leaf. We were working together on a project to characterize the rate of mutation that occurs when HIV is transmitted by blood transfusion. In addition to isolating the virus from the infected donor and recipient, detailed lifestyle data were collected on the donor as part of the research study.

Ed Leaf contacted me after he had interviewed Randy Johnston. He recounted the details of Randy's story and said Randy had consented to participate in the study.

The following week I met Randy. I repeated the medical interview as the study protocol dictated to confirm the accuracy of the epidemiological data collected. Randy reaffirmed that he had never used drugs, had never been transfused himself, and had had a monogamous relationship with his lover Jay for over five years. I obtained his consent to draw his blood to isolate and analyze his strain of virus and compare it to Matt's.

Randy was distraught, and said he hadn't slept in days.

"First I discover that I have HIV. Then I learn that while I thought I was doing a service by donating blood a few times, I infected other people." His hair was unkempt, he hadn't shaved, and he seemed on the verge of tears.

The fault lay not with Randy but with the donor questionnaire that the Red Cross had used in the early 1980s. It was seriously flawed, based on the prevalent presumption that AIDS was related to promiscuity and multiple sexual partners. Randy had answered the questionnaire honestly. I felt no anger toward him, only sadness to know how deeply guilty he felt and how one day he might face a death like Matt's.

Ed Leaf had referred Randy to the Fenway Health Center, an excellent community clinic near Randy's home in the Back Bay that was oriented to the medical and mental health needs of a largely young gay population. Randy would have considerable support services there and, he hoped, could better cope with his medical and emotional issues. I assured Randy that if I could help in his HIV therapy, now or in the future, I would.

MATT DID NOT IMPROVE. Sadly, there was nothing more to do. The fungus simply would not yield to our therapies. We followed his CAT scans and saw the multiple abscesses slowly expanding like balloons being blown up by small children at a party. The medical team was candid with Billy, but he persisted in ignoring our reports and ended each conversation with "I know with God's help Matt will be returned to me." I wished his words would be true, but knew that it would not be so.

I saw Billy every day at the hospital, holding his vigil next to Matt's bedside. We spoke at length after I reviewed Matt's medical condition. Billy found comfort in telling me detailed stories of Matt: his childhood without a mother present, his athletic abilities, how he had built himself back up after the chemotherapy, his recent interest in girls, his achievements in school and aspirations to attend college. As Billy spoke, Matt became more and more alive to me.

Billy also talked *to* Matt, recounting stories about Brighton in the 1940s, how he left school to join the navy, his courting of his mother, even the day she fell ill and passed away. He explained to the nurses and doctors who quietly watched this scene that Matt needed to know his past so that he would not make Billy's mistakes in the future. No one had the heart to harshly challenge his delusion beyond our honest reports on Matt's medical condition.

Matthew Joseph Jenkins died on the evening of August 23, 1989. Marv Samuels called me as I was preparing to leave the office. The conversation was brief. Matt's systems had been failing rapidly over the prior week, his kidney function declining, his lungs resisting the respirator, more of his brain tissue replaced by the expanding fungus.

I closed my eyes tightly for a long while after I heard the news. Although I knew that Matt was going to die, that everything had been done for him that could be done, I still felt a deep sense of failure, of guilt. We, his doctors, had failed Matt, unable to save his young life, a life that five years ago had passed through the shadow of death and returned to a promising future. We had also failed the living. Billy had believed in us, his son's "expert Harvard physicians," and this faith in our abilities had not been fulfilled. Our science was not miraculous enough to change reality. I reminded myself that we were not gods, not able to perform the instant miracles needed to cure an incurable disease. Still, I felt a profound sense of defeat, of loss.

Again I had to ask myself: Why Matt Jenkins? Why, after all he had gone through?

I opened my eyes. I again looked for an explanation from God that cannot be seen in the world around us. I knew that I wouldn't find one.

NO EXPLANATION, but a powerful response, came eight months later. It came from Billy. It arrived in the form of an invitation. On the third Sunday in April, beginning at two o'clock in the afternoon, the first fund-raising event of the Friends of Matt was to take place. A series of competitive athletic events was planned at

St. Sebastian's. Students would participate in relay races, basketball shooting, and distance football passing, followed by a baseball match between Matt's class and the teachers. Each team would be sponsored in the events: you checked off a pledge of ten, twenty-five, or fifty dollars on the reply card to the invitation.

The money raised would go to support special services for children with cancer or AIDS at the Children's Hospital: purchase of a second customized van to transport the physically disabled; accommodations for indigent families who lived far from Boston and needed to stay in town during their child's hospitalization; and subsidizing one child with AIDS and one with cancer to go to special summer camps in New Hampshire for boys and girls with these diseases.

Father Daley's parish would be holding a bingo game at twenty-five dollars a head following the athletic events. Refreshments were to be provided gratis by Billy's bakery. His employer had pledged $25,000, and the goal of the fund-raiser was to match this initial gift.

Enclosed with the invitation was an off-white button, the size of a silver dollar, which had a photo of Matt at its center. The picture was taken well after his recovery from leukemia. He appeared healthy, and was wearing his trademark Celtics cap and warmly smiling. In a semicircle crowning Matt's photo were the words FRIENDS OF MATT in bold black type.

It was clear and chilly that April day. Large cumulus clouds floated slowly across a sharp blue sky, alternately darkening and illuminating the pale concrete of the schoolyard as the sun was masked and then revealed. The towering chain fences enclosing the playground were decorated with maroon and gold streamers, the school colors. Posterboards with Matt's photograph created to promote the fund-raiser were hung on the side of the school building like icons at a shrine. Ladies from the PTA and Billy's fellow drivers from the bakery were stationed at tables loaded with sticky buns, M&M cookies, and chocolate chip muffins. There were pitchers of orange juice, cans of soda, bottles of Gatorade, and tall stainless-steel urns with perked coffee. Father Daley had set out wicker church collection baskets at each food station to hold the money paid for the refreshments.

Billy stood proudly at the corner of the schoolyard, orchestrating the event. He was in constant motion, signaling his fellow workers from the bakery that more pastries were needed at the tables, calling out for additional plastic cups for the drinks, instructing the novitiates from the Brighton rectory to gather the collected money and deposit it in Father Daley's strongbox inside the school.

There was a huge turnout in support of the event: nearly all the teachers and students from the school and their families; neighbors from Brighton who knew the Jenkinses or heard of the fund-raiser through the church; Marv Samuels and many nurses from the hospital; and several of the Red Cross technicians and scientists from my lab who were working on the research project in transfusion AIDS. Everyone wanted to show support, to demonstrate how deeply moved they were by this tragedy.

The schoolyard resonated with the sounds of people greeting one another, ordering food and drinks, debating the outcome of the baseball match, praising Billy's energy and skill in creating what appeared to be a successful first event. The excited shouts of the scurrying children formed brief bursts of steam as their breath condensed in the cold air.

I slowly walked to the corner of the schoolyard where Billy stood. I saw Matt in my mind's eye, lying in silent coma in the ICU, Billy seated at his bedside, stroking his son's pallid hand. I remembered Matt's wake, Billy standing silent next to the closed casket, not acknowledging the sympathies offered by neighbors and friends, a deep bitterness carved on his masklike face. I had tried to find a remnant of life in Billy's eyes, but they were cold and dead, his fixed gaze seeing through me and through all those around him as if we had ceased to exist.

Billy soon noticed me. He abruptly halted his orchestration and moved determinedly forward. We stood face to face. Billy offered a soft smile. He drew from his pocket the button with Matt's face and pinned it on my jacket. Tears filled our eyes. We embraced each other tightly like brothers. The hard metal of the button pressed deeply on my chest.

Billy had refused to let the disease that had taken his son also take from him his love of his son, his friends, his church, his community. He had forgiven me for failing, for not having the science to cure what was incurable. Billy would not rely on God to provide a miracle for all the other children suffering from cancer or AIDS. He would do everything he could to improve their lot in this imperfect world. That would be his form of prayer.

I sensed that Billy would always be there for me, that he had given me strength and courage, that his acts of kindness to help relieve the suffering of children like Matt would keep my heart from breaking. I had felt the undefeated force of life in Billy's arms, and knew that the breath of schoolchildren would be sustained, that our world would endure.

Debbie

DEBBIE THAYER WAS STRUGGLING to contain her pain. It was deep and visceral, coursing in powerful waves from the crests of her hips down into her legs. She moved cautiously in her chair, and finally found a position which, at least for a while, lessened the pressure on her bones. She exhaled a brief sigh of relief and wiped the perspiration from her pale forehead with a small cotton handkerchief.

I studied Debbie's features, her drawn cheeks and lackluster slate blue eyes. I tried to imagine her face as it once was, in expressions of joy and laughter in her work on Cape Cod as an art and drama teacher at a small private school for retarded children.

"Of course I'll give you a prescription for morphine," I said in response to her stated reason for the consultation. But as I extended my hands across my desk to touch hers, Debbie withdrew from my gesture of concern. I awkwardly returned my hands to the desk, picked up a pen, and wrote out the prescription: MS Contin 30 milligrams bid.

"It's a slow-release preparation, one thirty-milligram capsule taken in the morning and one in the evening. If the morning dose doesn't control the pain through the day, you can take an extra dose at noon."

Debbie nodded in understanding.

"Try to eat lots of fiber to keep your bowels regular, since morphine can make you severely constipated."

"I know its side effects," Debbie replied as she put the prescription in her tote bag. "Rob Major, my Tao healer, already warned me. He gave me *gan cao,* a Chinese licorice, which will help my digestion."

I paused a moment and decided to make one more attempt to change her mind.

"You're sure you won't reconsider? Radiation to the involved areas of your hips would melt the tumor masses in a matter of days. There is good chemotherapy that can keep the breast cancer at bay."

"With all due respect, Dr. Groopman," Debbie replied, her tone rising in intensity but retaining its well-bred New England accent, "there is no 'good' chemotherapy, or radiation for that matter. Chemotherapy didn't prevent my cancer from returning. Nor did it cure my mother or my two aunts." Debbie paused, and fixed her brightening eyes on mine. "The Tao has powers beyond what any Western medicine can imagine. I am going to be healed."

DEBORAH THAYER HAD JUST TURNED THIRTY. She was born in Plymouth, Massachusetts, the only child of Bradford Thayer and Alice McIntyre. Her father's line could be traced to the Pilgrim ships that had come to the Cape in the 1670s, a few decades after the *Mayflower.* Her mother's family were Scot Presbyterians, hardy farmers who had arrived along Boston's South Shore in the early 1800s. She had been raised in a traditional New England family, keenly aware of the attributes of honesty, hard work, and propriety.

Debbie had been an excellent athlete and, in addition to being a distance swimmer and runner, was an avid equestrienne. Recently, her disease had made these activities too painful to engage in.

Her mother had died from breast cancer at the age of thirty-six, when Debbie was ten. Her two maternal aunts also developed the disease, a few years after her mother. They had succumbed as well before the age of forty. Her father, who had raised her alone after her mother's death, was alive and healthy, and managed a successful chain of hardware stores on Cape Cod.

Because of her family history, Debbie had been evaluated since her teenage years by Dr. Arlene Roy, a gynecologist on the Cape. She had instructed Debbie in how to perform a self-examination, and Debbie was meticulous in doing so each month after her menses subsided.

"I was terrified when I felt the lump," Debbie said, working to maintain a calm tone. "It wasn't like other lumps I had felt before. This one was hard and irregular, like a small rock had grown in my breast. I immediately contacted Dr. Roy."

Debbie knew from Dr. Roy that many young women in their twenties developed lumps in their breasts. Most were small cysts that waxed and waned in size over the menstrual cycle. But her previous nodularities were more easily compressed and movable. Debbie knew that this one had the cardinal warning signs of cancer.

Debbie's mammograms were not helpful in distinguishing between a benign and a malignant mass. This is the case for most young women, since the density of the young breast creates a background that often obscures the lesion. So Dr. Roy decided, rightly, that it was too risky to observe the lump passively through another menstrual cycle and hope it would disappear. It felt too worrisome, and Debbie's family history was too threatening.

Dr. Roy referred Debbie to an older surgeon, Dr. Lawrence Ratcliffe.

"I didn't like him at all," Debbie confessed. "He seemed so cold and distant. He answered every question in one or two words. But I was too frightened and too in awe of doctors to look for other options."

I had received Debbie's complete medical records in preparation for her consultation with me. Her pathology report from 1991 stated that her breast cancer measured two centimeters at its greatest width and had already spread to the lymph nodes under her adjacent arm. The attached operative note dictated by Dr. Ratcliffe detailed a modified mastectomy. He stated that he had offered the alternative approach of radiation with preservation of the breast but Miss Thayer had opted for the mastectomy.

Debbie described to me how, at the age of seven, she had learned with her own eyes what the word "mastectomy" meant. It was an oppressive August day, and her family had decided to go to the Plymouth beach for the first time since her mother's recent surgery.

"Mother did not dare wear a swimsuit and chose a billowing white cotton dress with long sleeves and a high neck."

Debbie spied on her mother as she changed. The scarred skin of her chest had a pearly white glare, and the convexities of her underlying ribs pressed outward like the exposed bulwark of a rotting ship. Debbie had turned away, both repulsed and fascinated by the vision of what lay beneath the exterior of our bodies.

Over the ensuing months, as her mother adapted to her new condition, she became less secretive about her appearance. Some mornings she would ask Debbie to fetch her breast prosthesis from the bureau dresser where it was kept during the night. Other times her mother would hug Debbie tightly without her prosthesis in place. Debbie could feel the unnatural imbalance in the hug, one side of the chest full and soft, the other sunken and bony.

Debbie realized her mother wanted her to experience her changed form and learn something important from these intentional acts. Was it that a woman was more than her body, and that her pride could not be taken away by a surgeon's scalpel? Or was it a more practical lesson, a lesson of the strength of silent suffering, taught to prepare Debbie for the price she might one day pay for the heirloom of her mother's genes?

Her mother had died before Debbie was old enough to articulate these questions and hear their intended answers.

Radiation had been another matter. Debbie recalled her mother's burned chest wall, red and blistering after the cobalt treatments, her harsh whistling breath and spasms of uncontrolled coughing from her inflamed lungs filling their home with a cacophony of pain. The radiation had been given to her mother to try to kill any resident cancer that might not have been removed by the surgery.

Nearly a year passed before her mother could breathe quietly while at rest. And she was never again able to exert herself without becoming winded.

"So I chose to go ahead with the mastectomy," Debbie explained, "because the operation seemed to have no lasting effects on Mother, while the radiation did."

But she now realized it had been a terrible mistake. She felt horribly and irreparably mutilated by the surgery.

Debbie grimaced as she described to me the impact of breast cancer on a young and unmarried woman.

"I felt I had no future. At a time in my life when I wanted to meet someone, to find love and marry, I felt too afraid even to try. What kind of man wants a twenty-six-year-old without her breast? And even if somehow I found love and married, how could I risk having children and cursing a daughter with breast cancer?"

My heart was heavy. Likely destined from birth to develop this devastating disease, Debbie was frightened, confused, desperate. When I feel such pain from my patients' suffering, I channel it into productive action—using my medical and personal skills to diagnose, treat, and comfort. But Debbie had built a solid wall of denial around herself, believing the magical promises of an alternative healer, like a zealot in a cult. She had come seeking the morphine from me only because by law it had to be prescribed by a physician.

Why bother to confront her denial and offer toxic treatments like radiation and chemotherapy if there was no cure? What really was going to be gained? Wouldn't I only cause Debbie to suffer more as a victim of my therapy? Why not simply indulge her belief that the powers of the Tao would cure her? Didn't this give her spiritual comfort and a chance to die in peace?

I had asked myself, and been asked by others, such questions many times over the past two decades of caring for people with incurable illnesses like cancer or AIDS. Their answers depend upon each individual's specific condition.

To treat for the sake of treating, when there is no hope of the toxic drugs having a significant effect on the disease, is an all-too-common practice among physicians. It is rationalized as giving the patient and his loved ones comfort from the appearance of *something* being done, but in truth it only increases suffering. I would not condone such a course.

Debbie's case was different. Radiation and chemotherapy would be expected to shrink the tumor and control the disease. They might provide a remission lasting on average two to three years. During that time Debbie would likely feel good and be able to pursue her life.

There was another reason not to indulge Debbie's belief in a magical cure. Although her faith in the Tao seemed to provide shelter from the natural fear of debility and death, it was in fact a fragile and temporary refuge. Her denial would ultimately be shattered by the inescapable reality of a growing cancer. The promise of the Tao would be proven false. She would probably die feeling failed and forsaken.

The more I thought about Debbie's situation, the more determined I became to breach the wall she had erected and help her.

DEBBIE RETURNED A WEEK LATER for an appointment. I had purposely scheduled it at a short interval not only to monitor the effects of the morphine but also to learn better who she was and how she had arrived at such an extreme position.

I was pleased to see that Debbie moved more easily and was less pale. Two capsules of the long-acting morphine were enough to control her pain, and she had returned to work at the school.

"Thank you again, Dr. Groopman," Debbie stated with a warm smile. "It makes a world of difference for me to be back with the children."

After I examined her and refilled the prescription, I asked her if she would like me to explain more fully the biology of breast cancer. In part I wanted to learn how much she understood about the illness, but I also knew that acquiring knowledge of what was happening in one's body often worked to solidify a person's resolve to make a difficult decision.

"I've done some reading in the past, Dr. Groopman, but a lot of the language is technical and confusing."

Debbie knew that in 1991 she was one of more than 150,000 women in the United States who developed breast cancer. Although a woman had a one-in-nine chance of developing this malignancy over her lifetime, her family history put her at higher risk, close to 40 percent.

She was familiar with the most important factors, beyond family history, that determine a woman's risk for breast cancer: age of onset of menses, age at first pregnancy, and number of children conceived. Debbie had undergone puberty at an average age of thirteen and had never been pregnant. The longer a woman was exposed to the regular hormonal fluxes of the menstrual cycle—the earlier puberty occurred, the later she conceived her children, or did not conceive at all—the greater her risk for breast cancer.

I explained that this was because the female hormones stimulated reproduction of the epithelial cells in the ducts of the breast glands. With this sustained hormonal drive to reproduce came a greater chance for genetic mutations to occur, since mutations happen mainly when cells divide.

"Now you're getting into less familiar territory," Debbie said. "May I take notes?"

I gave her a yellow legal pad from my desk as she took a pen from her bag. I was pleased by her request, a sign that she was engaged by the information and willing to learn how modern science understood the nature of her condition.

I went on to describe how much progress had been made over the last decade in identifying genes which cause the transformation of a cell from normal to malignant. The main instigators are those genes which normally promote ordered growth, but when mutated, unleash a manic phase of reproduction. Such genes are called "oncogenes," for cancer-causing genes.

Debbie duly noted this on her pad.

Another type of gene associated with cancer is called a "tumor suppressor." The suppressor is a disciplinarian to the oncogenes, restraining them, making sure they don't become hyperactive during the cell's reproductive cycle. If the tumor suppressor gene is mutated, it no longer effectively limits the oncogenes.

Yet a third set of genes participates in the physiology of cell growth. These genes mediate *apoptosis,* a Greek term signifying programmed cell death.

Apoptosis means that each cell has a finite life span. Its demise is programmed into its genetic blueprint from its birth. Some cell types have very short lives, like the neutrophil, a white blood cell which combats bacteria and lasts only six hours in the circulation. Other cells, like memory T cells, which arise after vaccination, survive for decades. Certain cancer cells have been found to have mutated apoptosis genes. Programmed cell death does not occur on schedule. This allows the cancer cells to accumulate in the body while their normal counterparts die.

"Which of these genes are relevant to my cancer, or my mother's and aunts'?" Debbie interrupted.

"It's hard to say without analyzing the tumor that developed in each one of you. But in familial breast cancer, there's been a recent breakthrough."

A gene called BRCA1, which doesn't seem to fit into any one of the known categories of cancer-associated genes, has been discovered to be mutated in families like Debbie's with a history of breast cancer occurring before the age of forty.

The normal BRCA1 gene contains more than 100,000 bases of DNA and produces a protein which limits the growth of cells in the breast. When BRCA1 is altered by mutation, the protein is not made in its functional form and the cells grow without this brake. Why it takes decades for the effects of this unrestrained growth to cause breast cancer is not yet understood. But the discovery sets the stage for one day trying to prevent the cancer in afflicted families by administering the normal protein or an equivalent treatment and restoring order to the environment of the breast.

"Regardless of the cause, the mutated cancer cells act like bomb-throwing anarchists," I continued.

"I like that image," Debbie interjected. "I'll use it to create pictures in my mind when I do my visualization."

On her first visit, Debbie had explained to me that she could will the good cells of her immune system to destroy the evil cancer cells in her bones. This would help purge the tumor from her system. Rob Major was instructing her in this powerful technique.

I was disturbed by Debbie's statement but didn't want to get sidetracked from presenting the science, so I just lifted my eyebrows to indicate skepticism that visualization could eradicate cancer cells.

"Malignant cells grow without restraint," I pressed on, "disregarding the normal borders of tissues, spreading into organs where they don't belong."

In the case of breast cancer, the transformed cells spread first from the breast through its lymphatic channels to the lymph nodes under the adjacent arm, as they had in Debbie's case. They often lurked in the body after surgery, and could not be detected by even the most sophisticated X rays and scans. If unchecked, they spread further to take up residence in lung, liver, bone, or brain.

"That was the rationale for the chemotherapy you received after the mastectomy. It was intended to kill any residual cancer cells before they could spread and take root."

"But it didn't," Debbie bitterly retorted.

"No, it didn't. And I'm sorry it failed. But that doesn't mean it can't help now. And it's the only effective option."

Debbie glared at me in cold silence. I saw that my effort to use science as a springboard to a rational discussion of therapy would not succeed.

"Tell me what it was like, the chemotherapy," I said gently. "I may help more if I know what you went through."

Debbie hesitated, looking at me with lingering anger.

Debbie put the notepad to her side, capped her pen, and returned it to her bag.

"Two years ago, I felt I was being thrown from pillar to post," Debbie began, her gaze still icily fixed on me. "I didn't question what I was being told. And I didn't know where else to turn, what else I might do."

Dr. Charles Dell, her oncologist, had presented detailed data about the risk of breast cancer returning after her mastectomy. He had said the odds were such-and-such. The numbers played out so-and-so. This research study had shown a "reduced risk ratio" of "x," and another of "y." By giving so-called adjuvant chemotherapy, the "actuarial survival" improved. The statistics had appeared in her mind like numbers on a roulette wheel, spinning and spinning until they formed a blur.

The doctor never explained, specifically, how Debbie *as Debbie* fit into this whirlwind of technical terms and data. Not once, she noted, did he mention her by name in all these calculations of life and death. Nor did he ask her how she felt about all this frightening information he was conveying, how it fit in with her understanding of her own body and life. He just flatly told her what the odds were and how *he* would bet, in his detached professorial tone.

For six miserable months in 1991, she received three different drugs: cyclophosphamide, a noxious poison that lowered her white blood counts, removed her hair, and irritated her kidneys and bladder; methotrexate, another horrible chemical, which antagonized vitamin B and made her flesh blister; fluorouracil, a drug that had ulcerated her mouth and denuded her intestines, so she was unable to eat and had relentless diarrhea.

"It was a horror. And one that I do not have to suffer again."

"We can prevent many of those side effects now," I replied. "There are potent antinausea drugs, and natural proteins like G-CSF and erythropoietin that protect your blood cells from damage. Not that I'm painting a rosy picture. Toxicities are still frequent, but they are less severe and more manageable. And there are newly discovered chemotherapy drugs like Taxol that work better against relapsed breast cancer than what existed two years ago."

"No," Debbie flatly asserted, "it doesn't matter. I will never submit to chemotherapy again."

She paused a moment, and her tone became softer. "It is impossible to express how grateful I am to have Rob Major and to learn the Tao and avoid such misery. Sometimes I wonder whether some guardian angel, perhaps even Mother in heaven, steered me to this path."

It was not the moment to push her further. The tension felt just moments before had only slightly eased. I would learn more by quietly listening. Debbie seemed to sense my openness, and went on to tell me how she found her healer.

"It was a week after I learned from Dr. Dell that the aches in my bones were because the cancer had come back. I was with Kristen, my student teacher this semester. We were working on a special project in class, making designs with the children on cardboard paper using twigs, leaves, and stones they collected from the school's garden."

Debbie recounted how she was able to put her disease out of her mind as she worked and saw the joy on her pupils' faces. After class, as she and Kristen began to clean up the discarded leaves and stones from the art room floor, the pain in her hips and shoulder exploded in full force. It came on so quickly, and was so severe, it made Debbie feel faint and nauseated. Kristen noticed Debbie's pallor and unsteady stance.

"Kristen asked me what was wrong, was I sick? I was reluctant to answer. In my family no one is supposed to complain about pain, especially to someone whom you know only professionally. But I broke down and told her the whole story."

Debbie recounted how Kristen had listened patiently, not interrupting once, holding Debbie's trembling hands in hers. When Debbie was done, Kristen told Debbie it didn't have to be. She didn't need chemotherapy. She could be healed naturally.

Kristen explained that she wasn't a Christian Scientist, which is what Debbie first thought, but believed in spiritual healing. Her boyfriend, Rob Major, was such a healer. He had a practice in East Cambridge.

Rob's background was in clinical psychology. He had an undergraduate degree from Amherst and a master's from Yale. But after a few years in practice, he realized that he had not really been taught how to heal in these prestigious schools. So he had traveled to Nepal and Tibet in search of this knowledge. In the East he had learned that the way we in the West saw the world was false. It did not comprehend how all the elements of the universe were linked. It ignored the vital harmony of the body and mind described in the ancient Chinese writings of the Tao.

Rob had told Kristen of a great many cures of people who had been told by their doctors that there was no chance—people with cancer or AIDS or colitis or neurological diseases. Kristen said these were not really miracles, just the results of knowing how to harness the powers of the self to heal.

Debbie admitted to me that she was suspicious at first. She wondered whether Rob was a quack, some failed psychologist who now took advantage of vulnerable people with incurable diseases.

"But I was feeling alone, afraid, completely hopeless. And Kristen didn't seem conniving or dishonest. What did I have to lose, I thought. A day's time to travel to Cambridge and some money? So I asked Kristen to arrange an appointment."

Rob's office was in East Cambridge, far from the familiar environs of Harvard Square, where Debbie liked to shop. The neighborhood was poor, with many new immigrants. Pentecostal churches dotted the narrow streets, their storefront entrances crowned by large hand-painted signs in Spanish. She passed row after row of triple-decker wooden houses with peeling paint and rickety porches, windows in need of cleaning, and untended lawns.

Debbie had wondered whether her trip had been a mistake. Probably Rob was some charlatan, like a palm reader, making money from unsophisticated immigrants. She was tempted to turn back, but realized there was really nothing to return to.

Rob's office occupied the first floor of a double decker. Debbie described how, once she entered, she felt at ease.

"It's not like the antiseptic atmosphere of Dr. Dell's office. Rob's waiting area is decorated like a living room, with plenty of light, a comfortable couch, upholstered chairs, a coffee table, and plants. It seems silly now, but I had expected someplace dark and mysterious. There is no incense, no icons, no background music with chanting mantras that you might expect in the office of a healer."

Rob emerged from his office shortly after she arrived. He was tall and lean, with long brown hair in a ponytail and a thin mustache that curved down at the corners of his mouth in what her father called a "Fu Manchu." He was dressed in a green corduroy shirt and beige chinos, and wore Nike running shoes. Around his neck was a large silver ball with a mirrored surface that looked curiously like a Christmas ornament.

Rob smiled and took her hands in his. Debbie recalled how his grip was firm and sustained. He introduced himself, saying he had heard a lot about her from Kristen before she had become ill, and had looked forward to meeting her, although under different circumstances.

She was distracted at first by the silver ball hanging from Rob's neck. Debbie could see her reflected face on its surface, wide and flat, as in a fun house mirror. It made her think she was captured by the object, and was resting her head against Rob's chest.

Unlike the many doctors who had been involved in her case since the diagnosis of cancer two years before, Rob spent little time inquiring about the details of her family and her medical history. He told Debbie he knew from Kristen about her mother and aunts, and remarked it must have been terribly hard growing up with so much pain. He also stated that he was aware of her chemotherapy, and although Debbie had not informed Kristen of the details of these treatments, which drugs she had received after the mastectomy, the doses, and for how long, Rob did not request this information. He dismissed her prior treatment with a grave shake of his head.

Rob's questions were very different from those of the doctors. Each query, about her diet, breathing pattern, and dreams, was asked in a conversational manner, without the terse intensity that characterized the medical checklists of Dr. Ratcliffe and Dr. Dell.

Debbie paused thoughtfully, and then added: "I felt he was trying to sense who I was, what I was made of, not just where my disease had spread."

After the interview, Rob explained that he would work with Debbie to restore harmony within her body. It would mean not just taking herbs or receiving acupuncture or any other physical treatments, but primarily teaching her spirit how to heal her body. The Tao had the potential to cure her, to restore her to the state she was in before the cancer appeared. But it only worked if she believed in its truth and power.

This had made Debbie tense, she confided, because as desperately as she wanted to be healthy again, she wasn't sure she could force herself to believe in the Tao. Rob Major noticed her hesitation. But Debbie was impressed that, unlike Dr. Dell, who adopted a punitive tone when she doubted his beliefs, Rob offered in an understanding voice that it would take time to learn and to believe.

"He spoke from the heart. I was gripped by the feeling that I did not have to die, that with his wisdom I could live again."

Debbie stopped and looked into my eyes for a reaction. I had set my face as attentive but impassive. Now I measured my words, knowing my frank approach had failed before.

"I know a little about Chinese medicine," I began. "Many of its techniques promote wellness. Exercise, meditation, stress reduction, and diet are often neglected in modern Western medicine, and can improve health.

"But I just can't see how the Tao can combat *alone* a disease like cancer without rational Western treatments. There is just no scientific basis for seeing the world of illness this way."

"One day," Debbie answered plaintively, "you'll realize how indebted I am to Rob for not only healing my body but also my soul."

I asked Debbie how much Rob charged for her visits.

Debbie's face flashed with anger, and I immediately realized that my remark was a mistake. Before I could correct it, Debbie said Dr. Roy had asked the same question. It revealed the arrogance and antagonism of medical doctors toward a healer who was not "one of their own."

"Dr. Ratcliffe charged me three thousand dollars to remove my breast," Debbie acidly stated. "Dr. Dell charged two hundred and fifty dollars each time he gave me his poisons. And no doctor has cured me, or for that matter my mother or aunts. But they never hesitated to send me and my family huge bills. Rob's healing sessions cost one hundred twenty dollars each, and they're more than worth it."

I felt like a fool, and quickly apologized. I told Debbie I had been thoughtless and misspoke. But during two decades of medical practice caring for patients with cancer or AIDS, I had encountered many charlatans who preyed on desperate people with severe illness and were expert in taking their money. She should understand where my remark came from.

Debbie's face relaxed a bit. She said she appreciated my apology.

"You should know that Rob is helping me beyond this disease. I am learning how to be in better harmony with my self."

Through Rob's teachings, Debbie realized she had long seen herself as defective, even before her tumor and her mastectomy, before she became aware of the poisonous seed of breast cancer in her family. She had never felt happy with who she was, and had desperately wanted to escape her identity. Perhaps that was why she had learned art and drama, as a means of imagining and assuming different characters.

"And when my cancer returned," Debbie said in a soft and hesitant voice, "I was forced to face my deepest fear: that I would die without coming to terms with who I really am."

The Tao taught that no defects, regardless of how deeply rooted, were beyond repair. She now believed that one day she would be able to accept who she was and not feel the desire to escape her self.

With that affirmation, our appointment drew to a close.

I sat deep in thought at my desk after Debbie left. I was unsure how to proceed. The goal of giving her treatment that would relieve her suffering and possibly recapture several years of productive life was still foremost in my mind. But I realized that it was not so simple to dismiss what Rob Major was doing for Debbie.

In a trying and frightening period of her life, Debbie was deriving important inspiration and comfort from the teachings of the Tao. In this way, it was like any other religion or creed that supports us in times of suffering and trouble. The breathing exercises, visualization, and meditation calmed her spirit during a time of constant anxiety and turmoil. The Tao's principle of harmony was being used to help resolve the conflicting elements in her life that had been destructive to her self-esteem.

But I still feared for her future, when the teaching's magical powers were proven false by the reality of a spreading cancer. Would Debbie blame herself for lack of sufficient faith? Or would she die in regret, feeling cheated by Rob Major and bitter at having wasted her remaining time?

I wondered whether I should contact Rob Major and explore these questions directly with him, but concluded it was too risky. It would likely have resulted in a heated confrontation, since he had so sharply drawn the lines between alternative and conventional treatments. At that point, such a conflict would only have threatened my already fragile relationship with Debbie.

I did not really know how to care effectively for a patient like Debbie, under these conditions, because we understood the world in such radically different and opposing ways.

I knew I would be facing this dilemma more and more often. Our society's fascination with mysticism is a rapidly growing phenomenon. Bookstore shelves are overflowing with volumes on New Age spirituality, near-death experiences, and spontaneous healing. Talk shows on TV and radio tout sensational and unchallenged claims of miraculous cures.

Many patients are attracted to these beliefs and stories. Debbie was extreme in her total rejection of conventional treatment, but she was hardly alone in expressing a deep and unmet need for spiritual help to cope with the debility of disease and the fear of death. That was what I had to be attuned to, and be prepared to address.

The failure was not the patient's but ours, the medical profession's. There was a time when the physician was paramount in providing emotional support. He knew each member of the family as a person, often from the moment he brought a life into the world until he assisted in its passing. He functioned not only as a scientist skilled in the diagnosis and treatment of disease, but also as a priest and a friend, privy to the intimacies of his patient's heart, giving counsel and comfort as he accompanied him or her through the vicissitudes of life.

But many doctors seem to neglect this now. They have become so focused on the scientific and technical aspects of medicine, on sophisticated CAT scans and computer-designed drugs and cloned genes and recombinant proteins, that they ignore the patient as person.

There are no high-tech scans or laboratory tests to examine the fear and pain and turmoil in a patient's heart. It takes words and thoughts and, perhaps most critically, time to care for a patient's spiritual needs. And, as Debbie intimated, many doctors avoid this aspect of care by claiming they don't have the time. They say they are fully occupied with just solving the myriad medical problems of their patients.

I had learned why Debbie had become bitter and angry, first at the injustice and misery of her disease, then with the failure of her physicians to take the time to seek and care for her inner needs. The painful void created by this failure was readily filled by Rob Major.

. . .

OVER THE NEXT TWO MONTHS I saw Debbie weekly, each time listening to her reports of her healing with Rob, each time observing one more objective indication that the cancer was growing.

At one visit, when Debbie mentioned that her chest wall hurt during her tai chi exercises, I suggested we repeat her bone X rays. She, unexpectedly, readily agreed. As I mounted the films on the illuminated box on the wall of my office, I traced for her the ragged lucencies made by the cancer. They now appeared not only in her hips and shoulder but in her ribs as well. This, I explained to Debbie, was why it was harder to exercise and take her deep cleansing breaths.

The X rays showed that the cancer in her right hip had also expanded and was now impinging on the joint. When I asked Debbie if she had symptoms from this, she admitted that the pain and weakness in her leg had made it difficult to function at school, and she was spending most days at home.

But when I started to raise the issue of radiation, Debbie quickly said she hoped I wasn't trying to threaten her with what would happen if she didn't follow my advice, as Dr. Dell had done.

I replied that I never threatened a patient. I just wanted to help her, and hoped that by her knowing what was happening, she would consider what else might be done. Debbie abruptly ended the discussion by stating that soon the visualization would work, and her immune system would naturally heal her bones of the growing cancer.

Debbie next developed a bulge on her left flank with a surrounding hemorrhage into the overlying skin. Rob was concerned about this, informing her that the loss of *xue,* or blood, was to be avoided at all costs because it embodied her vital energy, or *chi.*

"After he examined me," Debbie reported, "he gave me a special salve to rub over the bloodied skin." Debbie paused, and surprised me with her question: "What do you think I should do?"

I told Debbie I was worried about two possible causes for this bleeding: her platelets, the blood cells that mediate clotting, may have been destroyed in the marrow by the invading cancer, causing her to bleed spontaneously into her skin; or she may have developed a metastasis to the abdominal wall that was intermittently bleeding.

Debbie surprised me again when she consented to take a blood test. Fortunately her platelet count was normal. But on examination, I palpated a rock-hard mass measuring five centimeters that was contiguous with her spleen and growing into the skin of her flank. It was clearly a new deposit of cancer. I explained it had probably grown into a small blood vessel, causing the hemorrhage.

"I'm pretty hopeful the herbal salve will melt the cancer," Debbie said weakly.

I did not hear the conviction in her voice that had been so clear in the past. But Debbie still did not permit me to pursue the issue of conventional treatments with her.

"I know you mean well, Dr. Groopman," she said, "but I told you that I am simply not going to consider chemotherapy. I really don't want to discuss it further."

I felt even more frustrated and anxious. The cancer was approaching a stage where it would soon grow beyond the reach of radiation and chemotherapy, and I had not found a way around the wall of her denial. I decided my only choice was to confront it again, this time more forcefully and head on.

So, a week later, on a humid July morning, as our next appointment drew to a close and I finished writing a renewal of her morphine prescription at a higher dose, I told Debbie that I feared she was going to die soon. I said this not as a threat but as a statement of fact.

The cancer was growing unchecked. No one could deny that any longer. Based on the usual course of the disease, it would so erode her bones as to leach out their calcium and unbalance her metabolism. This would draw her into a lethal coma. Or it would spread to her liver, lungs, and brain, irreversibly destroying these vital organs. I, and all the other people who cared for her, her father, her friends, her students, did not want to lose her.

I did not believe the Tao would cause her tumor to regress and cure her. I acknowledged that my conventional treatments were not likely to cure her either. But at least with conventional treatment we could hope for a remission where the cancer would be held in abeyance.

True, such imperfect therapies had failed her mother and her aunts. But Debbie had learned that she was not her mother or her aunts.

A remission lasting on average two to three years was likely in her case after radiation and chemotherapy. Still, Debbie knew that no individual was a statistic. There was also a small chance, perhaps a few percent, that intensive treatment would achieve a very long remission of a decade or more.

If Debbie were in that few percent of patients who lived for many years, then it was one hundred percent for her. And during that time, research might yield new and more effective therapies for her disease. This was not a false hope that I dangled before her. It had happened during the past two decades I had practiced oncology with other diseases, like lymphoma, leukemia, and testicular cancer, that were once uniformly fatal and were now often cured.

There were, of course, risks, serious risks. These had to be considered. The toxicities of the treatment could further reduce her function or even shorten her life. I did not think this was likely. As I had told her before, there were ways to protect her from those risks, but still, untoward events occurred.

I stopped, knowing I had talked a lot, and mostly about the clinical aspects of what might happen. Debbie had listened thoughtfully, and I took her attention as a sign that she was seriously weighing what I was offering and would not reject it out of hand. But before I finished, I wanted to say something that had been weighing heavily on me since we had first met.

"Debbie, I feel as if we, your doctors, have largely failed you. So often we focus on treating the disease and don't pay attention to the person, the pain and fear in his heart and soul. I can't undo the past. But I'll do everything I can to help in the future."

Debbie cautiously said she understood what I was saying. After a meditative silence, she elaborated on what the future might hold:

"Dr. Groopman, I understand myself, more than anything else, as an artist. I feel pleasure most deeply when I paint. I want to be able to return to my art, to sense that energy again.

"I deeply love Father and my friends—"

Debbie stopped in mid-sentence, and her eyes quickly welled with tears. She composed herself, drying her eyes with a small handkerchief that she carefully refolded and placed in her tote bag. "It would have been a gift, to me, to Father *and* to Mother, if Mother had lived longer. I believe the time I might gain with Father and with my friends would be meaningful.

"And you know how much my work with the children at the school means to me. It's been awful not to be there. If the cancer were controlled, I could work again."

Debbie paused to fix a tuft of straw-blond hair that had strayed from her bun. I noted how her slow, pained movements still retained their grace and poise, despite the limitations imposed by the cancer in her bones.

"It's not just these special things I think of. What I daydream about most is simply having a normal, ordinary life—swimming again in the bay this summer, or riding along my favorite trails in Falmouth. I think about what might sound silly or unimportant, like being able to go to the market and lift a bag of groceries without help, or walk Father's new dalmatian and have the strength to restrain it by the leash.

"I feel that if there are ways to control the pain, so I'm not constantly suffering, and so long as I don't lose my mind, I have reasons to live. Many, many reasons."

I reached out and held Debbie's hands tightly in mine. This time she did not withdraw. I said that all this was possible. Most people do not realize how we can be fulfilled even when we are limited by disease. They assert they would rather die than put up with the hardships of treatment if there is no cure. But they are rarely the ones confronting death. They view it from the outside, with a theoretical detachment.

Debbie listened to my words with an uncertain expression and, after a thoughtful pause, asked in an unsteady voice what *specifically* was I offering? She said doctors spoke in generalities, and the patient was left to meet the devil later in the details.

I first presented the various treatment options, the specific chemotherapy drugs that could be considered to control the rapidly advancing cancer. I then described their expected side effects. I delineated the doses of radiation and how they could be administered more safely with new computerized calibration techniques, avoiding the burning and damage to surrounding tissue that her mother had suffered.

I then outlined what I thought was the best chemotherapy regimen, emphasizing how they were derived from natural sources. This included Taxol, a recently approved drug that was purified from the Pacific yew tree. We would also administer G-CSF, a natural protein that would protect her bone marrow from the toxicity of chemotherapy, keeping her white blood cell count high enough to prevent infection. I ended by stating that it would take at least four to six months of intensive treatment to achieve a remission. Then, she could be free of treatment and free of disease for months to years.

Debbie listened very attentively as I spoke, and after I finished, we sat for a long time in silence. But then, almost more as a sigh than as a statement, she said again that only the Tao held out the chance of *cure*. She did not want to give up that hope.

I responded that I did not want to take away the hope she derived from this philosophy, but time was slipping by, and I could no longer delay informing her with blunt honesty how I saw things.

"Dr. Groopman, I don't know. I just don't know. I feel so drained I can hardly think anymore. I often wonder whether it might just be easier to give in and die."

Debbie paused, her eyes looking past mine at something distant and perhaps indistinct. I felt the hope and energy that I had touched when we talked about reasons to live, the emotional spark that had finally ignited between us, slowly fading. But then she refocused her gaze, and seemed to rally.

"Deep inside I don't want to die. I want so much to live."

I reached out again to hold her hands, signaling that I would be there for her to try as best as I could to make this happen. I sensed the time had come to seal our agreement to treat her. I asked if she had talked with Rob yet about the progress of the cancer.

Debbie told me that she had already asked him how he viewed the tumor's growth and how he planned to continue to fight it. He had responded that natural healing only worked when the person fully believed in it. Debbie had admitted that despite her best efforts over the last months to fully embrace the Tao, she had felt lingering doubts about its absolute truth. Rob concluded these doubts were probably preventing her from being cured.

I looked hard into Debbie's still-moist eyes.

I confessed, as Debbie had suspected, that when I first heard about the teachings of the Tao, I was ignorant and dismissive. But during the past months I had made a real effort to learn more. I had read several books on eastern medicine and philosophy: Daniel P. Reid's *Chinese Herbal Medicine,* Haven Trevino's *The Tao of Healing,* and sections of the *I Ching.* I had discussed their principles with other patients who had adopted some of their teachings.

I had been truthful with Debbie when I had told her that I appreciated many of the Tao's positive attributes, how it helped to cope with the suffering of illness by promoting wellness. And I had seen how Debbie had drawn psychological insight and emotional comfort from it.

"But when disease worsens, the Tao tries to sustain the illusion of unlimited powers to cure by implicitly blaming the victim of illness for his own demise. The tenet that only true believers will be fully healed is, to my mind, pernicious and destructive."

Alternative healers like Rob Major, I continued, readily place responsibility for the failure of conventional treatments on the doctor's shoulders and then place responsibility for the failure of their healing on the patient's. Rob Major was wrong to imply that Debbie was responsible for the unchecked growth of her cancer. Attributing this to Debbie's imperfect will, to my mind, bordered on the obscene. It meant that she deserved her death because she could not reach the level of faith where miracles happen. I would condemn in the same terms a fundamentalist minister or rabbi who interpreted disease as a punishment for imperfect belief.

There was another aspect of the Tao that rationalized its failure to cure while sustaining its claims of truth. This was the belief that it didn't matter if a person lived or died because material life was an illusion, so physical healing was an illusion. Only spiritual "cure" had meaning.

"But physical healing does matter, as you know, and life is no illusion. It's nihilistic and wrong to deny you the chance to gain time and be fulfilled by asserting that this life and your death are insignificant."

After I finished speaking, Debbie disengaged her hands, her eyes now dry.

I could feel her withdrawing from me as she averted her gaze from my face to the rows of scientific texts that lined the shelves behind my desk. We sat for several moments in numb silence. I waited for her to regain her focus, but, without another word, Debbie painfully lifted herself from the chair and slowly made her way out the door.

I called her at home in the middle of the week, but her father said she was resting and couldn't come to the phone. I called again on Friday morning. Debbie did not return my calls.

I worried that I had lost her. Did she conclude that my harsh criticism of the Tao and of Rob Major further endangered her cure by feeding her doubts about her faith and her healer? Or had the mounting debility of her disease and the realization that there was no cure caused her to surrender to despair and forgo any treatment?

I was deeply relieved when Debbie arrived the following Tuesday for her scheduled appointment. She had spent the morning with Rob and looked a bit stronger. She told me the increased dose of morphine had helped to control her pain better, and she was finally getting a few hours of uninterrupted sleep. The Chinese herb was keeping her bowels regular.

"Rob is upset with me. I assume you will be as well. But I want you both to understand and support my decision."

She had thought about my impassioned argument against the Tao for its tenets of blame and its nihilism. But she concluded I was wrong about both.

The Tao did not really say she was responsible for the progression of her disease. Debbie interpreted the lack of faith to mean the lack of sufficient understanding of its primary principle of harmony, its insight that within the negative was to be found the positive. This, she now realized, enabled her to be treated by chemotherapy. Within the negative poisons that I could administer against her cancer were to be found the positive forces that would work with her own body to heal it.

Similarly, within the apparently negative view that life was an illusion and death didn't matter was a liberating, positive message. It was really saying that the fear of death was an illusion, because death was a part of life. There was no frightening border between the two, just the illusion of such. Death would be as natural and known when it arrived as life was now.

Rob Major didn't agree that her decision about chemotherapy was true to this philosophy. But he was wrong.

She would take Taxol, the potent new drug that I had recommended. No denying it was chemotherapy and toxic, but it was a natural product of the Pacific yew tree. Within nature's deadly poison was to be found its opposite, life-giving health.

She also had learned more about G-CSF. It appealed to her not only because it was a natural protein but because it worked from within, boosting her own immune system. This, too, was in concert with the wisdom of the Tao.

"But I will *not* take radiation," Debbie asserted. Her face tightened and her voice increased in strength. "This is nonnegotiable. Not only because of what happened to Mother. I find its negative effects outweigh any of its positives."

Debbie finished speaking, and waited expectantly for my reaction.

I took a deep breath. She would finally begin some effective treatment.

I told Debbie I disagreed with her rejecting radiation, because its effects were immediate and definitive in limiting the local growth of her cancer. She was taking a real and unnecessary risk.

"I understand the risk, Dr. Groopman, but this decision is mine and mine alone to make."

I nodded in agreement: it was her decision, and in the end I would abide by it.

Although I appreciated how difficult it had been for Debbie to overcome her fear, accept the reality of her condition, and find common ground for its treatment, I doubted her logic was consistent with the Tao. There was an element of sophistry, of convoluted reasoning, that was required to bring her to this compromise. Yet this was not a flaw. Paradoxically, it was a newfound strength.

Life is more complicated than our beliefs, and we most clearly realize this and become expedient when we face death. Many patients I had cared for had made pragmatic decisions that seemed inconsistent with the philosophy of their prior lives. Our desire to live is so powerful that it obscures the apparent conflicts and contradictions of mind and heart. This provides an adaptive advantage that increases our chances of survival.

I told Debbie I would call Rob Major and tell him the details of the Taxol program and try to establish a working relationship with him. Meanwhile, I would set up an appointment for the next day in the chemotherapy clinic. I explained that Taxol required premedication with corticosteroids and then was given as a three-hour infusion. Debbie should arrive first thing in the morning. I was anxious to treat her.

Debbie smiled and said she was ready to be healed.

DEBBIE DID REMARKABLY WELL with the treatment. Within two months the tumors in her bones had shrunk to a quarter of their original size; by five months there was no evidence of disease. She did experience hair loss and fatigue with the Taxol, but no major toxicities beyond these.

"I might fancy myself a brunette with curls," Debbie joked as she made plans for a wig. "More daring than my former look of a blond schoolmarm with a bun."

She returned to work full-time and actively pursued her passions of painting and sports. After much negotiating, I gave permission for her to return to riding, so long as she was cautious and did not jump.

Over the winter Debbie and her father went for long canters along the deserted misty trails of Falmouth. During those outings, they talked about her youth, what each remembered of the pleasures and suffering they shared with her mother, and their thoughts about the future.

Debbie still saw Rob Major, who continued to object to her treatments with me.

"I'll take from each of you what makes sense to me," she had reaffirmed.

I didn't agree with many of her choices, but I was relieved by her assertiveness. Her growing self-reliance signaled she was reclaiming a part of her person that had been ceded in the past to her doctors and, more recently, Rob Major.

Debbie was in remission some twenty-two months, after which the cancer returned. It spread rapidly through her liver, bones, and brain. Debbie requested comfort measures only, and I supported her wishes. There was no chemotherapy that would meaningfully help at this advanced stage.

Debbie died at home, with her father in attendance, during the last days of 1995. She had suffered very little pain, the morphine that I prescribed along with the rising calcium level in her blood blunting any sensation of discomfort. Although I was prepared for her passing, I still felt the anguish of losing such a young and vibrant life.

I have thought about Debbie many times in the years since. I learned from our struggle how to communicate better with the increasing numbers of patients who share her interest in alternative treatments and eastern philosophy.

Debbie's desire for her body to use its own powers to cure her breast cancer curiously came to mind when I heard the outcome of recent experiments from my laboratory. We had discovered a gene called "CHK" that is dormant in normal breast tissue and is switched on in breast cancer cells. In early test-tube studies, we had observed that CHK could block the growth-promoting effects of the onco-genes. Why would CHK be switched on in a cancer cell and not a normal cell? Could the body be invoking a protective mechanism in an attempt to rid itself of the growing breast cancer, an attempt which for some reason fails? If that were true, we reasoned, then ma-nipulating the cancer cells to produce more CHK might abort the development of the tumor.

In early 1997, we took an important step forward in this research. Human breast cancer cells that we had genetically manipulated to overproduce CHK failed to grow in mice, while the unmanipulated cells formed huge tumors. Translating this into a clinical therapy for women with the disease is still an uncertain prospect, but the princi-ple seems true: natural forces of the body in the form of genes like CHK may be harnessed to eradicate certain breast cancers without surgery, radiation, or chemotherapy. The healing that Debbie was seeking may one day be made real through the miracle of science.

Alex

ALEX SPOKE like a conspirator, out of earshot of the emergency room nurses, his thick Swiss accent cloaking his whispered words.

"Help me to die quickly. Please, Jerry. Your word you gave me."

I purposely ignored his plea and continued with his examination.

Alex's blue eyes were puffy and inflamed, his skin blistered and lobster red, his joints swollen and tender. His temperature was charted at 105° F. The nurses had just bathed his burning flesh with rubbing alcohol, which rose in a halo of intoxicating vapors. I felt slightly faint, partly from the fumes, partly from the hour, awakened at 2 A.M. at home by the emergency call and arriving at the hospital shortly thereafter. I steadied myself by gripping the sidepost of his bed.

"I want to die. When I am still myself. I do not want to wait until I am sickly wasted. I have seen too many friends like that. *Das ist kein Leben.*"

I translated in my mind: "That is no life." He was right: for many, AIDS in its advanced stages was hardly living. But the pneumocystis pneumonia diagnosed four days before had been Alex's first clinical manifestation of the disease after carrying the virus without symptoms for many years. I had prescribed Bactrim, a sulfa antibiotic, and his pneumonia had begun to improve. Tonight he had returned to the hospital with what appeared to be a severe allergic reaction to that treatment. The inflamed eyes, blistered skin, swollen joints, and elevated temperature were all consistent with that diagnosis. His electrocardiogram and blood tests showed no toxic effects of the allergic reaction on heart, kidneys, or bone marrow. The partly treated pneumonia could be readily cured with alternative antibiotics. The allergy would quickly subside with steroids. How could I help make this the end when I understood it as just the beginning?

"*Der Alex,*" I said softly, using his diminutive, "this is only an allergy to the antibiotic I gave you. You'll be better in a few days. It makes no sense to die now."

His face immediately registered the pained anger of betrayal. I had long been counted on as a friend and ally, and now, at a moment of need, I was abandoning him.

"We had an understanding," Alex said, seething through clenched teeth. "You do not have the sickness. You do not have to watch yourself decay, as I do, at the age of forty-three. I wish to end my existence. You have no right to deny me that!"

"You cannot make clear decisions at this moment," I shot back. "You are fevered and frightened. You want to throw your life away. I won't let you. It's wrong."

Alex grabbed the rails of his stretcher, poised as if to leap from the litter and attack. I moved my hands over his wrists, locking them under my powerful grip.

"Are you some god who decides who lives and who dies?" Alex spat in fury.

"At this moment, yes."

IT WAS CLOSE to 4 A.M. as I drove along Longwood Avenue back home to Brookline. I doubted I would be able to go back to sleep. My nerves were on edge, my heart in turmoil from the confrontation. It had ended in bitter silence, Alex turning away from me, burying himself in his thoughts.

Alex had his new companion, Andrew, accompany him to the hospital. I had informed Andrew what had happened, and he had tried to comfort Alex with soothing phrases: It will be O.K.; just rest; let the new medicines begin to work. But Alex had responded with the same unforgiving silence he had visited on me.

The last ivory rays of a full moon illuminated the facade of the Harvard Medical School facing Longwood Avenue. The school was built at the turn of the century, modeled on a Greek temple, its five massive columns rising nearly four stories, its broad steps elevating the entrance some twenty feet above the ground. The intent of the founders was clear: this was a place of great importance, where the powerful gods of natural science and human healing were to be worshiped.

Were the school's columns Doric, Ionic, or Corinthian? I could never keep the differences straight. Alex, an accomplished architect, of course would know. But he would not so simply answer my question. He would want me to understand the building as he did, as a creation, virtually animate. He would explain how the neoclassical style reflected the aspirations of an emerging industrial America, its vision of itself as heir to the grandeur and intellect of the ancient Greeks. He would touch the marble pillars and gauge the physical composition of the stone, its resilience and range of coloration, and explain why it had been selected for a building of this type, in this climate and location.

I felt a searing pain penetrate my core. Here was a vibrant, sensitive, engaging person—pleading to be put to death.

The medical profession has its codes for easing the dying person's passage: "Expedite the process"; "Help nature take its course"; "Palliate maximally." Each aims to mask the stark reality of the act.

The "understanding" Alex referred to was established early in our relationship, as it is with most patients. Great comfort is gained from knowing there could be humane limits to the seemingly endless dimensions of suffering. When we reach these limits, my charge is described in stylized euphemisms: "no further measures will be taken" and "you will be made comfortable."

Such scenarios are rarely as simple or neat as they might sound. Because, as Alex had said, it is an act of God performed by mortals.

When the decision is made, I order the intensive life support withdrawn, and, if there is pain, an infusion of morphine begun. As I watch the breathing quiet, the flesh slowly cool, I am invariably seized by a sharp moment of doubt. Had everything been done that could have been done? Was there really no longer any reason to live? My fallibility is never more apparent to me than at that moment.

The reality is very different from its portrayal by Dr. Kevorkian with his "death machine" and "assisted suicides." I read the reports of his exploits carefully in the press, particularly the profiles of his subjects. While he deserves credit for drawing attention to an important hidden issue, I mistrust his sangfroid dramatics. What for me is an agonizing process is made to appear glib and uncomplicated. What if a patient is simply depressed, or if the diagnosis is mistaken, or if some further therapy might improve the condition?

Alex had specified clearly what he saw as incompatible with continued life. If he were to become permanently and completely neurologically impaired, paralyzed, blind, demented, he wanted no intervention other than narcotics to lessen the pain and allow him to die. This had been our agreement. I concluded that I had not breached it. What had changed to make Alex so ready to die?

I ENTERED ALEX'S HOSPITAL ROOM just after noon of the next day. The allergic reaction had largely subsided. His skin was no longer flaming red but a soft pink, as if he had been harshly scrubbed during a warm bath. His eyes were relieved of their swelling and rested comfortably in their deep wells. I noted on his chart that his fever was barely 100 degrees and his other vital signs were normal.

Although Alex could not have gotten more than two or three hours sleep, if any, he appeared as he always did, well groomed and composed, his sandy-brown hair neatly combed, his sculpted, aristocratic face washed and shaven. He greeted me with a warm, gracious smile, seated in bed wearing a rich blue silk dressing gown and a tightly bound sash, reading an article in *The New York Times* about the growing competition in America between Sotheby's and Christie's. Fresh-cut flowers were tastefully arranged in a vase on the windowsill. His lunch was set out before him. I noticed it was not hospital fare but from Rebecca's, a Boston café. Andrew sat quietly at the bedside, reading a book in Spanish by an author I did not recognize. For all the world, it appeared that I had come into the bedroom of a country gentleman enjoying a leisurely day.

Alex eagerly extended his hand. I shook it, and noted how much cooler and drier it was. After we exchanged the usual greetings, I took an inventory of his physical condition: How was he feeling overall? Did he notice any side effects from the new antibiotic, Mepron, against the pneumocystis? Were the steroids changing his mood, making him anxious or hungry? And had he gotten any rest, given that after he was sent to the floor from the emergency room, he had been visited by teams of nurses, interns, and medical students, each examining him, reviewing his medical history, and executing the treatment plan.

Alex listened intently to each question, and gave considered, succinct answers. He acknowledged he was much improved. He had noticed no untoward effects of the steroids on his mood, and couldn't say he was unusually hungry, since he always had a hearty appetite. Knowing the hospital cuisine was "limited," he had instructed Andrew to bring him more palatable yet healthy foods: pasta with fresh vegetables, sourdough bread, and a fruit drink. Alex noted that the take-out lunch was surprisingly well made. Yes, on his first admission to a hospital he was struck by its noisy and restless character. There was little rest or privacy to be had.

Andrew stood up from his chair at the word "privacy." He gestured to leave, but before doing so, said haltingly that he had not properly introduced himself the night before. I took his measure: in his mid-twenties, with a pensive and reserved demeanor, curly short-cropped hair, thick wire-rim glasses, prominent bowed nose. Like Alex, he was dressed with care despite the travails of last night, wearing pressed gray slacks, a stiffly starched white shirt, and a beige cashmere vest.

Andrew did not resemble the other young men who had accompanied Alex to his office visits over the preceding five years. Alex called those young men "houseboys." They were Andrew's age, in their early twenties, but of a different appearance, androgynous and fawning.

Alex would never allow them to enter my office and be privy to his affairs, firmly instructing them to remain in the waiting room. When our consultation was completed, he would dispatch them to do chores in the city, buying odds and ends for his house in Gloucester or posting packages to Switzerland. He always went alone to the pharmacy to fill a prescription or to the laboratory for his blood tests. These "houseboys" came and went with the seasons, like the objets d'art Alex acquired at auctions. With their departure, Alex would briefly mention some incident, that they had stolen petty cash, or failed to efficiently discharge their duties, or become drunk and "useless" on the weekends. He said he would soon find "new help" and dismissed the departure lightly, but I detected a sullenness in this usually ebullient man until the next one appeared.

I easily engaged Andrew in conversation. I learned he was from Wellesley, had graduated last year from Brown with a degree in comparative literature, and currently was in New Haven, preparing for a doctorate in Spanish and Portuguese at Yale. When he finished talking, Andrew politely excused himself and left the room.

"He is very kind," Alex stated, an adjective I never heard him apply to the previous "houseboys." "And he of course agreed with you last night."

"Do you today, or are you still angry with me?"

"I could never stay angry with you, Jerry. I will abide by your decision—for now." Alex paused pensively. "I did learn something last night."

I allowed his statement to be suspended between us so he could complete his thought.

"I learned that although I greatly fear death, there are moments I fear living more."

Before I could probe deeper, Alex stated plaintively, "Please do not ask why."

A LEX QUICKLY AND FULLY RECOVERED from both his pneumonia and the allergic reaction. We changed his anti-HIV medications, beginning a new drug called ddC in lieu of the AZT and ddI which he had been taking. The Mepron was continued against pneumocystis as a prophylactic therapy in addition to aerosol treatments with another antibiotic, pentamidine. Alex tolerated these drugs well. Within a month he was back to his vigorous regimen of daily exercise, leaving his seaside mansion in Gloucester early each morning and cycling, running, or hiking along the beaches and rocky hills of that quaint community along Boston's North Shore. He took on two new architectural projects: a townhouse renovation in Zurich and the construction of a ski chalet in Vermont. He was excited about them both, and asked for permission to travel back and forth between the two continents, which I readily gave, knowing work was therapeutic for him.

Andrew accompanied him on some of these work-related trips. He became increasingly apparent in Alex's life. He traveled up from New Haven each weekend, arriving late Friday afternoon and departing early Monday morning. He would miss class to make special weekday trips to Boston to accompany Alex to his medical appointments.

Andrew was remarkably attentive to the details of Alex's condition and therapies. He recorded Alex's symptoms on a list which he handed to Alex, who would then read them to me. Andrew also came prepared with his own questions, wondering if special foods or extra vitamins might increase weight and energy, whether the sheepdogs that Alex was bringing over from Switzerland carried parasites which might endanger someone with AIDS. He also regularly solicited my opinion of research developments in HIV that he followed on the Internet. At the end of each visit, Andrew dutifully noted when Alex's prescriptions needed refilling and arranged for Alex's next blood tests and appointment.

Alex clearly enjoyed the intelligent attention given him by Andrew. Over time, he sought Andrew's participation not only in his illness but in the great range of political and economic issues which he liked to discuss during his medical appointments. Would the civilized world watch the genocide in Bosnia without intervening, and if we did intervene, what should be done? How might the geopolitics of the Continent be changed by the European Union and how might his native Switzerland maintain its neutrality? Where was contemporary art headed, and was too much power wielded by the Whitney Biennial? How should education be restructured in Europe and America so a permanent underclass would not be created in our technology-driven society?

Alex, with Andrew seated at his side, one day seized upon an unexpected subject, introduced by informing me that Andrew was Jewish.

"I am embarrassed to say I am ignorant about Judaism, and interested to learn how it corresponds and contrasts with my Catholic heritage."

He remarked he had not known any Jews in Switzerland except for the Baers, a powerful banking dynasty that associated with his family strictly on business terms. He chided Andrew for not knowing the history of the religion or the derivation of its tenets in greater depth.

Alex was specifically interested in the Jewish concept of suffering, how the Book of Job was understood, and whether the pain incurred in this world was a preparation for the rewards of an afterlife. He was surprised to hear from me that of all the issues wrestled with by the rabbis in the Talmud and later, the meaning of suffering was one that they concluded was unanswerable. It remained an enigma why suffering in this life had to be; it was not rationalized by an afterlife. Indeed, heaven and hell were not prominent in Jewish belief, and purgatory did not exist.

"How then to describe my current state?" Alex humorously challenged.

I tried to use his remark as an opportunity to air my question from the night in the emergency room. I asked Alex to expand on his thought, to explain how he entered purgatory, and why he had sought a premature exit. But Alex deftly closed the subject.

"It's just a silly metaphor, unless you're a child terrified by visions of fire and brimstone. Let's end by saying I'll stay where you now see me."

Some six months later, in the autumn of 1992, I stopped in Switzerland after a research conference in Paris. It was in his native environment that Alex found the setting to answer me.

He was in Zurich to check on the progress of his townhouse project and had prevailed upon me to visit him on my way home. Unfortunately, he added, Andrew had to stay in New Haven to prepare for exams and would not accompany us on a tour of his homeland.

I had never seen Zurich, and Alex was an irrepressible guide. At daybreak, we were already walking the narrow cobblestone streets of the old town, Alex pointing out the Zunfthausen, the original medieval guild halls where the prominent families, including his own, still met for meals, continuing to the Grossmünster, the church where Zwingli had broken with the pope and declared his Reformation, and ending at the Peterskirche.

"The Peterskirche, built in the thirteenth century, still boasts the largest clock face in all of Europe," Alex said as he pointed to the forbidding black tower. "It dominates Zurich, saying 'die Zeit fliegt immer,' time is flying, always."

He checked his watch against the time on the Peterskirche and said we would be late for lunch if we didn't cut short the tour of Zurich and head into the mountains.

By midday, we arrived at Einsiedeln, the Benedictine monastery

where Alex had been educated. It was the home of the Black
Madonna, still on display for the veneration of pilgrims after ten centuries. Alex explained he had been sent to the monastery at the age
of nine, as every male of the Roesle family had been for generations,
to receive a classical education from the guiding hands of the monks.
He still knew many of the order, and as we walked through the
stone halls, Alex would greet each with a silent formal bow.

He led me to the far end of the building, the air thick and dank
between the roughly quarried brown stones. We passed dozens of
doors that opened onto identical cells until we reached the one
he had occupied. It was empty. I noted the bare stone floor, two
wooden pallets made up with tight-cornered white sheets and coarse
brown wool blankets, a single basin to wash, and a slit in the thick
wall that permitted a narrow shaft of light to enter.

"The younger boys live in a large common dormitory, but the
older students share these cells. It was to prepare us to enter the order, to live as the monks do."

We moved on down the hall. The heavy air was soon permeated
by the rich sweet smell of baking bread. Alex brought me into the
dining area. He explained that everything in the room was built by
the monks and students from the surrounding woods. There were
rows of unfinished plank tables and adjoining rough benches.

"The splinters are there for a reason," Alex whispered, with mock
seriousness, as I shifted uncomfortably on the bench.

He handed me a thick slice of coarse black bread and a slab of goat
cheese on a heavy metal plate.

"There also may be a few pebbles still in the bread. Be on guard."

A small heavyset monk, in his seventies, with rheumy eyes and a
few wisps of fine gray hair left at the back of his neck, appeared with
a plate and joined us. Alex greeted him warmly and introduced him
as Pater Odelie. He had been Alex's primary tutor, in Greek, Latin,
Hochdeutsch, the great books, and catechism. Although he spoke no
English or French, he seemed determined to engage me in an intelligent conversation. I struggled to respond to his inquiries about my
background and work, trying to transmute my *shtetl* Yiddish into
comprehensible Swiss German by imposing a singsong lilt on the
words and desperately searching my memory for the Germanic
equivalents of words that were derived from Hebrew or Russian.

Alex was enjoying my difficulties, mischievously grinning like a boy who has succeeded in his practical joke. When the lunch mercifully finished, Alex dutifully cleared the table, depositing our plates and utensils in a large sink at the end of the dining hall. Pater Odelie told me he wanted to show me their library, which housed the best collection of medieval and Renaissance manuscripts in all of Switzerland. Although the monastery had been sacked and burned many times, most recently by Napoleon's soldiers, the books had been saved each time through the cunning of the monks.

"They are better at saving books these days than souls," Alex said softly in English, out of Pater Odelie's hearing.

Pater Odelie escorted us to the vaulted chamber that was the library, took a large bound volume, and placed it at the end of a long polished oak reading table. He opened it casually, and my eyes were drawn to an illuminated picture of a man emerging from the earth. Only half consciously did I assimilate the familiar calligraphy. Before I could comment, Pater Odelie began to speak, chanting in his melodious Swiss German accent ancient words that I knew by heart.

"Va-yivreh eloheim et ha-adam b'tselmo—"

Pater Odelie paused and looked expectantly at me, he the teacher, I the called-upon student.

"And God created man in His own image," I translated for Alex from Hebrew into English. I then continued where Pater Odelie had left off:

"—b'tselem eloheim barah ohto." Again, for Alex, I said in English: "In the image of God created He him."

The monk nodded his head somberly, and closed the medieval Hebrew Bible.

WE SLOWLY NAVIGATED the twisting mountain road in Alex's Mercedes, descending through miles of black fir, the dense unconquered pagan forest drinking in the cool November sunlight.

"I hope, Jerry, you didn't mind taking so much time in the monastery. It was a special treat for Pater Odelie. He receives few visitors, and he is a very kind soul."

I said I had enjoyed the visit, that it was a unique experience. I had never been in a monastery. It felt like moving back in time, the silent monks sitting in their cells studying, the simple communal food, the furniture and utensils made by hand in the carpentry and metal shops. I imagined little had changed in that contemplative world for a millennium. I still could not get over the exchange with Pater Odelie.

"Sadly, he is the only monk left who knows Hebrew. The others have all died, and it is no longer taught. When I called to arrange our visit he was excited to meet someone who knew the language."

Alex was silent for a long moment, and then softly added: "He was my confessor as well as my teacher. He chose that passage from the Creation for a reason."

"Really? It seemed he opened the Bible randomly."

"Nothing an elder Swiss monk does is done randomly," Alex gently corrected. I waited for him to elaborate, but he lifted his brow to signal that I should guess.

I thought for a while. God created man in His own image.

"To say all men are God's children and make me feel welcome? As a Jew in a Catholic monastery?"

"Yes." Alex nodded. "To you he was offering ecumenical friendship. But he had you read the repetition as well: 'In the image of God created He him.' Pater Odelie was communicating at once to us both."

I told Alex I didn't fully comprehend Pater Odelie's intent.

"To me, he was giving comfort. Also as a child of God. Comfort, but not forgiveness."

We entered into a steel gray fog that had settled over the lower valley at the outskirts of Zurich. I was surprised by the abrupt change from the penetrating sunlight of the higher elevations. Alex said these mists were common in the late autumn afternoons, the temperatures falling quickly and the moisture from the Lake of Zurich condensing in the encroaching cold.

I sat silently, not wanting to distract Alex from the concealed twists in the road that seemed to spring from nowhere. He adeptly guided the vehicle as if he were an experienced mariner returning home through a storm, anticipating threatening obstacles before they fully came into view.

After fifteen long minutes, we emerged from the mist into the stone-gray November twilight of the city. Alex relaxed his tense grip on the wheel and began to speak again.

"If it were not for Pater Odelie, I might have gone mad. I showed you the cell I lived in. I did not want to leave home, but knew that every male in my family had for centuries. I was a sensitive and timid child unprepared for such a cold, demanding prison. We were awakened before dawn, then prayed, ate a meager breakfast, studied, did our physical work in the surrounding fields or the carpentry and metal shops, then prayed again, and at the end of each day confessed before retiring for bed."

Alex said at first he confessed to Pater Odelie the usual sins: he had spoken in anger, or forgotten his evening prayers, or been slothful. But he knew that to receive absolution he also needed to confess the sins that he kept tightly locked in the dark recesses of his heart. So he summoned the courage to tell Pater Odelie what he had wanted to hide from God.

He sinned in his dreams. There he was visited by large hairy creatures, apelike demons who approached him with protruding male organs. Their strong arms held him in a moist embrace as they entered him. Other dreams were not of creatures or really men, but of their isolated parts, buttocks, penises, mouths, suspended in black space and inviting him to know them. These visions terrified him, but also tortured him with excitement, and he would awake trembling, with his bedsheets stained.

Pater Odelie had instructed him to pray to the Holy Virgin. Her healing presence filled the monastery, and if his soul truly desired it, she would lift his misguided lust.

But prayer did not change his dreams. Worse, the more he concentrated in prayer, the more his fantasies permeated his day. He could not resist stealing glances at the boys around him. When they bathed and dressed together, he was overcome by the beauty of their form, his face flushing from his feverish desires.

"I believed I was destined for the fires of hell, even though in Einsiedeln I never had physical relations," he said with an anguished voice. "It was clearly written in the Holy Laws of the Old Testament. To lie with man as with woman is an abomination. And Paul the Apostle, in Romans and in Corinthians, preaches that men who consort with men like they do with women are cut off from the saved.

"It didn't matter that Pater Odelie absolved my sin, saying 'go and sin no more.' Or that he purposely gave me strenuous tasks that kept me late in the fields, so I did not bathe or undress with the other boys. When I confessed to him that I could not purge myself with prayer or work, he took me on long walks in the woods. I remember his slow thoughtful pace, the way he took my hand in his and told me of Christ's special love for the priest, the celibate who is the exemplar in man's fight against Original Sin. He encouraged me to become a monk, to withdraw from the outer world and find peace within his walls. But I knew I could not follow his path."

I watched Alex's eyes fill with tears as each painful wave of memory broke.

"I thought once I left and reentered the larger world, I could force myself to live normally."

He took his degree in Basel in law and finance, as was expected by his parents. They introduced him to young women of high social and financial status with the intention that the right match would soon be made. On dates, several of these young women invited him to touch them, but Alex found no pleasure in that.

"I knew inside I had no true desire for a Beatrice who could guide me away from the waiting Inferno."

So, at the age of twenty-one, Alex began the "final descent." He, an educated and refined young man, fluent in six languages—Greek, Latin, German, French, Italian, and English—knowledgeable not only about his studies of law and banking but also about painting, sculpture, history, literature, and music, entered the subterranean world of alleys and bars and bathhouses. His sexual encounters were with men who could have come from his dreams: anonymous, experienced as body parts, not as whole human beings. And when this furtive coupling was done, he would return alone to his quarters at the university and cry from debasement and loneliness.

There was one other person in his family who also was alone, Alex explained. It was his Aunt Vreni. She was in her forties, a soft-spoken intelligent woman who never married because of her condition, multiple sclerosis. Vreni had had this disease ever since Alex could remember, and she began to deteriorate rapidly while he was at university. Alex observed as her gait became broad and lurching, the reach of her hand feeble and inexact, and, to Vreni's great embarrassment, control of her bladder and bowels uncertain. Alex became devoted to her, and she to him.

"Aunt Vreni knew firsthand what is great suffering, and saw its marks on my face."

He would often spend Sunday afternoons with her in her garden in Kusnacht, overlooking the curved verdant valley leading north to Zurich. Still in his stiff church clothes and shined black shoes, he found a brief respite from the torment that was his life: his monotonous work as an apprentice lawyer at his father's bank; his coerced dates with the daughters of landed Catholic families; his humiliating trips into the homosexual underworld. In Vreni's garden he was free to share his other dreams, the dreams of what he hoped would sustain him. He believed he would find meaning and fulfillment in life through objects of beauty that embodied man's creative imagination.

"Aunt Vreni was intellectually challenging, although she never went to university. Like nearly all Swiss women of her generation, she was self-educated, reading the books her brothers gave her from their classes."

Vreni debated with him the great question that Alex knew had been raised by the philosophers of ancient Greece: Is meaning inherent in beauty and its physical forms, or does it only exist when man experiences those objects which uplift his spirit? Since Vreni held the latter to be true, she asked what human experiences he would link to the objects of beauty he so desired.

Alex explained to Vreni that he could not answer her question until he had changed the direction of his current life. His first step would be a new career. He intended to leave banking and become an architect. Then he could experience the pleasure of creating physical structures that melded his Swiss love of purpose with the Greek ideal of beauty.

"Aunt Vreni cautioned me to wait. I had no independent funds, and she feared the consequences of opposing my father's plans for me."

Vreni soon took a sharp decline. She became completely paralyzed and confined to a wheelchair. She then developed recurrent bacterial infections from her atonic bladder, followed by inflammation of her optic nerves, robbing her of sight. Alex spent every evening nursing her, administering her medicine, encouraging her to eat, comforting her with words of affection. Yet there was no improvement despite high doses of antibiotics, steroids, and vitamins. It was clear to everyone, including Alex, that she would soon be gone.

Days before she died, she told Alex she had been able to endure all she had because of him, that she loved him as she had loved no one else in her life. That familial love had fulfilled her life. She had also long known he was different, that he was homosexual.

"She said she would help me to become free."

Alex understood Vreni's words only after her death. She had left the entirety of her estate to Alex, estimated at some 15 million Swiss francs, or about 10 million dollars. Her will stated he could use the funds as he wished.

"We were two cripples, she in body, I in spirit. Her gift was to be my crutches through life."

Alex entered into an uneasy détente with his family. He left the bank over the angry protests of his father, and studied architecture, first in Zurich and then at Harvard's Graduate School of Design.

"I considered staying in the U.S., a more liberal and anonymous society than my own, but felt the pull of language and culture, so I returned."

He opened a successful architectural office in Zurich. Feeling he was gaining control over his life, Alex stopped his journeys into the underworld and brought a young man, Peter, to live with him in his townhouse near the dominating Peterskirche clock. Alex described Peter as striking in appearance, with jet black hair, doe eyes, and a muscular build. Peter was often mistaken for a model, but actually was a physician. They had met by chance in a park in Zurich, Alex drawn by his exquisite beauty.

Peter came from a poor family and was eager to establish a lucrative medical practice. Alex lent him money to set up an elegant office in a prime location. Although living with Alex, Peter regularly bestowed his sexual favors on older men who returned his affections with expensive gifts. Alex tolerated this infidelity with quiet pain, and tried to give Peter enough money and possessions so that he would not stray. Alex acknowledged that despite all he offered, he knew he would never succeed.

"It is the way most gay men are," Alex said with embarrassment.

In the spring of 1986, Peter decided to be tested for the recently discovered AIDS virus, HIV, at the Kantonspital where he had trained. He had promised to tell Alex the result when it was available.

Alex never heard the words, but the outcome was clear. When Alex returned that evening from his office to his townhouse, he found Peter sprawled in the living room. He had shot himself in the head with the rifle he—like all Swiss men—kept, as a reservist in the army.

"From the moment I developed pneumocystis, my mind could not leave that scene of Peter. As a medical doctor, he knew what it meant to have HIV. He could not endure living with the bug, just waiting for the sickness to come. I thought I was stronger. I had endured the monastery. I went to be tested, and when I learned I too was positive, decided to live until I became like Aunt Vreni."

Alex paused and searched my face for understanding. His basis for setting the limits of living defined in our "agreement" was now apparent. But my question from the night in the emergency room was only half answered. Alex seemed to read my thoughts.

"As my fever rose from the allergy, my eyes blurred and my joints would not move. I panicked, believing I was entering into Aunt Vreni's condition. My world collapsed around me, like a building falling in on itself in an earthquake. I searched around in the rubble for a strong arm to lift me up from the suffocating debris. There was none. All the beautiful things—the paintings and furniture and statuary—were shattered as well.

"I realized more deeply what Aunt Vreni had been saying. Those objects of beauty no longer had meaning. They could not hold me up against the blows of a life of illness. I needed more than objects. I needed a person. I had been that person for Aunt Vreni. No one was there for me."

I reached for Alex's trembling hand.

"You would not help me to die and I did not have Peter's courage to do it myself. So I am condemned to this purgatory until the time comes to descend."

I SETTLED DURING LIFTOFF into the soft leather of the Swissair seat and watched the rectangular green fields surrounding the Zurich airport become a distant blur. Alex had stayed with me until the final moments at the gate, and I had surprised him by embracing him warmly as I said good-bye. I had spontaneously expressed my growing feelings for Alex, a person for whom I had developed deep affection, his mind sharp and engaging, his heart genuine and giving. And so pained.

I thought after that hug how physical affection between men was part of my upbringing. It was natural to kiss my father, uncles, and brother, to be embraced by male cousins and friends at birthdays and holidays, to dance with men at Orthodox weddings and bar mitzvahs.

I recalled the very early years of the AIDS epidemic, before HIV was discovered, when a possible infectious or environmental cause of the disease was sought in the lifestyles of gay men. During the medical interviews, I was shocked and confused as I listened to graphic details of the subterranean world of gay sex. There was a compulsive frenzy evident in the numbers of sexual encounters, totaling a hundred or more per year for many of the men. These were usually anonymous, and as in Alex's case, consummated in bars, alleys, and parks. I maintained my professional composure as I listened to descriptions of practices that offered no apparent dimension of affection.

For the first time in the decade since I had heard such stories, Alex had shown me what, for some, was behind the practices and mores that were so foreign and perplexing. I compared Alex's sexual development with mine. As a teenager, hormones racing at a fevered pitch, I had fantasies that might be analogous to Alex's: dreams of pulchritudinous women offering me their bodies with no dimension of complicating emotional relationships. In college, like most of my peers, I had sought easy sex, sleeping with girls I had just met, the "free love" of the 1960s happily accessed without payment in feelings. But after a few years, this grew thin, repetitive, boring. I left it not with guilt but with the understanding that I wanted to find something more sustaining.

What if that search was made impossible, if it was stifled by a society that gave no permission or respect to the yearnings of my heart and soul? Marked as defective and damned, aberrant in creation, a mistake that opposed the correct flow of nature's demands and desires, Alex had fulfilled the biblical prophecy that was set out for him. Would I also go underground in my quest, believing that the damned did not deserve love in the light of day? Or would I rather accept the alternative Pater Odelie had offered, the sublimated safety of celibacy? Alex had concluded that while this might save his soul, it would not give meaning to his life. So he had sought a third solution, in the ideal of beauty, to answer the cries of his tortured heart. But physical beauty had failed him, its pleasing illuminations quickly extinguished by the cold breath of approaching death.

I awoke as the plane glided over the Boston harbor, skimming the black asphalt runway in a seamless approach. During sleep, I had returned to the events in the emergency room. As the scene replayed itself, I no longer asked why Alex was so ready to die. I awoke wondering how to help him live.

I HAD NO IMMEDIATE ANSWER, only knowing I wanted to give Alex time, as much time as medical science could possibly provide. I hoped that, during that time, a solution would be found.

And I knew that my clinical goal was not a simple one. Alex had very little immune function remaining. His T-cell number had fallen to below 50, some one tenth of normal. Despite the preventive antibiotics, he was still vulnerable to a host of infectious pathogens and to cancer. And, although I might juggle his anti-HIV medicines, at this advanced stage of immune deterioration, they had minimal benefits.

My fears were soon realized. Alex developed a series of bacterial pneumonias, with streptococci and haemophilus, microbes hard to eradicate despite prolonged treatment with potent antibiotics. The long courses of antibiotic treatment caused overgrowth of fungus in his mouth and a toxic colitis. These complications required therapy with yet other antibiotics.

While on business in Switzerland in 1994, Alex called urgently, his voice trembling as he described the abrupt onset of large black spots obscuring vision in his right eye. I instructed him to return immediately to Boston. Peering with my ophthalmoscope, I saw the heavy bloody tracks of cytomegalovirus infection. The right retina was completely destroyed, the virus having eaten deeply into its matrix. The sight in that eye was permanently lost.

Alex acquiesced to having a permanent catheter placed in his chest to administer daily intravenous ganciclovir, the noxious drug needed to treat cytomegalovirus. It had to be given for the duration of life, or else the infection would reactivate and spread to the other eye and then to his liver, brain, and bowel. So Alex became tethered each day for several hours to this intravenous medicine.

Shortly after the cytomegalovirus infection, Alex developed severe diarrhea that did not appear to be related to his prophylactic antibiotics. He became ashen and gaunt, his weight falling from 155 to 130 pounds. He could not sleep more than a few hours at a stretch before awakening with abdominal cramps and running to the bathroom.

After several weeks of this misery, we diagnosed the cause of his diarrhea as microsporidium, an unusual parasite that once primarily affected livestock and now was seen as an opportunistic infection in AIDS. The colitis abated completely with albendazole, an experimental antibiotic. Alex gained some weight but remained weak and gaunt.

He endured all this with a remarkably stoical demeanor, revealing no anger or bitterness, his quiet suffering occasionally punctuated by black humor. Pointing to the catheter that penetrated his sunken chest, the bruises on his forearms from the multiple blood tests, the fixed nonseeing right eye, he remarked more than once, "Now you see the stigmata of the fallen saint."

Through all this, Andrew was at his side. He had left Yale before finishing his doctorate and moved to Gloucester. Andrew spent the day meticulously arranging Alex's multiple medications, the prophylactic antibiotics, the ganciclovir treatments for cytomegalovirus, the albendazole for microsporidium, the azithromycin for bacterial pneumonia, as well as a new anti-HIV medication, d4T. He encouraged Alex to eat as best he could, cooking the foods Alex digested easily—pastas, fish, bread pudding. He made sure Alex rested when needed, and tried to distract him from the constancy of his condition and its therapies by brief trips out of the house to auctions, museums, and antiques shops.

Alex, with a weak chuckle in his voice, began to refer to Andrew as "my wife," a term that at first made me uncomfortable. But with time, I came to see it was only because it was a female appellation, not because their domestic arrangements differed in any substantial way from those of heterosexual spouses. As with a married couple, there were moments of temper and distance, appreciation and affection, stubbornness and coaxing, as they worked to fit themselves into a joint life. Tragically, it was a joint life permeated by sickness and debility.

IN THE AUTUMN OF 1995, a lottery was held to determine who would first receive the newly developed protease inhibitors. This lottery was necessary because the initial supply of the drug was low and the demand great. Designed partly by human imagination and partly by computer simulation, the first drugs succeeded in clinical trials beyond anything anyone expected. Combinations of these inhibitors with the older nucleoside drugs like AZT and 3TC lowered levels of HIV in the bloodstream on average a hundred- to a thousandfold; in some patients the virus became undetectable even using the most sensitive tests. In concert with these dramatic reductions in viral levels were increases in T-cell numbers and clinical improvement: marked gain in weight and energy, and reduced occurrence of opportunistic infections.

Alex won the lottery to receive the first of the protease inhibitors, called saquinavir. It was developed by the Swiss pharmaceutical company Hoffman LaRoche. Of the forty patients I had submitted who qualified based on their very advanced states, only two were fortunate enough to be selected.

"I never expected my Swiss compatriots to rescue me," Alex quipped as he began his first treatment.

Within weeks, he said he was feeling better than he had in a decade. His wasted form began to fill out, his ashen color returned to its former robust hue. Alex changed not only in body but in spirit.

"I consider again for the first time in years that I may live," he allowed.

After four months on the drug, filled with energy and a sense of well-being, Alex ventured to make concrete plans for the future. With Andrew, he visited select properties in Boston's Beacon Hill neighborhood, seeking a space where they might open a business in antique and modern furniture of the highest quality. They traveled to New York, London, and San Francisco, assembling an inventory for the store. They combined assets and approached banks for long-term financing of the project.

Alex decided to formalize his relationship with Andrew. Because they could not marry, he adopted Andrew as his son. Alex also worried that his family would not respect his will, and would try to seize his assets.

"When the time comes, hopefully many years from now, I want to pass on the freedom that came with Aunt Vreni's gift," he explained.

By late spring, after some nine months on the protease inhibitor, Alex's viral load in his blood fell from its initial level of 425,000 to 17,000. With this drastic reduction in HIV level, Alex's helper T cells rose to above 50 for the first time in two years. He gained so

much weight that he announced excitedly he was planning a cele-
bratory shopping spree for a new wardrobe.

At first I resisted the joy that welled in my heart as I watched Alex
return to such a vigorous life. I was strangely unsettled by the striking remission of his disease, uncertain how long it would last. But
Alex's clinical improvement was so profound that I finally admitted
that yes, a miracle of science had occurred, his AIDS had gone into
remission. And I began to share Alex's dream that he might live, and
live long, and live well.

In May 1996, Alex developed fever. It was at first low-grade,
hovering for a week around 100 degrees, but then sharply rising to
104. I examined him and could find no obvious source of infection.
After two weeks the high fever did not abate. Alex tried to sustain
his many daily activities, refusing to cancel appointments related to
the planned business and its financing. But Andrew and I prevailed
upon him to give in, at least until a diagnosis was made. Now pros-
trate from the raging temperature, rising only to travel to see me for
tests, Alex looked to me desperately, the way a starving child looks
for the nourishment he once enjoyed and never imagined would be
taken away.

I considered both infectious and malignant causes for this sudden and worrisome development. I wanted to find the cause of
Alex's fever quickly, treat it, and return him to health. I cultured his
blood, urine, feces, and bone marrow for bacteria, mycobacterium
(tuberculosis-like microbes), cytomegalovirus, herpes virus, syphilis,
fungi, protozoa, and parasites. He had chest X rays to rule out pneumonia, CAT scans of the abdomen and pelvis to check for lymphoma or abscesses. I performed an MRI scan of the brain and spinal
cord to assess the possibility of a malignant, infectious, or degenera-
tive process of the nervous system. The ophthalmologist who examined his one functioning eye searched the retina for a recurrent
infection and found none. After three weeks, I was at a loss to explain his fever.

Alex began to lose weight rapidly, dropping some twelve pounds
in three weeks. His face again became drawn and pale. As I watched
Alex leave my office, Andrew's arms supporting his withered and
frail form, I sank into my chair, feeling weak and faint, a dry, sour
taste welling up in my mouth.

I did not often feel this way when confronting illness. Like all doctors, I had been conditioned during my medical training not to react viscerally to a patient's pain and suffering. Otherwise, my judgment would be impaired and my effectiveness limited in responding to the needs of my patients. But in this instance, I felt I had absorbed Alex's raw suffering and it was threatening to overwhelm me. I was unsure how to contain it or expel it.

It was not just his suffering that jarred me, but the sense that I was failing him. I was responsible for sustaining his life, and if it could not be reasonably sustained, then our understanding was to allow for a death with the minimum of pain. Without a diagnosis, I was navigating blind, unable to chart an appropriate direction. I had arrived at the deepest point of despair that a physician can reach, the netherworld of uncertainty.

Unsolved cases such as Alex's often end up being diagnosed only at autopsy. There was even a didactic exercise, almost a game, in academic teaching hospitals, based on cases that eluded diagnosis. The exercise was conducted as a so-called "clinical pathological conference," or CPC. It involved the ruminations of a clinician who first analyzed the data available when the patient had been alive and then offered a diagnosis. This diagnosis was confirmed or rejected by the findings obtained during the autopsy by the pathologist. Indeed, every week there was a CPC published in *The New England Journal of Medicine*, the most prestigious publication in clinical medicine.

I had served as a clinician in a *New England Journal* CPC, and had gotten the diagnosis right. It was a heady experience, first standing before the Harvard faculty in the amphitheater at the Massachusetts General Hospital, where the exercise was conducted, and then again several months later, having the whole medical world read in the *Journal* your intellectual dissection of the case and applaud your skill in solving the mystery which had been unsolved by the treating doctors. Now, my confidence was nowhere to be found, undermined by my failure to identify the cause of Alex's deterioration.

The thought of learning the diagnosis from a pathologist performing Alex's autopsy sickened me. Although I tried to block the image from my mind, I visualized him as a corpse supine on the cold metal of the autopsy table. The sharp scalpel of the prosector would cut open his yellowed flesh as the pathologist searched for the hidden cancer or infection that had thrown his internal thermostat out of balance, accounting for the raging fevers.

I pulled myself back from this morbid daydream. I concentrated again on the image of the living Alex, gaunt and weak. His illness seemed to taunt me, that I would never figure out what was wrong, would never effectively treat him, would never restore the quality of his life.

I would not be comforted by the rationalization that, despite the respite from the new protease drug, Alex had AIDS, that there was no cure, that in the end a few weeks or a few months did not matter. There would be no psychic peace, for Alex, or Andrew, or me, if he died without our knowing why. Not every disease is treatable or curable, but I believed that every disease should be discernible.

When Alex returned to the office at the end of his fifth week of fever, I noticed a subtle change in his drawn face. There was a slight droop to his left cheek and eyelid. I carefully tested the cranial nerves that control the muscles of the head and neck, and believed I had at last found a clinical abnormality. The fifth and seventh left cranial nerves were impaired. Was there a growing abscess along the route of these nerves that caused this? Or was a brain tumor not seen on the previous scans now emerging from its hiding place?

I explained to Alex that we would repeat an MRI scan of his brain, and then perform a spinal tap, with analysis of the fluid for microbes or cancer cells. He closed his eyes in exhaustion and nodded in assent.

With Andrew holding him on one side and I on the other, we carried Alex to the scanner. No abnormality in the brain or along the tracks of the cranial nerves was seen. We then transported him to the emergency room. There, I learned that the worst had occurred. A thick, viscous fluid dripped slowly from the needle inserted in his spine. Under the microscope, I saw it was laden with cancer cells.

I stood mute by Alex's bedside, feeling as if the dimension of time had collapsed, four years converging into a single moment. I tightly gripped Alex's fevered hand in mine, as Andrew gently stroked his other. I finally found the words to tell Alex what I had found, that he had a cancerous meningitis due to lymphoma, meaning his brain and spinal cord were bathed in the cells of this aggressive tumor. The cancer cells released toxins that accounted for his raging fevers. And because the lymphoma cells were swimming through his nervous system and had not yet aggregated into masses, the MRI scans did not detect them.

"Alex, you always insisted I be totally honest with you, regardless of the information. There is no cure for this cancer."

Andrew began to cry, the tears flowing down his long thin face. Alex looked up at him, his vibrant blue eyes wide, his smile soft and comforting.

"*Mein Schatz,* don't cry. Please don't cry, Andrew. It will be fine. You and I, we will be fine."

I gave Andrew time to compose himself, and then recommended to them a palliative approach: first, medications to reduce the fevers, including steroids, which might have some temporary effect against the lymphoma; and then, if needed, comfort measures should there be significant pain or neurological impairment. I assumed our "agreement" would soon be invoked, and stood ready to help Alex die with the minimum of suffering.

"There is no other treatment, no chemotherapy for lymphomatous meningitis?" Alex asked.

I replied that chemotherapy could be administered, directly into the spinal fluid around the brain, but it was toxic and of minimal benefit in cases such as his. I reiterated that lymphomatous meningitis in AIDS was incurable, and usually resulted in paralysis as the tumor choked the nerves to the arms and legs.

Alex pressed harder. Did anyone ever respond? Could any time be gained?

I answered that responses were rare, and that the time gained was best measured in a few weeks to months.

Alex listened to my words with a calm and distant look in his eyes. Then, in a clear and unwavering voice, he declared: "I want to be treated. I choose life."

ANDREW AND I FINALLY LOCATED a small corner table at Rebecca's Café. It was crowded with lunchtime customers from the surrounding medical area, students, nurses, patients and their families seeking culinary relief from the bland cafeteria food of the hospitals. We were meeting for the first time since Andrew had returned from Switzerland, where he had scattered Alex's ashes on a lake in the majestic Eingadine region Alex so loved. I could see the strain around Andrew's deep blue eyes. He had not left Alex's side for a moment during the long awful weeks in hospital as Alex had struggled to survive the toxic chemotherapy and rapidly advancing lymphoma. At each step of the treatment, I had questioned Alex, restating the side effects of the drugs and the extremely remote chance of benefit, but he had forcefully reaffirmed his desire to be treated aggressively so as to live as long as he could, despite the pain.

"So many times in the past he had told me he wanted simply to be put to sleep, to avoid the degrading final stages of the disease," Andrew continued. "But he chose otherwise. And apparently not out of fear."

"He was not afraid to die," I agreed. I knew this because I had bluntly asked Alex, concerned that his tenacious insistence on toxic treatment reflected this common fear.

"I never thought he would want to go through all he did," Andrew flatly stated. "And he never complained or showed anger. He put all his energy into comforting me, and you. He loved you, Jerry, like a brother."

I felt my chest tighten, my eyes become moist.

I vividly recalled the scenes in Alex's hospital room, Andrew sitting close to the bedside, gently stroking Alex's wispy skull, the fine brown hair gone after the chemotherapy, whispering words of love in his ear.

"I'm here, Alex. I'm with you, now. I'll always be with you. And you with me."

I also recalled Andrew's torment, revealed only in private, that we were torturing Alex with our therapies. He painfully questioned the wisdom of continuing along the path Alex had chosen. I too felt conflicted, knowing that the chance of success was remote while the likelihood of toxicity and increased suffering was great. But Alex had been rational and clear in his wishes, and I explained to Andrew that until we reached the point of invoking our "agreement," his decisions were to be respected.

I returned my focus to the present and asked Andrew if he had begun to make plans.

He bowed his head, softly saying he needed more time to piece his life back together. He had left his studies and his work to devote himself to Alex. While Alex was on the protease inhibitor, he had regained hope and made concrete plans about the future. All that needed to be rethought.

Andrew confessed he was exhausted, not only from the travail of

Alex's final illness and death, but because he was already besieged by Alex's family. They were furious about the adoption and maneuvering to contest the will. It was hard to mourn and to take the time to reconstruct one's life while dealing with the personal and legal attacks of Alex's father and siblings.

I thought if Andrew had been the "wife" Alex jokingly called him, there would have been no contest from the family.

We left the pain of recounting the circumstances of Alex's treatment and the current turmoil with his family, and told each other stories that neither knew. Alex's spirit suffused our dialogue, his energetic, playful voice echoing in our minds.

I thought how, following that night four years ago, I had stood confused, uncertain why Alex had been so ready to die. Listening now to Andrew, it was clear why, when the end approached, he had been so desperate to live.

Elizabeth

WHAT NOW? I asked myself with annoyance as I opened Elizabeth's letter. I prided myself on not only being a doctor to my patients, but also a friend, a partner working in unison toward common goals. But with Elizabeth, each interaction—whether correspondence, telephone call, or office visit—made me feel like an adversary in a long-running contest. She would probe my strengths and weaknesses, maneuver for advantage, and then press to have the upper hand.

And it was a Tuesday, a long and tiring Tuesday, as nearly every Tuesday was, the day of the week devoted to most of my clinical duties. Mornings were spent with people with AIDS, afternoons with those battling cancer or blood diseases. I usually saw fifteen or more patients over the course of the day, rarely breaking for lunch or attending to anything else but their care.

I looked out my office window over the Boston skyline, the fiery August sun almost set, the city clothed in the soft pink silks of a summer evening. I was already late for an end-of-the-day meeting planned in my lab, and her letter forced me to delay.

Seever Estates
Edgartown, Martha's Vineyard
22 August 1987

Dearest Jerome,

I trust you are not wilting in this ghastly heat wave. All the fuss in the *Globe* about the city eventually becoming a greenhouse from global warming! If that hellish time comes, I shall retire to my island estate here and escape the fate suffered by my fellow townsfolk.

The summer passes once again without much drama. I finally divined what's missing and it's not only my blood cells, which is all you really care about. Does that remark make you wonder whether I was a good girl and went for my transfusions at the Vineyard Hospital?

Did she? If not, she's more than two weeks late by now and could be dangerously anemic.

At my age I can enjoy only Six of the Seven Deadly Sins! The dinners, the teas, the garden parties are all great opportunities for Vanity, Envy, Anger, Avarice, Sloth, and, of course, Gluttony. Among my set, the last is considered the most egregious. But with my condition, I don't give a damn if eyebrows rise when I ask for a second helping of dessert. I confess that I have gained at least six pounds since I last saw you in June. Will you scold me about my weight at our next appointment?

Noted on margin of her letter by me: Gained 6 lbs. No apparent metabolic effects of her disease, e.g., loss of appetite or weight.

Perhaps my summer would be less of a bore, and I'd be thinner, if Lust, the Seventh Sin, arrived. But I'm not holding my breath.

Get to the point, Elizabeth. Did you keep your appointment to be transfused or not? The time I spent arranging it with the Vineyard Hospital to be convenient during your summer stay!

I saw our Boston minister, the Reverend George Brooks, at a cocktail party last week. He said he's here escaping the heat, but I know the real reason.

You see, I knew in advance he was fund-raising for his pet project, our church's homeless shelter near Tremont Street.

When it comes to money, our minister is like one of those heat-seeking missiles. And despite the cool sea breezes, *that* heat is to be found on the Vineyard during the summer. Most of my friends have already been solicited. The Seever Foundation will of course contribute, partly because it's in our charter to give to Congregational church needs, partly because he is a dear man, although a bit insipid.

One more well-meaning supplicant, from the president of Smith College to the curator of the Museum of Fine Arts, cultivating Eliza-beth and jumping through hoops to receive support from the Seever Foundation.

The funds I inherited from Father just keep on growing like perennials under the green thumbs of those clever men on State Street.

Father told us that everyone always wants something from people like us. And Father was *never* wrong.

How many times had I heard that line? What did I want from Elizabeth at this moment? To tell me she had been transfused as planned.

It is so tiresome, this myelofibrosis. I still like to tell friends it is "my-low-fibrosis," like it sounds, and have them wonder what's wrong down under. Then I explain that my sarcastic na-ture scarred my bone marrow so that it doesn't make much blood. You dispute that and claim that scarring of the marrow doesn't come from one's personality. But you don't know where it comes from in my case, do you? So I'm as likely to be right as you!

Back to her favorite topic: that no doctor knew why she had developed this rare marrow disease, and we are not as smart as we think we are.

Now, down to business. My secretary will call your office girl Youngsun after Labor Day to schedule my regular fall ap-pointment. One thing we should address at that visit is that I seem to be having minor aches in my lower back. Not every day, but often enough to be a bother. It's probably just arthritis, or maybe my new pounds weighing me down. But remember to remember it in case I don't.

Cheers,
Elizabeth

Again an intentional provocation, not at all subtle. Elizabeth purposely didn't confirm she was transfused. Now I was concerned and obligated to find out. Youngsun was finishing her paperwork for the day and I asked her to contact Elizabeth in Edgartown and inquire whether she had received her three units of blood at the Vineyard Hospital. With Youngsun calling, I could make most of my meeting.

About forty minutes later, I was paged in the lab. Youngsun had reached Elizabeth, but Elizabeth had dismissed her call: "Inform dear Dr. Groopman that I don't discuss the details of my medical condition with a secretary. He can spend another dime and call me himself if he's so anxious to know."

I HAD FIRST MET ELIZABETH two years earlier. She had called for the appointment herself, saying she had been diagnosed with a serious blood disease and needed to be seen "immediately." I set up a consultation for the next day, assuming it was an urgent matter and expecting to receive a fax or call from her primary physician.

When she arrived, she introduced herself as Elizabeth Seever, instructing me to drop the married name "Pierce," since her husband was dead and she had never been really that fond of him. Elizabeth was a tall and full-bodied woman of sixty-four with cool blue eyes, a thin smile, and puffed silver-gray hair. She dressed with care, her sharply cut clothes chosen to flatter her ample figure, her double-strand pearl necklace and emerald earrings tasteful, but meant to be noticed.

Having no records, I asked who had referred her, since I had not yet heard from her doctor. Elizabeth responded that it was *not* Walter Page, her internist in Cambridge, but a *very, very* important person at the Harvard Medical School who said I was an expert in her unusual condition, myelofibrosis.

"It's a matter of some discretion who sent me."

There seemed to be little need for mystery, but Elizabeth made me feel it would be rude to ask further. She then told me that, before I learned her medical history, she wanted to know mine: what medical school I attended, where my internship, residency, and specialty fellowship had been served, what faculty rank at Harvard I held. She listened carefully: medical school at Columbia College of Physicians and Surgeons; internship and residency at Massachusetts General Hospital; specialty training in blood diseases and cancer

medicine at the University of California at Los Angeles, Boston Children's Hospital, and Dana-Farber Cancer Institute. I was now a chaired professor and chief of the department of blood diseases and cancer medicine at the hospital. Stating she was "pleased" that my background was "as advertised," she said she wanted to know more about my "pedigree."

"Groopman is quite an unusual name. Is it Dutch? Has your family been here long?"

"It is Dutch, and it is an unusual name," I politely replied. "Actually, we're the only family I know of in the U.S. with that name. We're Jewish. My grandfather was originally from Kiev, in Russia. He escaped a pogrom in the 1880s and made his way to Amsterdam. The name 'Groopman' was acquired there. He came to America in the early 1900s."

"What a charming story! Well, we say in Boston that the mayor should be Irish, the barber Italian, and the doctor a Jew. We'll see, won't we?"

I sat speechless, uncertain how to respond. We had just met, she as a patient in need, I as the doctor she had sought out. Was her remark a benign attempt at upper-class humor or a provocation?

If I ignored it, it might appear to be a sign of weakness or shame about my identity. If I reacted sharply, it would divert us from the focus of the visit—her health—and I would not fulfill my role as a physician.

On the wall next to my desk hangs a drawing of a man with a full black beard and white turban seated in an ornate palace. Two parallel columns of Hebrew and English calligraphy form the pillars upon which his chair rests. I directed Elizabeth's attention to the picture.

"That man is Moses Maimonides, a physician and rabbi who lived in the twelfth century. He worked in the court of the sultan of Cairo by day and cared for the destitute of that city by night. His books on science and faith influenced generations of thinkers, including Saint Thomas Aquinas and Islamic theologians. He began each day with the prayer that forms the two pillars:

> *Deem me worthy of seeing,*
> *In the sufferer*
> *Who seeks my advice,*
> *A person*

Neither rich nor poor,
Friend nor foe,
Good nor evil.
Show me only the person.

I imagine Maimonides would concern himself with the competence, not the religion or race, of his mayor or barber or fellow physician."

Elizabeth smiled coolly, commenting that it was "a lovely sentiment." I nodded in agreement, wondering, in her case, if I would be able to fulfill this prayer, and what I would eventually see.

THE BLOOD DISEASE that Elizabeth suffered from is relatively rare. It is characterized by overgrowth of fibroblasts, the cells that form scars, in the bone marrow. Instead of providing a supporting nest within the marrow cavity for the developing blood cells, the fibroblasts become a suffocating blanket that chokes off cell production. That usually results in a low red blood cell count, or anemia. Patients then experience fatigue, dizziness, or shortness of breath due to the reduction in oxygen normally carried by the red cells. A low platelet count may also occur, predisposing to bleeding, since platelets are essential in blood clotting. The leukocytes (white cells) may be diminished as well, increasing the patient's susceptibility to infection. Aside from anemia, which required regular transfusions to prevent symptoms, Elizabeth was fortunate in having had low but stable leukocyte and platelet levels that put her at only minor risk for infection or hemorrhage.

As the marrow space is closed off by the dense scarring, the developing blood cells are forced to depart like refugees expelled from a conquered homeland. These expelled cells enter the circulating bloodstream, desperate to find a welcoming shore. Most take up residence in the spleen, creating new settlements of ectopic blood production. These colonies of growing blood cells cause the spleen to enlarge massively. In most patients, the spleen eventually becomes so overcrowded that blood can no longer be made there effectively. New settlements have to be founded in the liver and lymph nodes. These tissues eventually become congested as well.

Occasionally, exposure to a volatile solvent such as benzene or toluene results in myelofibrosis. Elizabeth told me she had majored in art and painted as an undergraduate at Smith, but had minimal contact with these solvents. She preferred watercolors to oils, and abandoned painting soon after college when she decided she lacked real talent. Her only current contact with art, she dryly informed me, was adding to her already substantial collection.

Radiation was another cause of marrow scarring, but Elizabeth had no known exposure. She also had never been given thorotrast, a radioactive dye used as a contrast agent for X-ray studies, which was found in the 1950s to damage the marrow and lead to fibroblast overgrowth.

Certain nutritional deficiencies, such as lack of vitamin D, and infectious diseases like tuberculosis could cause myelofibrosis. Elizabeth tartly pointed out she was "hardly a consumptive waif" and since childhood had taken a full glass of whole milk each day with her breakfast.

The most common cause of myelofibrosis was not environmental, dietary, or infectious. It developed because of the misbehavior of a population of blood cells. The culpable cells had mutated and lost control of their genetic program, wildly pouring out proteins called "growth factors." These protein growth factors caused the adjoining fibroblasts to form dense scars.

Acute leukemia often developed from these deranged blood cells. In that case, the whole marrow was whipped into an intoxicated frenzy, the fibroblasts forming even denser choking scars, the malignant white cells proliferating madly. Treatment of acute leukemia occurring in conjunction with myelofibrosis was notoriously unsuccessful. Even if the leukemia was eradicated by chemotherapy, the outcome was dismal: a marrow that was a scarred wasteland, producing practically no blood at all.

I had published several articles in the late 1970s on myelofibrosis. My laboratory had characterized which growth factors were produced by the leukemic cells and had described in biochemical terms how this destructive orgy was unleashed in the marrow. The research had received wide attention in the hematology community, and I suspected it was this prior work that had led the "*very, very* important person at the Harvard Medical School" to recommend that Elizabeth see me.

Only after I had completed her medical history did Elizabeth produce a photocopied letter from Robert MacPhearson, a respected older Boston hematologist at the Mount Auburn Hospital. It stated that, after thorough evaluation, she carried the diagnosis of "idiopathic myelofibrosis," or scarring of the marrow without an apparent cause. It included a paragraph describing how she had been informed of the risk that acute leukemia would develop, and that she would require close medical follow-up.

"I do not like MacPhearson," Elizabeth asserted when I had finished reading his letter, "even though we travel in the same social circles. He's too ancient and unimaginative to figure out why I have this silly condition. And he's bossy—a doctor from the old school."

I disagreed in carefully chosen words. "Despite his age, he's a sharp diagnostician with excellent clinical judgment."

I could imagine why Elizabeth didn't like him, and vice versa. He was a busy, blunt patrician who would not put up with the kind of behavior I had already witnessed.

Elizabeth's physical examination was as expected for a patient with myelofibrosis. Her conjunctivae, or inner eyelids, were not the normal rich cranberry color but a pale salmon hue because of her low red blood cell count. Her enlarged spleen extended some eight centimeters below her ribs. Normally, the spleen is the size of one's fist, and safely situated under the protective shield of the lower ribs. Her liver had grown, as well, into her mid-abdomen. But there were no signs of bleeding, no blood blisters in her mouth or areas of bruising on her skin.

I tried to speak reassuringly to Elizabeth, explaining that, based on the relevant medical history, physical findings, and blood test results summarized in Dr. MacPhearson's letter, there were no signs of acceleration of the disease to acute leukemia and no major complications beyond her anemia.

I had expected her to be pleased with my positive assessment and recommendation that all she required were occasional transfusions to maintain her red blood cell count, and B-complex vitamins to keep her sites of blood production well nourished. I would follow her closely, what in medical jargon was termed "watchful waiting."

"Just vitamins and transfusions for my anemia, like what old MacPhearson said? Only 'watchful waiting' as you call it? That's not a very satisfactory response. No clever pill to stop those pesky fibroblasts from growing? 'Watchful waiting,' indeed! We Seevers are not used to *watching,* we're used to *doing.*"

Elizabeth abruptly stood up from her chair.

"Dr. Groopman, good day. I shall have to find another specialist who can do better than your passive approach."

With that she left my office.

I felt a guilty sense of relief. She would find another doctor, one whom she might pressure into prescribing a nostrum even if it had no effect on her disease. I had many patients to care for, a laboratory to run, classes to teach, and countless other responsibilities. Elizabeth would consume a great deal of time and energy, commodities in short supply.

But three weeks later she returned, having received the same recommendation of "watchful waiting" from two other hematologists. Hearing the same news four times over finally convinced her she would only be told of a "cure" by a charlatan.

"I'm not so stupid as to place myself in the hands of a shaman," she explained. "So here I am again, back in your office."

After her return, I gave Elizabeth the benefit of the doubt, hoping that the friction I felt during the first visit might be explained by her anxiety about the uncertain course of her condition and the lack of specific therapy. And there were occasional moments when I enjoyed her company. She was educated in the arts and literature and could speak intelligently about a wide range of painters and authors. She had a particular interest in Degas, and his sketches of dancers formed the centerpiece of her collection. She confided she had dreamt of being on stage, a ballerina, from the time she was a little girl.

"I tried to dance, but sadly was made like Father, large and horsy. Now I sit in my study and gaze at my collection. I imagine myself as Degas's subject, in complete command of my mind and my body, both moving in sublime synchrony."

But such moments were overshadowed by her arriving chronically late to appointments and failing to appear for scheduled blood tests and transfusions. After each incident, I would politely but firmly request that she be more attentive to her schedule, and have more consideration for my time and the time of my staff.

"I don't mean to be a pill, Jerome. It's just so many things come up."

But on the heels of such halfhearted apologies flowed a deluge of criticisms about the hematology clinic and the nurses. Nothing was done to her satisfaction: not the insertion of the needles to draw blood or infuse it; not the time it took for her blood to be typed and the correct number of pints ordered; not how her vital signs, pulse, blood pressure, and temperature were monitored prior to and after the transfusion. Elizabeth was not only carping to me but also aggressively expressing her complaints to the staff.

I decided I had to deal with the situation more effectively than I had.

"Elizabeth"—I opened in a serious tone during a routine visit in the early autumn of 1992—"we need to talk about a difficult but important matter."

"Is this the bombshell we've all been awaiting, Jerome? That I have leukemia and will die a miserable death? Won't my son and daughter love that! Finally released from their golden handcuffs when the Seever trusts can be accessed."

"Thankfully, Elizabeth, you don't have leukemia. The problem is that many of the staff find it more and more difficult to take care of you."

Elizabeth recoiled with a grimace of disdain.

"Difficult? I *am* difficult, dear doctor. I've been difficult since the moment I was born. But it's their *job* to take care of me. That's what they're paid good money for."

"It is their job to take care of you, and everyone who is ill. But it's not their job to . . ." I hesitated, searching for the right word. Not convinced I'd found it, I decided to just state it as it was. "You're not going to like what you hear, but what I say is for your own good."

"Oh, how wonderfully patronizing, Jerome." Her eyes chilled and her reedy voice ascended in tone.

"It's not patronizing," I replied evenly. "It's simply that what you may do inadvertently can be taken otherwise."

"Don't make me secretly sweet, because I'm not. Just spit it out, already."

"You can't treat the medical staff like servants. You have to respect their sensitivities and needs. Your lack of compliance with schedules and procedures is disruptive to their work."

"I see."

Elizabeth paused for a very long time, averting her eyes from mine. She was surveying my office, first the books on my shelves, then my children's drawings saved from kindergarten and addressed to "Daddy" mounted on the wall, and finally the array of family photographs on my desk. Elizabeth picked up one, of my wife and sons and newborn daughter, which stood in a small silver frame.

"Lovely family. Pretty little wife. Are you a saintly father as well as a faithful husband?"

I felt anger well up in me and fought to contain it, knowing that if it spilled over, the purpose of the meeting would be lost.

"What's your point, Elizabeth? My role as a husband and father has nothing to do with the issue at hand."

She responded with a cold smile.

"Oh, really? It has a great deal to do with the issue at hand. As a doctor you delight in the role of in loco parentis. And we patients are your timid children. You tell us what to do, how to do it, when to do it. This blood test, that X ray, this transfusion, that medication. And God forbid if we forget our manners in front of Daddy!"

I was fed up with Elizabeth, her sarcasm, snobbery, and abuse of the staff and me. I tried to calm myself, breathing deeply and slowly, trying to dispel the fury that threatened to shatter my control. My voice trembled as I struggled to find words that were rational and professional.

"I understand the frustration and bitterness of being ill. But those feelings do not give you license to be rude. This discussion is not about my being 'Daddy.' It's about your treating very hardworking and dedicated people with a modicum of respect and appreciation."

"No, it's not. It's about power and control. Admit it! You men of medicine are men of guile. You are taught to manipulate the patient in every word and action. Even now you are thinking what *you* want me to know, and phrase it in a way *you* think is right for me to hear. Daddy knows best, isn't that how you play the game?"

I opened my mouth to speak, but Elizabeth cut the air sharply with her hand to signal she was not finished.

"I'm not one to cede power. I enjoy it too much. I have power because I have money, a great deal of money. My family has been in New England since the time it was given that name. Important people come knocking at *my* door asking for *my* help all the time. Smith wants an endowment in fine arts. My minister wants me to save souls by filling stomachs. The Museum of Fine Arts wants my Degas collection. On and on."

Again I tried to speak, but Elizabeth signaled she still had not finished by raising her index finger.

"And I wish to point out that the Seever Foundation has given considerable funds to your venerable hospital and the Harvard Medical School. Did you know that, young man?"

"I do. Still, Elizabeth—"

"Still what? 'Treat the staff like servants.' They *are* servants. I am used to servants. Frankly, I can't imagine living without them."

Elizabeth shook her head forcefully in apparent disbelief. She had run into me like a speeding locomotive and then quickly braked to a stop, her statements about servants released in a final screech.

I forced myself not to respond, to take the time to cool off and consider my reply.

Her attempt to use the gifts of the Seever Foundation to the hospital and Harvard as a lever to bend me to her will would not work. Over the years I had met many prominent people in positions of power, men and women with great fortunes, high positions in industry, government, the arts, academia. They entered my world under unique circumstances, when they were sick, and often desperate, with a disease for which there was no simple cure. Although on a rational level they would admit that there were dimensions of life, such as illness, beyond their control, many who had never experienced it before clung to the illusion that their case would be different, that the power they possessed would triumph, as it seemed to in virtually every other sphere.

"I'll give you two million dollars if you cure me of AIDS," I had been told early in the epidemic by a real-estate magnate from Philadelphia. When I called to discuss his case with colleagues who already had seen him during his national tour of HIV experts, each recounted the same offer. It was a poignant, pathetic gesture, as if life had this single currency which was negotiable across all its realms.

Many such VIPs received surprisingly poor medical care. One would expect them to buy or access the best, but several destructive factors often coincided to make it otherwise. They fell prey to their own ego and arrogance, accustomed to being in a position of total control and believing they knew best about everything. But they were also preyed upon. This was the ugly underbelly of medicine. Physicians and hospitals vied for such patients, for the status and money they brought with them. As Elizabeth had asserted, people always "want something from people like us," and here it was donations and publicity.

The sacred aim of Maimonides' prayer came again to mind. To see wealth or power was to worship idols, the idols of material possession and human ego. To see the person meant to search for the part of man which is created in the image of God, that sacred spark which exists in us all, and which would remain when the flesh of the body and all its worldly trappings are lost.

I had a perspective on wealth and power drawn from a tradition that offered not only the sober prayer of Maimonides but also the irony and insight of the *shtetl*. Money, I was instructed as a child, was undoubtedly useful and important, but it had its limits. Never allow it to make you into a fawning fool. This caveat was captured in a Yiddish proverb learned from my grandmother: *"Az men hot gelt, iz men i klug, i sheyn, i men keyn gut zingen."*

Loosely translated, it means, "With money in his pocket, a man is wise and handsome and always sings on key."

But I could not dismiss Elizabeth's broadsides as merely the rantings of a controlling dowager. There was truth to her charge of in loco parentis. What was missing was the qualifying element of what kind of parent a doctor should be.

I remembered when, gravely ill after my back surgery, I had thirsted for a doctor who would be like a caring parent able to guide me back to health. Comfort and strength were drawn from doctors who were experienced, devoted, decisive, loving.

Love Elizabeth? The thought seemed absurd. What was clear was that I had the responsibility to provide her with care *and* have peace prevail between her and the staff.

"Think of it pragmatically, Elizabeth. You gain nothing by compromising your care by missing appointments and blood tests. There is no advantage in alienating the staff with your remarks. If you have problems or concerns, address them directly to me. I'll try to improve the situation. Consider it, Elizabeth, if only pragmatically."

The conversation worked only in part. In the clinic she carried herself with a cool and formal distance, offering the minimum in civil words: Good morning. Yes, you infused the blood in that arm last time. Thank you and good day. But her confrontations with me continued, although she now stayed above the belt, avoiding the sensitive territories of religion and family.

ELIZABETH ARRIVED, as promised in her letter, shortly after Labor Day. I had called her from my lab and confirmed she had gone to the Vineyard Hospital for the transfusions, as scheduled. She had glibly brushed aside my concern, saying it was "an oversight" not to inform me of that in her letter.

She was tanned and well coiffed, in a cream-colored suit with a blue and gold Hermès scarf tied at the side of her neck—so as not to obscure a broad gold choker that formed a sweeping V beneath her full throat.

"Do you like it?" she asked.

"What?" I responded, not knowing which part of her costume I was to have noted.

"The gold choker. It's new and special."

"It's very nice," I offered.

"That's the best you can come up with? You are rather uncreative with words. Stick to science."

"Why is it special?"

"Aha, why is it special? I shall give you a clue. I lost not only the six pounds I gained early in the summer, but four more as well. Ten pounds in the last three weeks. That's the clue."

I had noticed that Elizabeth's face had become more trim.

"Is your appetite still good?" Occasionally with myelofibrosis, after a long period of stability, there were acute increases in the size of the spleen and liver. These enlarged organs exerted pressure on the stomach, diminished appetite, impaired digestion, and thereby caused weight loss.

"You are a dense ninny! My appetite is sinfully good. Don't you have my little letter pasted in my chart like a crib sheet for this visit?"

I nodded that I did.

"Well, look at it! The clue is there. What missing sin could be substituted for gluttony to make me happy?"

I referred back to the letter.

"Lust?"

"Slow but sure you are. Enough silliness. I'll cut to the chase, since you *are* a busy man."

Elizabeth paused for dramatic emphasis and proudly announced:

"I have a beau. A fine sixty-seven-year-old widower. He lives life intensely. He loves sailing and tennis, drinking and laughing. But he's not just a sportsman. There are hordes of those in my set. He has a rather good knowledge of art and literature. He says he adores my wit, my *authenticity*. I met him shortly after I wrote to you. And I hate to admit it, but I'm actually feeling *happy*."

"Why shouldn't you?" I replied, wondering what her "authenticity" was.

"Because, my dear Jerome, I can't recall the last time I really was. It's been so terribly long. And certainly not since I developed this nuisance of an illness. Of course, sometimes I think it's just a silly infatuation, and we'll tire of each other. But who knows?"

Elizabeth opened her large patent-leather handbag and drew out a piece of neatly folded white paper.

"Now, before we go on to the tedious discussion of my illness, I need to inform you of my itinerary. We shall travel to London for a week, then Paris for a few days, and on to Venice. Venice is open-ended. I haven't booked a return ticket yet. Isn't Venice the most romantic city you've ever seen?"

I replied that I had never been to Venice.

"Then you have lived a deprived life. We'll probably skip Rome. Too crowded and dirty. But we may return via Nice."

She said she didn't want to bore me with too many details, but informed me her friend's name was Jedidiah Raines, nickname "Jed," from an established Virginia family—old money, and lots of it. She didn't have to worry that he was interested in her for her wealth, because he had more than she.

"Was your father wrong, then?"

"Father was *never* wrong, young man. He just seems not to have been always right." She smiled slyly and continued.

"Jed's wife died three years ago of breast cancer. I met him at the Edgartown Yacht Club at a cocktail party. I liked his look: a beefy man, broad shoulders, drinks his whiskey without ice. I later learned he played football at Yale. But despite that, like I said, he has a brain. And there's a gentleness to him. Not that he's a pushover. He's a banker, and those men have to be terribly savvy. Believe it or not, your ornery patient finds a touch of softness quite fetching."

"I'm happy for you, Elizabeth."

"No one is happier for me than I. Now, on with the show. Do you think lust, or dare I say it, love, will unscar my marrow?"

I told her, unfortunately, no.

We moved on to discuss her medical condition. Before the transfusions at Martha's Vineyard Hospital, she had had symptoms of dizziness and fatigue, attributable to her anemia, and they had been resolved with her transfusion. She would certainly need to be transfused again before her trip, and given her planned itinerary, also in Europe.

One of my former trainees, Jean Balieu, was on the faculty at Hôpital Saint-Louis in Paris. I would contact him and ask that her blood counts be checked and that she be transfused with the appropriate number of units. I emphasized that she should be diligent about keeping her appointments and reporting any change in her symptoms while abroad.

"Fine. I'll behave and prove I deserve parole."

I skimmed her August letter again and inquired about her back pain.

Elizabeth asserted it was minor, just some aches, all in the lower back. It came on if she lifted something heavy or twisted too suddenly, so she tried to avoid doing those things.

"The seventh sin"—Elizabeth smiled saucily—"doesn't seem to bother it. I suppose it's a touch of arthritis. Nothing that would stop me from traipsing across the Continent with Jed, I assure you."

Her physical exam revealed some localized tenderness in her lower back when I pressed on the lumbar vertebrae. When she was supine and I raised her straightened legs, the back pain was exacerbated. But the pain did not radiate down her legs, her reflexes were intact, her sensation normal, and there was no muscle weakness. Her spleen and liver were enlarged to the same extent as before. These organs were not likely to be straining her back.

"There's a hint, Elizabeth, of some process in or around the lower spine, since the discomfort was reproduced when I raised your straightened leg."

"Some *process?* Now don't get all clinical with me, Jerome. Just say in plain English what's wrong. Is it arthritis?"

"It could be. Or a bulging disc pressing on the nerves of the lower back. In light of your myelofibrosis, we also have to consider little islands of blood cells growing outside the scarred marrow. These blood islands can form localized masses in the lymph nodes of the abdomen and press on the back."

"I don't like the sound of that."

I explained to Elizabeth that I wasn't trying to scare her but wanted her to know all the possible causes. I didn't feel impelled to investigate it aggressively, since the pain seemed minor. But we shouldn't ignore it, either. I repeated an old medical adage: "When you hear hoofbeats, think of horses, not zebras." Common things are common. Mild back pain in a woman of her age would likely be arthritis or a disc problem. With stable blood counts and no further enlargement of her spleen or liver, it would be "a zebra" that islands of blood were forming around her lower spine.

"I see. So what tortures do you have in mind to figure all this out?"

I ordered an X ray of her lower back as a start. I reminded her to avoid standard arthritis medications like aspirin or Motrin. Such seemingly innocuous drugs interfered with platelet function and, with her low platelet count, could predispose to bleeding. One aspirin was enough to disable all the platelets in her body.

"I understand. I can put up with the aches. I'd rather not be a black-and-blue eggplant and—"

Elizabeth stopped herself in midsentence.

"I just remembered something silly, Jerome. Early in the summer I was drinking a bit too much. I took a few Alka-Seltzers for my hangovers. There's aspirin in Alka-Seltzer."

"You didn't read the package before you took it?"

"Now, don't get all in a snit. I know you instructed me to read the contents before taking anything. But one doesn't think of Alka-Seltzer as a medicine, just a tonic. I happened to read it after I had taken a few."

I asked if she had noticed any bleeding, especially upon minor trauma, like brushing her teeth or nicking her skin.

"Only once. I had a large bruise on my thigh, but I had been riding and thought I pressed too hard against the saddle."

"You were riding with the back pain?"

"Of course not! I stopped as soon as the pain came on. All that bouncing seemed to make it worse. And you'll be happy to learn that I slowed down on the drinking after I met Jed. A proper lady doesn't want to give a man the opportunity to take advantage, now does she?"

Elizabeth raised her eyebrows and gave an exaggerated girlish giggle.

It seemed as if no harm was done with the Alka-Seltzer. I asked her to avoid all alcohol, since it could limit platelet production.

"God! You're more of a puritan than Reverend Brooks."

The X ray of Elizabeth's lower spine revealed minor arthritic changes consistent with her age. There was no narrowing of the spaces between the vertebral bodies, which would have suggested a problem with a lumbar disc. The contours of the muscles supporting the lower back were sharp, without any suggestion of an overlying mass. I suggested she try some moist heat to reduce the spasm in her back, avoid any twisting or lifting, and report her ongoing symptoms to me over the next few weeks.

Elizabeth was relieved to hear this report. I emphasized that we still needed to follow her symptoms closely and that the plain X ray would not detect subtle abnormalities. She assured me that she would "be a good girl" and let me know immediately of any change in her symptoms.

BEEP! BEEP! BEEP! BEEP!

The repeated shrill cries of my beeper signaled an emergency page. It was shortly after 8:30 A.M., the last Tuesday in September. I had just entered the clinic and begun to review the patient list for the day. I immediately dialed the urgent page number.

"Dr. Groopman?" the flat voice of the hospital operator intoned.

"Yes."

"Connecting to an emergency call."

A faint mechanical click, then a fraction of a second of silence, and a breathless, panicked voice, which I recognized immediately as Elizabeth's.

"Jerome? Jerome?"

"Yes, Elizabeth."

"I can't walk. I'm paralyzed."

Paralyzed. The word hung suspended in my mind. What had happened? Did I miss something on her exam? Should I have gotten the MRI? There was no time to dwell on these issues.

"When did this happen?"

"Last night."

"Why didn't you call me then?"

"Because I had a date with Jed. My back went into a . . . a knot during dinner. I decided to tough it out. I came home. Canela, my maid, prepared a hot bath. It felt better. My legs were wobbly . . . weak getting in the tub. But I thought it was . . . because . . . I had three drinks. Jed didn't spend the night. . . . He has meetings in New York today."

Elizabeth paused, trying to catch her breath and slow her speech. "I woke up around five . . . and I couldn't feel my legs. Like they were still asleep. I needed to urinate . . ." She began to cry in stuttering sobs. "I needed to . . . get to the . . . toilet . . . but I couldn't . . . I couldn't get out of bed. I lost my water. Canela had to carry me . . . *soiled* . . . to the bathroom. It was awful . . . degrading. Jerome . . ."

"Elizabeth," I said in a firm, deliberate voice, "you are to come to the hospital immediately. I'll arrange an ambulance and I'll be waiting for you in the emergency room. Should I contact Jed or your children?"

Elizabeth was silent for a few moments.

"No, don't," she said, her voice steadying. "I don't want them to know what's happened until I know *why* it's happened."

"I understand. I'm here, waiting for you."

The stretcher carrying Elizabeth was wheeled quickly through the maze of the emergency room under the skilled hands of the attendants. Elizabeth lay on her back, a small blue embroidered pillow tucked under her knees. I assumed she placed it there to support her legs in a bent position—straightening them generally exacerbates back pain. Elizabeth's face was pasty and drawn, and her fine crown of silver hair now lay flat and dull over her temples like a Puritan's bonnet. She had no makeup on and wore no jewelry.

She looked up at me, speechless, her eyes wide with terror. I reached for her hand. The cool moisture of her palm sealed our grip.

"Let's move her from the stretcher to the bed," I instructed the surrounding nurses. They were adept at this maneuver and had already positioned a firm board under Elizabeth's back to stabilize her spine during the passage.

The undersheet of the stretcher was grasped at each corner, and Elizabeth was slowly raised like an infant in swaddling clothes and placed gently on the flat mattress of the bed.

"Keep the pillow under her knees so they're flexed and there's no tension on her lumbar spine."

Cathy O'Donnell, the ER nurse attending to Elizabeth, nodded her agreement, and then quickly wrapped a blood-pressure cuff around Elizabeth's fleshy upper arm.

"Elizabeth, while Cathy takes your blood pressure, pulse, and temperature, I'm going to examine your legs."

Elizabeth was silent while I examined her. There was virtually no muscle strength in her toes, calves, or thighs. Her reflexes were absent at her ankles, knees, and hips. Her ability to sense the light touch of a cotton swab or the sharp end of a pin was gone. Her rectal sphincter tone was reduced. These neurological findings were consistent with acute compression of her spinal cord at the level of the upper lumbar spine, and accounted for her severe back pain, the weakness in her legs, and her incontinence.

"Why can't I move my legs?" Elizabeth whispered as soon as I finished my examination.

"I don't know yet, Elizabeth. The suddenness of the back pain and the loss of strength and sensation in your legs suggest pressure on your lower spinal nerves. I've already arranged for an emergency MRI scan of the spine. That should give us a better idea of 'why.' "

"I cannot live like this. I cannot live paralyzed. I won't live paralyzed."

She started to cry, tears flooding down her wrinkled cheeks. I grasped her cold, trembling hand again in mine and rested my other hand lightly on her shoulder.

"We need to take things one at a time. We'll define what happened and then work to reverse it. Don't look too far ahead, Elizabeth. Don't think the worst. There's a good chance of restoring strength if we relieve the pressure on the nerves quickly."

Elizabeth dabbed her tears with a tissue offered by Cathy. She looked up at me and forced a brave smile.

The MRI scan showed a large ovoid mass measuring 4 by 6 centimeters located in what is called the "epidural space." The spinal cord is encased in a thick sheath called the "dura," which shields the fragile spinal nerves like the protective insulation wrapped around the wires of an electrical cable. The mass was situated on the surface of the dura and pressed inward, strangling the lower spinal cord. Its consistency could be inferred from the MRI scan: a mixture of old clot and fresh, unclotted blood. Elizabeth had had a small hemorrhage in her epidural space sometime in the past weeks to months and then bled massively the night before. I hadn't missed the spinal cord compression; it had occurred the prior evening with the second hemorrhage. I felt some tension leave my body, the anguished anticipation that I had made an error and caused a patient harm. But I quickly stopped thinking of myself and focused on the matter at hand.

I explained to Elizabeth that emergency surgery was required to remove the clot. I urgently paged Edwin Bass, a senior neurosurgeon. He came to the bedside, reviewed the history with Elizabeth, examined the MRI scan, and offered the opinion that she was likely to recover fully.

Elizabeth, as if touched by a magic wand, resumed her former persona.

" 'Likely,' Jerome? That doesn't sound quite good enough. I want you to guarantee it."

"There is no such thing possible. But Ed Bass is outstanding."

"I certainly hope so. Now, where did this blood come from? I didn't fall or get hit in the back."

I told her I wasn't sure. She may have an inherited arteriovenous malformation of the blood vessels around the spinal cord which spontaneously ruptured. There could have been trivial trauma to her spine that she didn't recall, and with her platelets so low, caused her to hemorrhage. We wouldn't know until she was explored during surgery.

"Well, let's get this show on the road. I knew my life now was too good to be true anyway."

It took most of the morning for Ed Bass and his neurosurgical team to evacuate the mass of old and new blood and remove the spinal cord from its grip. The freed spinal nerve roots were observed to be pale and flaccid, the pressure of the clot having choked off their blood supply over the past eighteen hours. There was neither any structural abnormality identified nor any evidence of trauma to explain the hemorrhage. The blood tests taken in the ER did not reveal a drop in her platelet count that might predispose to spontaneous bleeding.

Why, then, had the hemorrhage occurred? Perhaps the Alka-Seltzer had weakened her platelets, resulting in a small, contained hemorrhage during the summer. That would account for the old clot and her mild chronic back pain. The cause of the recent bleeding and subsequent spinal cord compression remained obscure, the only remotely likely factor the alcohol she'd been drinking.

I stood by Elizabeth's bedside as she slowly awakened from the anesthesia in the recovery room. She was pivoted on her side, so that there was no pressure on her sutured lower back. An intravenous line carried an enriched sugar and salt solution into her bloodstream and a catheter drained urine from her bladder. Oxygen was delivered into her nostrils by a translucent green mask strapped tightly over her pallid face. A monitor next to her bed showed a rapid but regular rhythm of her heart and a stable blood pressure.

"I . . . I guess . . . I'm still . . . on earth," Elizabeth strained in a hoarse voice as her eyes slowly centered on my face.

I took her waxy hand firmly in mine, pressing warmth into it.

"You are most definitely on earth, Elizabeth. The clot pressing on your spinal cord was removed. There was no malformed blood vessel or evidence of trauma."

She received this information and then slowly shook her head.

"Then why . . . why did I bleed?"

"I'm not sure. Perhaps the Alka-Seltzer and the alcohol last month weakened your platelets. That would explain the old clot. We don't know why you bled again last evening. Perhaps the alcohol again, though I really don't know."

Elizabeth grimaced in disgust. "I'm paralyzed . . . because of an Alka-Seltzer and . . . and a few vodka martinis?

"Oh, Jerome" she sighed. "Shakespeare understood . . . 'As . . . as flies to wanton boys . . . are we to the gods; they . . . they kill us . . . for their sport'—"

I pressed her hand more tightly.

"You're not dead, Elizabeth. There's a good chance your strength will recover."

Her eyes slowly shut, the heavy lids descending like the curtain at the last act of a play.

"Elizabeth?"

"I don't want . . . to open my eyes."

"Is the light bothering you? Are you nauseated from the anesthesia?"

She shook her head no.

"Are you in pain?"

"No. The narcotics have me floating."

I waited, noticing that the overhead fluorescent light made the droplets of perspiration on her forehead sparkle like a diamond tiara.

"I . . . I don't want to look at my legs. They're dead."

"Your legs are not 'dead.' It takes time for strength to return. The nerves are still in shock."

She opened her eyes and fixed her gaze on me.

"Jerome, listen to me. Listen closely." Her voice had become dry and commanding. "I . . . I know what I'm saying . . . and it's not the dope they gave me.

"I'm not going to live as a . . . cripple . . . wheeled around like some . . . pitied lump of clay. I . . . know my body. I . . . I can feel *inside* . . . the nerves were choked . . ."

I slowly shook my head.

"Elizabeth, it's impossible to know how much strength you'll regain. The clot was just removed. Healing takes time."

She shook her head weakly, closed her eyes again, and drifted into an exhausted, drugged sleep.

Elizabeth was discharged a week later. She had been given steroids to reduce the inflammation and swelling that results from pressure on nerves, and she was to begin a graduated program of physical therapy at home. Because of the effort required to come in to the office for an appointment, we arranged for a visiting nurse to draw her blood at home and monitor her medications until she was up to the trip.

I kept in close touch with Elizabeth by phone over the ensuing weeks. Our conversations were brief. Elizabeth was polite but made no attempt to expand upon her symptoms or question the outcome of her condition.

Two months later, shortly after Thanksgiving, Elizabeth arrived for her first scheduled appointment. My door barely accommodated the width of her wheelchair. A red and black crocheted afghan covered her legs and feet. Her cheeks were sunken and pale. She wore no makeup or jewelry. Canela guided the wheelchair to face my desk and then exited, softly closing the door behind her.

"Hello, Elizabeth. Did you celebrate Thanksgiving with the kids and Jed?"

"Are you ready to concede defeat now, Jerome?" she responded, bypassing the formality of returning my greeting.

"We're not defeated yet. This is a long war with many battles yet to fight."

"Oh, stop the asinine clichés," she spat out, her lip curling in disgust.

We sat silently for a few moments, each waiting for the other to speak.

"No response, Jerome?"

"They're not asinine clichés. There's still much to do. I understand from the agency you want to stop your physical therapy."

"You're well informed. I had that sweet young girl come to my home four times a week for almost two months. Two hours each session. I suffered her moving my dead legs and reciting her scripted pep talks. I took those miserable steroids for the inflammation around my nerves. I did everything you said to do. I was as good as good could be. And what was the result?"

"Elizabeth, I think you—"

"*Answer* me. Don't evade my question." Her voice was bitter and increasing in volume. "Answer me, *now.*"

I looked hard into her face, holding her icy blue gaze in mine.

"I'll answer *you,* but then you listen to *me.*"

She flinched momentarily and then regained her bitter grimace.

"The result, *so far,* is that the only feeling that has returned is pain and you are still paralyzed."

Elizabeth smiled and nodded her head in victory.

"And I know *exactly* what you're feeling, Elizabeth."

Her smile receded and she skeptically tilted her head. She began to speak, but I held up my palm to stop her.

"Yes, I know what you're experiencing, Elizabeth. I know it all. The electric shocks that burst in your back and race down your legs. The fear that you will never walk again. I know the anger that grips you from the moment you awaken. And I know the despair that empties everything in your world of pleasure and meaning."

"And how are you so intimate with this knowledge?"

"I was once a runner—"

"Do I have to listen to a 'Once upon a time' prologue?"

"You don't *have* to listen unless you want to, Elizabeth."

She folded her hands tightly together like a pupil in grade school, resting them on her afghan and looking blankly at me.

"I injured my back training for a marathon. It was before the days of MRI scans. The X rays suggested a bulging disc. I underwent surgery. The neurosurgeon removed the disc and fused the vertebral bones of my lower spine. He had told me I'd be running again in three weeks. I awoke, my legs frozen in excruciating pain. Every minor movement caused me agony. The surgeon wasn't sure what had gone wrong. It seemed I had bled around the spinal nerve roots when they were excavating the disc."

Elizabeth unfolded her hands and placed them symmetrically over her upper thighs.

"The Percocet they gave me for the electric shocks and spasms in my back made me feel stupid and nauseated, and didn't really control the pain. I had to lie on plastic bags filled with ice to numb my spine and hips to get some relief. I hardly slept.

"Pam, my wife, had to support me while I transferred to the bedside commode. I was trapped all day in my room until she came home from work. Then I crawled to have supper, lying down on the dining room floor.

"I was young, twenty-nine, a new assistant professor on the faculty. We had married less than a year before. My world fell apart. Because of the relentless pain, I couldn't work, I couldn't move, I could hardly think. And after two months, despite steroids and pain medication, there was no indication I would ever walk again free of pain."

"Is this true, or are you exaggerating the story to manipulate me?"

I told her it was all true.

Elizabeth pursed her lips and looked hard into my eyes.

"It's easy to preach a sermon when you're on the mount and not on the cross."

"I'm not preaching, Elizabeth, I'm *telling*."

Her face briefly softened and she asked me to continue.

"I became despondent. I wouldn't say depressed, because that's a clinical term. I was convinced that this would be my life, that I would spend the rest of my days incapacitated, in pain, unproductive. I began to lose hope."

"As I have."

"As you have."

"Now, am I going to hear your spiritual punch line? I know you're religious. Is this why? Did the divine hands reach down to heal your withered limbs while an angel levitated you from your bed of pain?"

Her face was flushed and her words flew from her mouth.

"Why so cynical, Elizabeth? Are you the only person ever to suffer and despair?"

"To me, I'm the only one who *matters*."

"One evening, Pam came home from work. I had spent most of the day staring at cracks in the ceiling, lying on the ice bags. I couldn't muster the energy to listen to music or look at the newspaper. I felt profoundly sorry for myself. I had taken some Percocet for pain earlier in the day and was just coming out of that fog. The electrical shocks were becoming more frequent in my legs."

I took a deep breath, grateful for how the mind suppresses the palpable dimensions of painful experience, allowing us to recall only an ethereal memory of the sensations suffered.

"Pam asked me how the day had gone, and I lashed out at her. All my anger focused on that perfunctory question.

"Pam listened to my tirade, and then said: 'Stop the pain medications. Stop lying in bed all day on ice. Force yourself to walk. Start physical therapy. Go back to the lab. Even if you have to lie on a stretcher and direct the technicians on your back, start to work again.'

"I thought she was crazy. I told her so. She moved next to me on the bed and hugged me tightly. I *felt* something in the warmth and softness of her body, something other than my pain, for the first time since the operation.

"While she was preparing supper, I began staring again at the cracks in the ceiling. I knew each one. I had counted them every day for two months. I could trace their paths in the white plaster with my eyes closed. And as I looked at the cracks in the ceiling a ridiculous thought came to my mind. I could decide which one to follow. There were the ones that coursed in the center of the ceiling, or the ones along the molding, or the ones that ran diagonally. I then realized what Pam had been telling me: I still had my will. I still could decide which path to take. It was just an illusion that all choice in life had been taken from me."

Elizabeth eyed me pensively.

"And you got better."

"I did. I'm hardly one hundred percent. I will never run again—it causes immediate pain. The nerve roots are tethered from the scarring of the operation, and a running stride pulls on them and sets off the electric shocks. But I can swim and even bicycle. I can't lift heavy things. Occasionally some innocuous movement triggers severe pain in my back and legs. Then I'm forced to rest in bed for a few days. Those episodes still frighten me.

"But I built my strength up. It took years, literally years. I went to physical therapy. I learned to walk again. I started along parallel bars in a hot pool and then graduated to a flat floor and eventually a few stairs. I pushed myself, painful though it was. I relearned how to do simple things in ways that didn't set off pain—get up from a chair, turn my torso, reach down to pick something up.

"Elizabeth, I was where you are. I had surrendered to bitterness and despair, believing I had lost my life. That doesn't have to be. Even in the most extreme circumstances, we can still make choices."

We sat together in silence. After a long moment, Elizabeth reached out her hands and extended them to me. I got up from my desk and came toward her, grasping them in mine.

"I haven't allowed Jed to see me since the surgery. He still calls. Sometimes I speak with him, other times I tell Canela to say I'm indisposed. He tries to be comforting, but . . . but I can't understand why he persists. Who wants to be attached to a cripple?"

Her rhetorical question hung in the air. I waited silently for her to continue.

Elizabeth disengaged her hands from mine, and drew a fine white lace handkerchief from under the afghan and wiped her tear-filled eyes.

"I keep one at the ready," she said, folding the moist cloth into a neat square. "I cry so much, Jerome. Alone, of course. We Seevers can't have people see us crying. They might get the wrong idea and think we're actually human."

New tears slowly collected at the corners of her eyes. She reached for my hands again and grasped them with surprising strength.

THE WINTER OF 1994 was a fierce one in New England. During January, Boston suffered successive storms that left several feet of accumulated snow as the temperatures rarely moved above freezing. The main roads were narrowed to one lane by gray mounds of ice deposited by the plows. In February, we were visited by freezing rain, which formed a treacherous glaze over the snowy base.

A mixture of sleet and wet snow had begun to fall the first Tuesday in March, solidifying the gloom that had encased the city since Christmas. I expected Elizabeth's appointment to be canceled, given the conditions, but Youngsun informed me that Elizabeth had called to confirm. She said she would not be dissuaded from venturing out.

There was a pair of sharp knocks on my closed office door.

"Come in," I called.

Elizabeth entered in her wheelchair, her red and black afghan draped as usual over her legs. For the first time in nearly five months, her hair was combed upward in a sharp bouffant. She wore her "special" gold V-shaped choker over a tight-fitting cream-colored satin blouse that accentuated her full bosom.

The hands that angled her chair deftly through the doorway were not Canela's, but large and reddish with thick tufts of gray and black hair. I looked up and saw a tall, broad-shouldered man with a full head of gray hair, tortoiseshell glasses, ruddy cheeks, and a soft smile. He sported a double-breasted blue blazer with a pressed white handkerchief in the pocket, and L. L. Bean rubber-bottom leather boots.

"Jed Raines, Dr. Groopman. Very nice to meet you." His voice was deep and confident, the Southern accent just perceptible in the drawn out "you."

He strode from Elizabeth's parked chair with his broad hand opened and thrust forward.

"Nice to meet you, Mr. Raines. I've heard a great deal about you."

"And I about you, sir."

His handshake was strong and indicated that it was ready to equal whatever pressure was applied to it.

"Oh, boys, let's not start one of those mutual-admiration-society dialogues."

Jed returned to sit next to Elizabeth, straightening the seams of his gray wool slacks as he sat attentively forward.

"I'm surprised you came out on a day like this. The roads are iced over, and we're getting another storm. Youngsun said you didn't want to delay until next week."

"I didn't, Jerome. Jed had arranged to come in with me, and I didn't want to make him reschedule."

"I would have gladly, Betsy."

"It wasn't necessary. A Seever isn't deterred by a little ice on a Boston street. Anyway, I wanted to get the green light from Jerome. And I *hate* to wait, you know."

"Green light?" I asked, wondering what requests were forthcoming.

"Really, Jerome, do be *patient* and let me talk."

Jed raised his pepper-and-salt eyebrows and turned to Elizabeth: "Darling, even Dr. Groopman is not spared your kind words?"

"Of course not. Now hush! I'm bursting to get this settled."

Elizabeth reached into the handbag, which was slung on the side of the wheelchair, and removed a shiny white sheet of paper.

"This is a fax from Donald Knowles. Donald is the senior curator of European paintings at the Metropolitan Museum of Art in New York. He has been a great friend of mine for years and does all the tedious 'leg work' for me in the art world, if you'll pardon the expression." Elizabeth chuckled. "I have decided to donate my Degas collection to the Met."

Elizabeth paused, her voice tentative.

"It is still a bit of a shock, to give away what I have doted on all my life. But in a curious way it gives me pleasure, a kind of pleasure I have never really gotten from all the monetary gifts from the Seever Foundation. And of course," Elizabeth continued, her voice regaining its usual even tone, "it will be very dramatic and glorious. You see, there is an upcoming international Degas exposition, which will begin in Paris and then travel to Madrid and New York. My gift will be the centerpiece, and the works have never before been shown to the public. Donald was thrilled. He arranged all the tiresome things, the insurance, shipping, and so on.

"The fax is a draft of the press release to be issued next Friday. The opening will be in June, June twelfth, to be exact. I would like to be there, in Paris."

Elizabeth smiled nervously.

"I should say *we* would like to be there. Jed is planning to go with me. Donald confirmed there is wheelchair access at the Grand Palais. From Paris, we'd like to go to Venice, if they can find me a gondola that won't sink from the weight of this leaden chariot!"

Jed reached out to take Elizabeth's hand.

"Now don't get all soft and mushy in front of Jerome. I don't want him to give permission for the trip out of pity for two star-crossed lovers. We need to know that it is medically safe for me to travel. I still have the name of that French doctor who can check my blood counts and fill my tank if it's low."

Elizabeth had not recovered any significant strength in her legs. The painful spasms in her back had largely abated, and the radiating electric shocks down her legs were less frequent. She had a physical therapist come three times a week to her home on Beacon Hill, but her efforts were directed to maintaining flexibility of Elizabeth's flaccid limbs. It was unlikely she would ever walk again.

"And your physical therapy regimen while you're away?"

"Oh, Jed is a master at moving my legs," she responded with a coy smile. "He'll keep me from turning into a contorted pretzel."

I thought for a few moments, and could see no reason to object. I said I would contact Dr. Balieu in Paris and make the arrangements for the blood tests and transfusion.

Elizabeth left the office with a warm smile, promising to call Youngsun to confirm the arrangements at Hôpital Saint Louis.

This had been first time I was not forced into a confrontation with Elizabeth, yet I felt strangely unsettled after the visit. I realized I did not trust her euphoria, her perky chatter, which gave the impression that her life had fallen back into place.

I recalled the similar burst of optimism that marked my initial departure from the apartment after Pam's imperative. I had imagined that I would soar through the upcoming struggle, as in a movie, a proud and confident hero admired as he smoothly vaulted over the bars of his debility. Then came the harsh reality, back in the outside world, where so many of life's usual activities required huge effort or were entirely impossible. I retreated into long periods of anger, frustration, and despair.

I had to learn to buffer those feelings and find the equanimity to persevere. Most important, I had to relinquish my pride and depend heavily on Pam, my doctors, my friends, both logistically and psychologically. Did Elizabeth understand that that would be true for her as well?

I considered telling her at our next appointment, as a warning to what she would soon be likely to encounter. For a moment the scene played out before my eyes: Elizabeth reacting indignantly that I would challenge her feelings, dare to burst her bubble, again be the all-knowing parent instructing her in how to modulate her emotions and behavior.

I feared I was being too negative. My view of Elizabeth had been colored by who she was before her paralysis. The extreme circumstances of illness did cause fundamental changes in the way people understood themselves, their property, and their relationships.

As a physician, I was charged to see not only what "the person" was but who "the person" could become. Elizabeth had intimated that her remarkable act of charity was "very dramatic and glorious," and thus might be seen as self-aggrandizing. But she was parting with possessions that had been assiduously acquired and jealously guarded.

I believed that her motives were mixed, that she had done this not just out of ego but out of consideration for others, and had experienced unexpected and unique joy in its giving.

In Paris, Elizabeth would return to life's stage, immobile in her chair, poignantly surrounded by Degas's dancing figures. I recalled that she once had imagined herself as his subject, but lacked the powerful equilibrium to challenge the limits of nature and its gravity. I sensed she was learning how to realize that dream, this time with her heart.

Elliott

"JERRY, IT'S ELLIOTT. In Jerusalem. I know it's early, but it's an emergency."

Emergency. I felt a burst of adrenaline race through my body.

It was still dark in the bedroom. The glowing red digits of the night-table clock read 5:03 A.M., making it just after noon in Jerusalem.

"What is it, Ell? How I can help?"

I imagined the worst—Elliott's wife, Susan, or son, Benjamin, injured by a terrorist bomb or a car accident.

"I have a growth of lymph nodes in my chest. It's interfering with my breathing. A few hours ago, my doctor told me I need surgery. What do I do?"

Elliott was transformed in my mind from one of my closest and oldest friends into a "patient." I mentally organized his particulars into the format of a clinical case: a forty-three-year-old previously healthy Caucasian male, nonsmoker, working as a journalist in the Middle East, with enlarged lymph nodes in his chest, considered for surgery.

"Ell, tell me first what happened, from the beginning," I evenly replied, following the principle that the best history of an illness is elicited in the patient's own words. That way, the physician does not prejudice the recounting and keeps an open mind to the full breadth of possible diagnoses.

He had first become aware of something wrong eight weeks before, during his regular early morning jog on the hills between West and East Jerusalem. It was a temperate spring day, the sun hardly over the horizon, the cool nighttime air from the Judean desert still lingering over the city. Elliott started at his house in the German Colony, at his usual pace, aiming to complete his regular four-mile course. But at the very first ascent, at the Bethlehem Road, he had been forced to stop.

"My chest felt tight, heavy, like there was a weight pressing on it. I couldn't get enough air to make it up the hill. I figured I was coming down with a cold, and walked back home."

I asked Elliott if he had had any fever or chills. None whatsoever; he had checked his temperature when he returned from the aborted run, and several times since. Cough or sputum? He had recently developed a dry cough, but without phlegm.

As I listened, I was creating a list of diagnoses in my mind. By my own convention, I always started with the worst category. In the case of a mass of lymph nodes in the chest, it would be cancer.

I considered the different types. First, cancer of the lung: Elliott had never smoked cigarettes that I could recall. But lung cancer also occurred from exposure to environmental toxins like asbestos, once commonly used in house insulation. I recalled that Elliott and Susan had renovated their house in Jerusalem three years before. Elliott could have been exposed to the material then, but the incubation period from exposure to lung cancer was usually much longer, a decade or more. Next was malignant lymphoma: very possible, and often involving the chest. Lymphoma was classified as Hodgkin's or non-Hodgkin's, and either type generally occurred in teenagers and young adults when centered in the chest. I moved down the list to the less common cancers. Thymoma, or cancer of the thymus gland: often associated with a disease called myasthenia gravis, which impairs muscle function. Elliott would not be regularly running four miles if he had myasthenia. Thyroid cancer: more frequent in women, and related to radiation exposure. Such exposure was remote for Elliott in his occupation as a writer. Testicular cancer: often overlooked and important to consider, since the embryonic testes originate in the upper chest and migrate during fetal development into the pelvis; vestigial deposits in the thorax can become cancerous in adulthood.

"Ell, you never smoked, correct? And you weren't in contact with asbestos during the house renovation?"

"Never smoked, except grass of course. A contractor did the renovation, and we were assured for Benjamin's sake that all precautions were taken when they stripped the old pipes."

I continued down my mental list to the second category—infection. Tuberculosis: quite possible in a world traveler now residing in the Middle East. Fungal diseases like coccidioidomycosis: prevalent in the Sacramento Valley of California, where Susan's parents lived and Elliott often visited. Toxoplasmosis: a parasitic infestation from cats, ubiquitous animals, but generally causing a self-limited flu-like illness. All three—TB, fungus, and toxoplasmosis—would have fever as a prominent manifestation, and Elliott had affirmed he had had a normal temperature throughout.

I ended my list with the category "miscellaneous," considering rare disorders like sarcoidosis. Sarcoidosis is a condition where the body becomes allergic to its own tissues, resulting in inflamed masses of lymph nodes in the chest. It is most common in African-Americans. There is scarring of the lung tissue, which would be evident on chest X rays in addition to the nodes. Sarcoidosis often caused red nodules in the skin and inflammation of the eyes.

"Any rashes or skin bumps? Do you have conjunctivitis or a gritty feeling in your eyes?"

"None of that, Jerry. I'm just totally winded. And not only when I try to run. Even walking fast, I feel the tightness."

Elliott had begun to worry when the chest tightness persisted through the week. He called his general practitioner, Jeremy Levy. But the doctor, also an American who had emigrated to Israel, was on military reserve duty out of the city. The covering physician had Elliott come to the office, but there he was not examined, not even his chest, just handed a prescription for erythromycin for a presumed bronchitis.

"Even though you had no fever or sputum?"

"Correct."

After two weeks on the antibiotic, there was no change in his symptoms. His regular doctor was still away. This time, the covering physician listened to his lungs and heard some wheezing. Elliott was told he might have asthma and was prescribed an inhaler. This afforded some relief, but he still couldn't make it up the hill when he tried to jog again.

"Finally Dr. Levy returned from the army. He ordered a chest X ray. After two months of this growing inside me."

I maintained my calm and even voice, even though I felt angry and anxious. My friend, a reliable person complaining for two months of a disabling symptom, had been incompetently evaluated. Critical time may have been wasted. For a fleeting moment I saw my father, gasping in the throes of heart failure, a general practitioner standing confused at his bedside. My father's life was lost because of medical mistakes. This memory painfully gripped me, and I forced myself to disengage from it and return my focus to Elliott.

"Did you have any blood tests? Did Dr. Levy describe what was seen on the chest X ray?"

"I'm not anemic and my white count is O.K. Susan had me get a copy of the X-ray report. It says, and I'm translating from Hebrew, so give me a minute: 'Enlarged mediastinal lymph nodes—' What's mediastinal?"

"Just medical jargon for the central area of the chest under the sternum, the breastbone."

"Right. 'Enlarged mediastinal lymph nodes measuring eight centimeters in maximum diameter and surrounding'—better English would be "encasing"—'the trachea and extending to the aorta. Compression of the right bronchus. Lung fields otherwise clear.' "

I paused to assess the information. The dimensions of the mass, the compression of his airway, and the adjacent surrounding unscarred lung, taken with the absence of fever or sputum, made cancer overwhelmingly likely.

I began to review my diagnostic list of cancers, but felt my concentration slipping. It was not the early hour and interrupted sleep. Rather, my focus was clouded by a collage of intersecting memories—Elliott and I lingering over coffee in his Manhattan apartment, talking about his aspirations as a writer at *Time* and mine as a future doctor; Pam in her bridal gown and me in a tuxedo joined with Elliott in a triangular embrace at our wedding; Elliott gently dabbing drops of sweet red wine in my firstborn son Steven's mouth to "anesthetize" him before his ritual circumcision.

The collage was erased by the sound of Elliott's quivering, plaintive voice.

"Jerry—what do I do?"

I paused a moment, then said: "Put Susan on the phone."

Susan, an émigrée from California, worked as a political and business consultant and was a coolheaded master of logistics. Her native American optimism had been mixed with an acquired Israeli toughness, so in a notoriously bureaucratic country like Israel she was able to make things happen quickly and efficiently.

"Hi, Jerry," Susan began. "We really don't know where we are yet. I checked out the surgeon Dr. Levy recommended at Hadassah Hospital. He's said to be good. And I know enough powerful people there to make sure Elliott gets special attention. But we want the best, the *very best,* so maybe it makes sense to come back to the States."

The "very best" in clinical medicine was not only expert physicians and technologically advanced hospitals. There were many of those to choose from, throughout the world. Serious illness demanded more. It was like a wild rodeo bronco, often exploding in unanticipated directions, stubbornly bucking to throw you off its back. The "very best" required tight and determined hands on the reins. There needed to be attention to every detail and nuance of diagnosis and treatment. Even seemingly minor errors—a misread CAT scan or a too rapidly administered medicine or the lack of an available catheter—could allow the situation to spiral out of control and be catastrophic. Who would exert such control in Elliott's case?

"I can't make the decision for Elliott and you. Medicine is quite good in Israel, although many new drugs are not yet available there. You need to be sure that the specialist in charge will be totally focused on Elliott's case, covering every aspect of the situation. You also have to consider the practical dimensions—your jobs, your insurance, Benjamin's school, and a host of other things holding you there."

Susan paused but a moment.

"But we don't have you, Jerry. We're coming to Boston. Expect us the day after tomorrow. I'll arrange to get seats on the next El Al flight."

· · ·

IT ALL HAPPENED in rapid succession. They arrived early Tuesday morning, just after my sons, Steven and Michael, left for school. Elliott was anxious and pensive, an ashen shell of his ebullient self. I embraced him forcefully, and could feel a weak shiver pass through his body as he tried to return my hug.

Susan quickly occupied herself with organizing their luggage in the upstairs playroom where Pam had opened the couch into a sofa bed. Benjamin, a cute three-year-old with jet black hair and almond brown eyes like his mother, immediately fell asleep after the fifteen-hour plane trip.

Elliott and I sat in tense silence during the car ride to my office, each absorbed with his own thoughts of what the day would hold. I had designated myself as his physician of record and arranged for blood tests, a CAT scan of the chest, and appointments with Peter Draper, a thoracic surgeon, and Tom Cramer, an anesthesiologist, in anticipation of surgery the following day. Before sending Elliott off on this schedule, I thoroughly examined him.

I moved Elliott's long auburn hair off his neck so I could palpate for lymph nodes. He still affected a bohemian look, the same look he had when we first met two decades before. We had been introduced by a mutual friend, Anne Albright, who brought us together because she was struck by how similar we were.

"You could be brothers, so tall, with those deep-set, soulful eyes," Anne had teased us over mugs of French roast coffee one Sunday morning in her Riverside Drive apartment.

But it was not just our physical resemblance that had struck Anne. She said it was how much we shared in spirit—our appetite for information, our sense of humor, our loquaciousness. Elliott and I had blushed at her bold praise.

"You look worried," Elliott stated as I removed my hand from his neck.

Just above his collarbone was a matted hard tongue of tissue. It resisted the compressive force of my fingertips. The mass was growing up now, from the mediastinum to the apex of his thorax. I had noted a subtle bulge in the veins in his neck, and a slowing of their rhythmic flow.

I hesitated in responding, not wanting to tell him what I observed. But I knew I should not deviate from my policy of honesty with a patient, even a patient who was like a brother to me and whose condition caused me deep anguish. If I did not tell the truth always, I would not be trusted when I had a truth to tell.

I explained that the veins in his neck were dilated, and this indicated "superior vena caval syndrome." The vena cava, the large vein that drains the blood from the upper body, was being compressed by the mass of nodes in his chest before it emptied into the right atrium of his heart. That backed up circulation in the brain and could cause increased intracranial pressure, manifest first as a headache.

"I've had a constant headache over the last few days, but figured it was stress."

I agreed that his headache could be due to stress, but the compression of the vena cava was contributing as well. By tomorrow we would diagnose the nature of the mass, and begin to treat it. That would decompress the vena cava.

Elliott looked knowingly into my eyes, and then returned my honesty with his own.

"Jerry, don't let me die."

I shuddered at his words.

I had cared for many patients who had intuited their own deaths. Sometimes it was obvious to all, to patient, physician, family. Then the disease was widespread, the treatment failing. But occasionally there was no clinical sign that pointed in that final direction. I had come to believe strongly in how a patient feels and reads his body. Beyond any objective tests, blood chemistries, cardiograms, or CAT scans, a patient's sense of impending death often proved true.

I gripped Elliott's exposed shoulder tightly, holding fast as I offered words of comfort. He was exhausted from the trip and from worry, I said, and should not rely on grim feelings in such a state. We did not yet know the cause of the enlarged lymph nodes. Once we made the diagnosis, we would embark on our course of action.

But as I continued with my reassurances, I studied the distant look in his eyes, and wondered whether he had indeed seen the arrival of life's last visitor.

"SCALPEL"—"SCALPEL"; "Clamp"—"Clamp"; "Suture"—"Suture."

We were well into the second hour of the operation. Peter Draper, the thoracic surgeon, had finished dissecting between the vital structures of the mediastinum—heart, aorta, lungs—and had just reached a dense band of inflamed fibrous tissue overlying the mass of nodes.

I stood slightly away. It was too distressing to watch a person whom I understood as I understood myself—as thoughts and feelings projected in the external form of the body—exposed as a conglomeration of tissues and vessels seeping blood and lymph.

I looked upward from the operative field. Elliott's lids were closed over his china blue eyes and his face rested in a motionless mask. He had been transformed by the anesthetic into that intermediate state between what we know as life and what we imagine as death, where consciousness and feeling are suspended. In this state, I pictured his soul waiting in the anteroom of time, ready to pass back into life should the surgery succeed, or exit on its voyage with death. As I gazed at Elliott's immobile form, I silently prayed for his return to life.

Elliott's life. I knew its intimate details, learned during twenty years of friendship.

He had been a child prodigy from an Orthodox Jewish family in Brooklyn, excelling in languages, mathematics, music. His father, whom I still deferentially referred to as "Professor Ehrlich," was a renowned scholar of medieval Jewish history; his mother was the principal of a Hebrew high school.

Elliott was one of the first students from his yeshiva to go to Harvard, where he graduated magna cum laude in American studies. Following in his family's professorial tradition, he began a doctoral program in Colonial history at Yale. But he found the academic life too quiet and staid, the dimensions of the ivory tower too small.

So he left Yale for a job at *Time* in New York. For a while Elliott had found it exciting. It wasn't the New York he had known— Brooklyn with its sedate, tree-lined streets with two-family houses and elderly denizens chatting on the sidewalks. It was Manhattan, with all its intensity, grit, and ambition. At *Time* he found many like himself, educated at Ivy League colleges, poised to conquer the larger world. It was when Elliott was at *Time* and I was a medical student at Columbia that Anne Albright introduced us.

Although Elliott had made a living at *Time*, what his parents called a "decent" living for a single person in Manhattan, after three years he felt unsatisfied. The thrill of seeing his name among several on a joint byline waned, and he did not advance to a regular national column or produce an article that was considered for a national prize.

In June 1976, as I was leaving New York for my internship in Boston, Elliott quit the magazine and set out for L.A. He hoped Hollywood would provide what Harvard and Yale and *Time* had not.

"You bring yourself wherever you go," his father reminded him. I recalled remarking to Elliott at the time that it was the kind of advice my father, had he been alive, would have offered.

I heard Peter Draper sharply announce that he had snared the upper lip of the mass and that the attending pathologist, Ned Waterman, should enter the operating theater. I watched Peter deliver a glistening cube of tissue from the deep cavity of Elliott's open chest. He placed it on a sterile gauze sponge and then cut it into three equal pieces. Ned Waterman quickly moved his pathologist's forceps onto the field and distributed each piece into a different receptacle: one flash-frozen in liquid nitrogen; one placed in a plastic container with fixative; the last dispersed into a cell suspension in a saline-filled tube.

Peter Draper looked up and nodded to me. It was a signal that all was proceeding smoothly. I relaxed a bit, feeling the tension in my legs ease, and returned to my thoughts of Elliott.

Perhaps he occupied such a special place in my life because, among all my friends, he was my alter ego. Through his odyssey I acknowledged my own restlessness, my own fantasies of taking risks in life, of deviating from the path of the "good Jewish boy."

When I left Harvard for my training in hematology and oncology at UCLA, Elliott was working as a script writer in Hollywood. He lived in a rundown cottage on a hill in Malibu, overlooking the churning Pacific Ocean. There, Elliott entertained glamorous women he met at the studios, charming them with his humor and warmth.

His quest was to write a film about the formation of the first-generation American identity. He searched for cinematic venues not only in urban centers but in the far reaches of the country, traveling to the remote Arizona desert, small towns of east Texas, the wild chaparral of Montana. As he reached more deeply into the diversity of American culture, he became ambivalent about his parochial background. Still profoundly bound up with the Jewish people, their triumphs and neuroses, he was nonetheless eager to stretch his roots—suspending his celebration of religious holidays, no longer keeping kosher, preferring the company of non-Jewish women.

Elliott was financially successful in L.A., earning a hundred thousand dollars or more a year on options and commissions for scripts. A few of his works became TV movies, and one was almost made into a motion picture, but was killed at the last minute by the studio that bought it. But the major project on the American experience—his serious work of cinematic art—never came to be.

The surgical team was closing now. The ribs were realigned and the final sutures placed in the overlying skin. Elliott soon would be re-formed as he had always appeared to me.

In the adjacent room, Ned Waterman, the pathologist, was already studying the slices of snap-frozen tissue to obtain an initial diagnosis. I exited the operating room to join him. As I sat at the two-headed microscope with him, I began to review in my mind the diagnostic list I had formulated, but my thinking stalled. I felt my deeper mind repelling my conscious aim, as when two magnets are brought together at the same poles.

I suspended my effort to review the diagnostic list and momentarily retreated into recollections of the past, before the emergency phone call some four long days before.

Elliott stayed in L.A. after I came back to Boston. We spoke often, and I heard the disappointment in his voice as he described deal after deal that did not come to fruition. Three years after I left UCLA, in the summer of 1986, Elliott decided he needed a break from Hollywood. He traveled through Europe and then to Israel, where his parents had retired. At a garden party in Jerusalem he met Susan. They fell in love, married, and Elliott started yet another life, in Israel.

Elliott told me how he looked forward to living in Jerusalem, how he imagined the city would be his "teacher." He believed that the radical change in culture from the superficial, narcissistic world of Hollywood to the ancient holy city would nourish his creative powers and facilitate his writing of a major work. To support himself he took a job as a columnist for a new English-language periodical, *The Israel Bulletin*, and a position teaching film criticism at Hebrew University.

"Look at those cells," Ned Waterman said.

Gazing into the aperture, I found it hard to comprehend that the tissue I was studying under the microscope was a part of Elliott. The magnified field should have been recognizable but was confusing, almost surreal. Large cells swirled and danced like the intoxicated moon and stars in the frenzied paintings of the mad Van Gogh.

"It's a T-cell lymphoma," Ned Waterman tersely concluded.

My heart sank.

I tried to sustain my emotional equilibrium and think about Elliott's situation in a considered, clinical way. I recited to myself the details of T-cell lymphoma, as if I were teaching on rounds with a group of medical students and interns:

T-cell lymphoma represents some 2 percent of adult lymphomas. It is aggressive, marked by invasion of vital organs, particularly liver, bone, and brain. It is generally of unknown etiology, as it likely would be in this case. Recently, a mutation in a tumor suppressor gene called p16 was found in T-cell lymphoma. The p16 gene normally puts a brake on cell division in the T cell, but when mutated, the genetic brake loses its traction and the cells are released in a headlong rush of growth. There is a rare form of T-cell lymphoma endemic in southern Japan and the Caribbean. It arises not from a mutation in the p16 gene but from infection with a virus called HTLV, an acronym for human T-cell lymphoma/leukemia virus.

I halted my didactic mental exercise, recalling that I had studied HTLV at UCLA in the late 1970s, while Elliott lived on the hill in Malibu. Could he have contracted this rare virus from one of his romantic liaisons? We would test him, but it would almost certainly be negative.

I paused, my mouth dry, feeling slightly nauseated. I envisioned the next steps. We would clinically "stage" his lymphoma, assessing by CAT scan and tissue biopsy where, beyond his chest, the cancer cells might be growing. Although it might be confined to the mediastinum, given the size of the nodes and the two-month delay in diagnosis, I suspected we would find it elsewhere.

Elliott then would require very intensive treatment. At least five different chemotherapy drugs administered together for nine months, followed by two years of so-called maintenance therapy with three more agents. The aim was to destroy every last lymphoma cell. The treatment would bring him to the cusp of death, damaging much healthy tissue—in bone marrow, liver, skin, mouth, and bowel—in order to purge the cancer completely.

My mind stumbled in its clinical mode as I considered the prognosis of a "forty-three-year-old Caucasian male, previously healthy, with T-cell lymphoma presenting as an 8-centimeter chest mass." The numbers would not hold together. Each time I approached the statistics on long-term survival, less than 50/50, my heart sank again.

I knew at that moment that I could not be Elliott's doctor. For the first time in my career I had reached my limits as a treating physician. I was unable to function with the clinician's necessary analytical detachment. I realized that my inability was not just because of our closeness. It was also because Elliott was too much a mirror of myself.

His situation had sparked memories of my father's death, of my youth as a student, and of my dreams as a physician-in-training. The arrival of Benjamin and Susan had made me consider how Pam would manage with our children if I were the one suddenly stricken with a life-threatening disease. In the operating room I had averted my eyes because I feared seeing myself as he was then, exposed for what we all are: vulnerable flesh and blood. Later, during his therapy, I would wonder how the poisonous drugs flowing into his veins would feel flowing into mine. And—I shuddered at the thought—I knew I would perceive the final throes of his death as a vision of my own.

I realized I could not trust myself to be his primary care provider, to walk each morning into his hospital room and see the suffering that had to be if he had any chance of surviving—the vomiting and diarrhea and hair loss and bleeding and fevers and infections and mouth blisters and skin sloughing and a host of other side effects from the treatment. I feared that his physical suffering and psychological anguish would color my judgments and cause me to make a mistake—a mistake that could cost him his life.

I would never forgive myself for that, as I never forgave the physician who failed my father. That physician did not know his limits. I knew that my father might have died even in the most competent hands and the most modern hospital. But then I and my family would have known that all had been done that could have been done, and we would live without added anguish or regret.

I could think more clearly now that I understood the basis for my inner conflict.

I decided I could not, would not, remove myself entirely from Elliott's case and medically abandon him. I desperately wanted to help.

I arrived at a solution. I would offer myself as a "physician once removed." My scientific knowledge and technical expertise would be brought to bear at each step of Elliott's illness as they might be useful. After the clinical staging of the lymphoma, I would identify a competent and committed oncologist. With this specialist, I would help set the treatment strategy and advise on the medical response to problems and complications—as they undoubtedly would occur.

I STOOD in the surgical recovery room, grasping Elliott's pale hand. Susan leaned over, wiping beads of perspiration from his forehead with a damp cool cloth. She took the news of his cancer without flinching. I sensed she had expected it from the start.

"Elliott will defeat it," Susan forcefully asserted. "I know him, how tough and determined he can be."

Elliott looked at her with measured appreciation. He whispered, his voice still heavy from the anesthesia, an echo of her sentiments: "I'm ready to fight. I want to live. Above all, for you and Benjamin. And my daughter-to-be."

I looked at her with surprise, and then understood. Susan had seemed heavier, her taut facial features subtly expanded, her waist wide. I thought it was the first changes of middle age, she being in her early forties.

Susan smiled softly at me.

"I'm just in the first trimester."

"Mazel tov," I congratulated them, wishing literally "good luck." The traditional phrase hung heavily between us. We would need all the luck possible for their unborn daughter to know her father.

Later that evening in his hospital room, after Elliott had taken his first nourishment and the effects of the anesthetic waned, we began to discuss the logistics of his care. I began by outlining the further staging that needed to be done, two separate biopsies of his bone marrow and an MRI scan of his brain followed by a spinal tap. We would begin a short course of radiation to the mass tomorrow to free the vena cava and restore the free flow of blood from his head.

I hesitated and then, in faltering speech, began to discuss the question of where he should receive his nine months of chemotherapy.

Elliott looked knowingly at me. Before I could broach the issue of my being his primary physician, Elliott asserted that it didn't make sense to be treated in Boston. Now that the situation was under control, we could think more pragmatically.

He reached for my hand, gripping it with considerable force. He said he knew I would be there for him every step of the way, and my presence meant a great deal, more than he could express. But someone else, whom I knew and trusted, should take over his case.

I rallied, feeling grateful he had read my feelings and relieved me of my conflict.

We analyzed the options of which location and hospital and medical team would be the "very best," and concluded Elliott should go to Alta Bates Hospital in Berkeley, California. A warm-hearted and skilled colleague, Dr. Jim Fox, directed its outstanding program in blood diseases and cancer. Jim, I knew, would make the personal commitment to Elliott's care. A key factor in this choice was Susan's family. Her parents lived in Sacramento and owned a condominium in San Francisco. Susan and Benjamin would stay there while Elliott was receiving treatment. When the new baby arrived, there would be the support and resources of nearby grandparents.

Before Elliott left, we administered two short pulses of radiation to the mass. Within forty-eight hours the veins of his neck had flattened, and his headache disappeared. It would buy enough time for him to make it to the West Coast and begin definitive treatment.

I contacted Jim Fox, reviewing Elliott's case in detail, and then sent him by overnight mail the pathology slides, copies of X rays, and the operative report. The lymphoma, as I had feared, had spread to the bone marrow, but mercifully it had spared his liver and brain.

Elliott began the chemotherapy regimen four days after leaving Boston. He developed the expected side effects from the treatment: nausea, vomiting, hair loss, mouth blisters, diarrhea, and then less common complications. First was chemical pancreatitis, an inflammation of the pancreas from the drug L-asparaginase. He suffered weeks of severe abdominal pain that bored into his midback, and wild fluctuations in his blood sugar as insulin production fell. The high doses of chemotherapeutic drugs also injured the small vessels of his circulation. Fluid transited from his capillaries and swelled the soft tissues of his arms, legs, and face. This was eventually brought under control by aggressive administration of diuretics and restriction of his fluid intake.

The repeated courses of steroids resulted in painful necrosis of the bone of his right hip. It was decided that Elliott ultimately would need surgery and an artificial joint. The steroids also made his lungs a breeding ground for a fungus called *Aspergillus*. This fungal infestation triggered spasm of his airways and severe air hunger. He needed oxygen, antibiotics, and bronchodilators.

Elliott stoically absorbed each awful side effect, and looked to his humor to diffuse his pain and fear. "I'm the Pillsbury Doughboy," he said when his body ballooned from the edema. "They say mature women like Susan love bald men," he quipped when his distinctive auburn hair was completely gone. With a raging fever and harsh cough from the fungal infection, his mouth ulcerated and his intestines unable to hold the little he took in, Elliott hoarsely concluded, "I think I finally outdid Job."

I stayed in close contact with Jim Fox by phone, fax, and e-mail. After receiving the clinical update, I would speak with Elliott. Our conversation developed a regular pattern, first mulling over the medical issues and then discussing his emotional state and the state of his family. I also visited him, using my frequent trips to scientific meetings in California as opportunities to see him in San Francisco or Sacramento.

Beyond clinical assistance, Elliott looked to me for hope. I told him all these complications were reversible, and we were very much on track with the lymphoma regimen. He began to ascribe to such words of support and reassurance a deeper significance, as if I were privy to a world of certainty beyond that of our senses. Susan, the hard-driving political operative, surprised me by also taking up this line. She regularly ended our joint discussions of his condition with the assertion "If Jerry says it will be O.K., then it will O.K., Elliott."

I felt deeply uncomfortable in such a role. I knew all too well how desperate we become facing life-threatening illness and its toxic treatments, and understood how we grasp at straws, wanting to believe that the doctor, with credentials and experience, can see the future clearly.

I tried to defuse their statements while still being encouraging, to gently restate the truth as I knew it, in scientific terms. I reiterated that the sum of the clinical data so far indicated that Elliott's chances were increasingly good that he would survive, but there were still major hurdles to overcome.

After his third course of the five-drug chemotherapy regimen, the mass of lymph nodes disappeared in his chest. After the fifth course, no lymphoma cells were seen on his repeat bone marrow biopsy.

With each positive advance, Susan and Elliott reaffirmed that I, like an oracle, had predicted everything would turn out fine, and my words were being proven true.

Elliott completed his eighteen months of intensive therapy. He then underwent complete restaging, with CAT scans of his chest and abdomen, bilateral bone marrow biopsies, and a spinal tap. There was no evidence of lymphoma. After so many invasive examinations, Elliott offered: "I always tested well, and this one was open-book."

Elliott was declared to be in complete remission. It would take five years of follow-up before it was safe to state he was cured—after that time, relapse was very rare.

"I will live with that uncertainty," Elliott asserted. "If I've learned anything from developing this disease, it is the fundamental uncertainty of all of life."

TWO YEARS LATER, in early June 1994, Elliott and his family visited Cambridge for his twenty-fifth Harvard reunion. I had never met his daughter, Tikva, now three years old. A petite and outgoing girl, she greeted me with a clever smile. Born after the fifth cycle of Elliott's therapy, when the lymphoma disappeared from his bone marrow, she was given her name as an expression of thanks. In Hebrew, *tikva* means "hope." Susan said the name embodied their tenacious optimism.

Elliott walked briskly with his family and me through Harvard Yard. Despite his artificial hip, he only occasionally depended on his cane to negotiate the inclines in our path. He was wearing sharply cut clothes he had purchased at Banana Republic in Berkeley to celebrate his complete remission: a white collarless shirt, beige linen pants, and a matching vest. His hair was thick and long, tied artfully in a pony tail. Susan remarked with a loving grin he was "Samson with his strength back."

Susan took Tikva and Benjamin for an early lunch while Elliott and I rested on the steps of Widener Library. We watched the preparations for commencement to be held the next day in the Yard, the stage arranged before Memorial Church, where the president, deans, and tenured faculty would be seated facing the graduates.

Elliott was in a reflective mood, moved by his return to a place he cherished, where every student was told he was one of the chosen, graced to attend America's most prestigious university.

He candidly shared his recent thoughts with me. He allowed that for the first few months after returning to Israel he was thankful just to be alive, taking each day as a gift. To eat without mouth ulcers and diarrhea, to breathe without oxygen pumped from a mask, to move his limbs without intravenous lines restraining them, this was enough to greet each morning with joy.

But now that he had fully resumed his former routine, writing at *The Israel Bulletin* and teaching film to undergraduates at the university, he was feeling deeply unsettled. During this reunion, he was realizing more forcefully than ever what had eluded him since leaving his alma mater. He wanted, finally, real success. Returned now to health, he was determined to obtain it.

I was aware we were moving into charged territory. We all want to succeed, and we usually define it in comparison to others, a problematic exercise. I feared that I might sound condescending or patronizing by saying this. Not knowing quite what to say, I remained silent.

"What have I accomplished?" Elliott continued as he gazed at the workmen hanging the rich crimson banners of each of Harvard's schools—law, medicine, business, divinity—from the poles of the stage. "This is what I have: a monthly column in a struggling Jewish magazine; two TV movies and countless unmade scripts; a part-time teaching job in cinema at Hebrew University.

"I know I almost died. It's not that I'm ungrateful for life. It's that I can't live on the edge every day, just thanking God and my doctors for my life. No one can live that way—it's a state of paralysis, a suspension of life. I have to deal with living again, in all its petty details—getting the kids to school and the car fixed and the taxes paid and the laundry done. And I have to deal with my larger issue—my desire to do something truly major.

"It was good to come back to Harvard, now, at this juncture in my life, after facing death. It energizes me to do what was always expected of me. And what I expected for myself."

He was thinking about finally writing a book. It was envisioned as a major work about the transformation of American culture. It would draw on the experiences he had had in a series of portraits of places in time: Brooklyn in the 1950s when the American dream was like a collective unconscious; Harvard in the '60s, the relinquishing of WASP hegemony, of New England gentlemanliness as authority was being challenged by the upheaval of Vietnam protests and experimentation with drugs; then the New York scene in the '70s, the rebirth of careerism, the social climbing, the attempt to find an anchor and direction; L.A., meaning Hollywood, the wanna-bes, the groveling, the raw crassness of money and fame. And finally the West Coast in the '90s, with the ascendancy of the wonks, computer nerds and their venture people, who have changed the way knowledge is received and processed by society.

"The experience of my cancer hasn't only made me want to do what I've always aimed to do—produce something substantial and important, a book that will be respected by the people whom I respect. I think I may have broken down the block to doing it. My illness has given me insights into myself that weren't apparent before."

Susan returned from lunch with Tikva and Benjamin, and we continued our stroll with them through the campus. We moved on to other subjects, the political situation, how the peace process was slowly but surely moving forward after the historic meeting between Rabin and Arafat. It was a time of hope and opportunity in Israel, and Elliott commented that, despite prior frustrations and failures, it was never too late for new beginnings.

ONE YEAR AFTER his Harvard reunion, Elliott had another opportunity to visit Boston. In addition to writing his biweekly column, he was now engaged in frequent travel as a public speaker. He had developed a reputation as a fresh voice in the Jewish intellectual scene. His commentaries drew on his considerable knowledge of Jewish history and tradition but added a modern secular slant. His subjects ranged from politics to cinema to books to religion. His readership in *The Israel Bulletin*, although select, was widely distributed throughout the Jewish world. He had addressed communities in Australia, Canada, and England already this year, and was now invited to New York to address a large rabbinical gathering. It was a special challenge, Elliott remarked, to "sermonize to the pros." He would come up to Boston midweek after his speech. Almost as an aside, he asked me to recheck his blood counts. On a routine visit last week with Dr. Levy, his general practitioner, his white blood cell count was noted to be just below normal.

"I'm at the tail end of a cold which I picked up from Tikva. Jeremy Levy thought this might have slightly depressed the number. You think it has anything to do with the lymphoma?"

I said I didn't. I agreed with Dr. Levy. Respiratory viruses often caused a minor diminution in the leukocyte count.

Elliott arrived looking strong and energized. There was a bronze color to his face from the Middle Eastern sun. His chest and shoulders were broad from his new passion, swimming. He no longer limped, having adapted to the artificial hip. We embraced forcefully, feeling the triumph that marked his survival. Pam and the kids welcomed him, as usual, with warm kisses.

Elliott did justice to a hearty homemade dinner, and rose early to read *The New York Times*. We spoke of the continuing move toward peace, how the redeployment in the West Bank was proceeding, and the chances that Rabin's Labor Party would triumph in next year's elections.

When we arrived at my office, Youngsun greeted Elliott with great excitement, and spent much time inspecting his photographs of Benjamin and Tikva.

Two hours later, I sat with Ned Waterman, the same pathologist who had reviewed the biopsy of Elliott's lymphoma. We systematically scanned the slide made from a single drop of Elliott's blood, which held thousands of white cells. Swimming among the normal white cells were several large ragged forms. These unkempt cells had bloated nuclei and bright pink splinters littering their cytoplasm. I looked at the face of my colleague across the microscope, how his brow arched and the muscles of his cheeks tightened. The diagnosis could be made by a first-year medical student, the morphology of the large, distorted cells was so distinctive. Elliott had acute leukemia.

I closed my eyes, the residual image of the leukemic cells lingering on my retinae. Then all I saw was deep blackness. I felt hollow, as if the darkness before my eyes had coursed down into the core of my being and emptied me of feeling. There was no anger, no pain, just a cold numbness, like the unfeeling shock of a person swiftly cut by a sharp knife who has no sensation of the wound.

Despite my emotional void, I immediately understood on a rational plane what had happened.

"Treatment-related leukemia" was the term applied to Elliott's condition, the cruel outcome of modern chemotherapy, which provided a lifesaving result at first only to trigger, years later, a second potentially fatal disease in an unlucky few. The drugs that Elliott was given to destroy the lymphoma had damaged the DNA of his normal bone marrow cells. Most of these cells had died from the trauma, unable to survive with an impaired genetic program; a few had accumulated, by chance, the necessary mutations to lead to the opposite of cell death—the unrestricted growth of cancer.

I returned to my office, where Elliott was waiting for me. We had planned to go to lunch at Rebecca's Café, the gourmet fast-food place near the medical school. He had spent the morning at the Harvard Coop buying T-shirts for his kids and wandering around his beloved campus.

"It's incredible how fast they grow," Elliott remarked as I entered the office. "Last year at the reunion, we bought them all sorts of Harvard outfits, and they've outgrown everything."

I agreed, saying kids grew like happy weeds, and then sat down. I looked into his soft blue eyes, knowing what they would soon see.

"Ell, I just returned from reviewing the slide of your blood test."

I paused. The cold emptiness that I had felt was now quickly replaced by searing pain.

I was tempted to hide behind euphemisms, to say there were some "abnormalities" noted and "further tests" would be needed. I had thought that might ease him into the news, the awful crushing news, that after all he had endured, he now faced more, much more—a treatment as intensive and battering as any that existed in clinical medicine. To definitively eradicate the leukemia and cure him, chemotherapy would not be enough. He now required a bone marrow transplant.

But I knew, as before when I had informed him of this T-cell lymphoma, that it was best for him to know everything, as soon as possible, in honest detail.

"Elliott, it appears your white count is low because you've developed leukemia."

Elliott paused after my words and then nodded knowingly, as if he recognized a familiar face. I had expected him to flinch from the harsh blow just delivered, to break down in tears. I was fighting to prevent myself from doing so. But he sat still and silent.

I took his silence as assent to inform him of what was needed to cure him, a bone marrow transplant, and what that meant, since it was often misunderstood by many laypeople. All the blood cells in his body would have to be destroyed. This would be accomplished by administering radiation, the kind of radiation that was called "total body" because it penetrated every millimeter of tissue, like the radiation from a nuclear bomb.

Once all his blood cells were destroyed, he would be given the most primitive marrow cells of a compatible donor. These primitive cells were called "stem cells," because they grew into all the mature blood components—white cells, red cells, platelets—and could reconstitute his entire hematological system.

I waited for questions, but his silence continued, and I wondered if Elliott was really processing the information, whether it was all too much and he was overwhelmed.

"Am I clear, Ell? I know it's a lot, coming fast and furious."

He finally spoke.

"What if there is no match for me, no one compatible to provide the needed stem cells?"

It was clear that he did understand, all too well, because this was the key issue. Even if he passed through the treatment for the leukemia and entered remission, he could be left in a netherworld of waiting, unable to proceed to the transplant. Desperate options were then considered.

"If, God forbid, there is no match, from your family or the worldwide registry of marrow donors, then there are two options. One is conservative—to live in remission from your leukemia, knowing it will come back in months to years. You are healthy and functioning during that time, and, we hope, research advances give us a second curative path before the leukemia returns. The second option is fraught with risk—an unmatched transplant. With an unmatched transplant, the stem cells grow into blood cells that will recognize the tissues of your body as foreign, and attack. This is 'graft-versus-host' disease—the unmatched transplanted blood cells are the 'graft,' and they charge against your liver and skin and bowel, as the 'host.' "

"And the outcome of the battle?"

"Not usually in favor of the host."

I retreated from this discussion to focus on the most immediate step, treating his acute leukemia. I said we should operate under the assumption that he would have a compatible donor—Michael or Simon, his brothers, whose genetically related cells would be unlikely to cause a severe graft-versus-host reaction. I reviewed the logistics and latest statistics on matched transplants, at each point emphasizing the positive edge he might have: his general robust health, his relatively young age, the diagnosis of the leukemia early in its evolution. I was functioning as I usually functioned, as a clinician, with calm and expertise and honest optimism in the face of a complex and frightening disease. I thought I was transmitting to Elliott a sense of determination and authentic hope.

But Elliott seemed to move all the clinical science to the side, and surprised me with his response.

"What is your *choosh,* your sense, Jerry? Am I going to live?"

Choosh is a biblical Hebrew word, meaning "sense" or "feeling." It is onomatopoeic, capturing the sound of a rush of breath that emanates from the deep reaches of the spirit. It is a word that speaks not of rational deliberation and assessment, but of inner vision.

I paused, not expecting to have a *choosh* but an *opinion* as a sober clinician, one drawn from weighing the factors that went in his favor and those that did not.

But within me I had *felt,* not calculated, a reply.

"My *choosh* is good. I believe you will make it, that you're going to live."

I stood from my chair and hugged him tightly, tears now streaming down both our cheeks.

I wondered if I had gone mad, whether the anticipated pain and loss from imagining his death was so great that, after I rebounded from the numbing shock of the news, my rationality had collapsed and I was retreating into delusion. Who was I to pretend to be a prophet, to have extrasensory perception? What did my *choosh* mean in clinical reality? Was I indulging myself and my closest friend in a convenient lie?

But it was not a lie. I had felt it, clearly and strongly. Deep inside me was a prevailing calm. I clearly realized all the obstacles and uncertainties that lay ahead—the induction chemotherapy for the acute leukemia, the identification of a compatible match, the preparation with total body radiation for the transplant, the tense waiting to see if the graft of stem cells would "take" in his marrow space and grow to repopulate his blood, then the risk of graft-versus-host disease. All the while, Elliott would be in a tenuous state—without an immune system—vulnerable to overwhelming and often deadly infections. He would be placed in an isolation room with special purified air and food, rare visitors allowed for short times and only under mask and gloves and gown, secluded as completely as possible from our world of ambient microbes while he lived without any bodily defenses.

But all these clinical realities faded under the powerful feeling that he would survive. I did not see light or hear words or otherwise hallucinate. And when I first heard his question, I assumed I would evade addressing it because in medical science *choosh* was meaningless.

But I had sensed that he would live, and it would have been a lie not to tell him.

"Let's call Susan," I said, anxious to move away from the moment of mystical feeling and focus on logistics. "We should figure out the next steps with her."

"She's probably back from work by now," Elliott replied, looking at his watch.

I dialed their number in Jerusalem, which I knew by heart, and as I listened to the flat ringing of the phone, wondered again if my experience of Elliott's illness was teaching me my limits.

ELLIOTT DECIDED to return to Jim Fox at Alta Bates Hospital in Berkeley for the leukemia therapy and the marrow transplant. Its clinical unit was state of the art, there was added comfort in knowing the nurses and the hospital routine, and the close-by resources of Susan's parents would again be of great help. Moreover, Jim had become not just his physician but his friend.

Susan flew to join Elliott in California, leaving Benjamin and Tikva in Jerusalem with Elliott's mother. The kids were in the middle of the school year, and it would have been disruptive to take them out of class. They were informed that Daddy had to go into the hospital again. They reacted appropriately, disappointed but with understanding, since Daddy had spent so much time in and out of hospitals during their young lives.

Elliott received high doses of Ara-C, a chemotherapy drug very effective against treatment-related leukemia but with terrible neurological side effects. He vomited for days despite powerful supportive antinausea medications, and then went into a swirl of vertigo as the Ara-C temporarily shocked his cerebellum, the balance center of the brain. He could hardly speak, lying with his eyes closed and his head immobile. These side effects slowly passed over the course of two weeks. Then his hair fell out, his mouth blistered, his bowels ulcerated, and his blood counts fell. He developed streptococcal pneumonia and required oxygen and high doses of antibiotics. It was all too familiar.

Through each blow Susan clung to my words like a sure lifeline, repeating as a mantra: "Jerry's *choosh* is that Elliott is going to live."

After six weeks Elliott passed the first critical hurdle—the leukemia went into remission. He was discharged from the hospital. A week later I was called by Elliott and Susan from her parents' apartment in San Francisco. Susan was the one to break the great news: Elliott's older brother, Michael, was an excellent match to be the marrow donor. She exuded determination, like a tank commander leading a charge.

"On to the radiation. Then the transplant. Michael's cells are perfect! Just a few more steps forward. Everything will turn out fine, just as you predicted, Jerry. Right, Elliott?"

Elliott had not spoken yet. There was a long pause before he affirmed Susan's words. Then in a flat voice, he simply said: "Right. Everything will be fine."

Later that night the phone rang. I was in the kitchen, unloading the dinner dishes from the washer. It was well past ten, the kids asleep in bed, Pam reading in the den before we would retire for the night.

"Jerry, it's Elliott." His voice was hushed.

"You O.K.? Why are you whispering?"

"I don't want Susan to hear me. She's watching TV in the other room."

He paused and drew a deep breath. "I don't know if I can continue. I don't know if I can go ahead with the transplant."

I could hear him trying to control the quavering of his voice.

"Why not? You've done great so far. You've come through the leukemia treatment beautifully. Michael is a perfect match. We're almost there."

"I'm not sure why . . ." He began to sob. "I just don't know . . . if I can . . ."

He paused to collect himself, and then continued, his voice still shaking.

"Susan and you and my parents and Michael and Jim Fox—everyone just expects me to do it. But I don't know . . . if I can fulfill your expectations."

I felt the distance of thousands of miles, the difficulty of finding the right words to reply without the benefit of seeing his face, touching his hand, following his eyes.

"Jerry, the transplant has become in my mind like writing my great novel or my major film script. The expectations that surround me—that have surrounded me all my life—everyone believing I could accomplish great things—it's all now focused on this. I just don't know if I can do it."

I paused to collect my thoughts. It was not my place to explore the degree of success or lack thereof in Elliott's life. That was not the critical issue now. What was critical was having him move ahead with the transplant, his only chance to be cured. I first tried an analytical approach, explaining to Elliott what I thought was happening to him psychologically, hoping the insight would comfort him and bolster his courage.

"Ell, it's normal to be frightened. Especially on the second go. It's like a soldier sent back to the front after surviving a first bombardment. You're still shell-shocked. You lose your nerve. That's natural, normal. I've seen this countless times with other people—a flood of self-doubt, all the secret insecurities rising to the surface and threatening to drown you.

"But you won't drown. We're all there supporting you, not with expectations but with love. I know Susan can be tough and drives you forward. It's her way of coping, her way of trying to keep herself, as well as you, intact."

"You don't understand, Jerry."

I heard him sigh, a desperate frustrated sigh.

"All my life I was expected to hit home runs, to slug it out of the park. Harvard. Yale. *Time.* Hollywood. But I'm not a home-run hitter. I hit singles—short grounders in the infield and pop flies. This time my life depends on a home run, and there isn't another chance at bat."

I continued to reassure him, that he was battle-fatigued, that Susan and I and Jim Fox and his parents were only trying to reinforce his will and confidence, not pressure him with expectations. But my words seemed hollow and I feared would be ineffective.

I paused to regroup my thoughts, and could hear Elliott begin to sob again.

I tried to see the impending transplant from Elliott's perspective and then modify that perception to make it more manageable.

"My words are just words, Ell. I've only seen it from the other side of the bed, the doctor's side. But I don't think it has to be a home run to score. It can be a series of base hits, one single after another. It may sound like a silly metaphor, but think of it that way. Break it down into a series of manageable pieces, instead of seeing it as a daunting whole. You've already proven with the lymphoma and the leukemia that you have the strength to swing the bat. You don't have to prove anything more, to yourself, to Susan or to—"

"Tell me your *choosh* about the transplant, Jerry," Elliott interrupted, his voice now more even and calm.

I sat silently, calling on my deepest feelings, seeking my inner sense of harmony or disharmony. It was again strange, because I did not resist his request. On a conscious level I wondered again whether this was all a game, my lack of resistance a way to extricate myself from a situation which had no ready solution. It was like a child's belief in the truth of fairy tales and the power of magic. I thought of the stories I had heard from my Hasidic relatives while growing up, of wonder rabbis, seers, diviners to whom the secret workings of time and space were revealed through angelic visitations and the study of mystical texts, *kabbalah*. I had been instructed by my parents to discount such tales as primitive and nonsensical. Was I assuming such a role for Elliott, or for me, or both?

But deep inside I had *felt* an answer, and offered what I sensed, not what I knew.

"I feel you're going to make it, Elliott. I really do."

. . .

ELLIOTT RETURNED to Jerusalem after the required one hundred days under observation in Berkeley. The marrow transplant had followed a remarkably smooth and uncomplicated course. His brother Michael's stem cells had found their niches in Elliott's emptied marrow space, and over six weeks began to spawn all the cells of Elliott's blood system. The growth factor G-CSF was given to expedite the maturation of the transplanted white cells, which reached normal numbers by week 10. There was no sign of graft-versus-host disease, and the medications that were used to prevent this complication were soon to be tapered off.

We had spoken several times each week during these critical one hundred days. After assessing the progress of the transplant, we discussed the biology and medical science that gave rise to the procedure. Elliott had brought a laptop computer into his isolation room, and in addition to e-mail and writing, had researched the history of the technique on the Web.

The Nobel Prize was awarded in 1990 to E. Donnall Thomas, now at the Fred Hutchinson Cancer Research Center, for developing marrow transplantation. It was the culmination of a remarkable story. The first eleven patients treated by Dr. Thomas had died within a few weeks. It was an extraordinary act of determination to persevere, to believe that the barriers to transplantation of human bone marrow could be surmounted.

The biology of the process is similarly remarkable. The rare stem cells, present only at a frequency of one in 10,000 donated marrow cells, could be infused into a recipient's vein, circulate through the body, home specifically to the emptied marrow space, and then grow to fully reconstitute our entire blood system—its billions and billions of cells that make up our immune defenses, oxygen-carrying capacity, clotting functions. It is a testimony to nature's astounding regenerative powers.

Elliott commented that beyond the exceptional history and biology was another dramatic dimension to marrow transplantation, one likely to be experienced only by the fortunate recipient. It was expressed by a verse from Leviticus: "The life of the flesh is in the blood." Within him, flowing in every tissue space—heart and brain and muscle and gut—were the life-giving blood cells of his brother Michael.

"I feel as if I've been reborn, like I participated in a new form of creation, joining the hand of God with the hand of man."

While I rejoiced in Elliott's metaphor, I somberly remembered what it had taken to bring bone marrow transplantation to the sophisticated state it now enjoyed. Some two decades earlier, when I was a hematology fellow at UCLA, bone marrow transplant was still in its infancy. Dr. Thomas had just passed the first hurdles and achieved sustained grafts. A transplant unit was established in our department. There were many, many failures which now would have been successes. Little was known about how to optimally administer total body irradiation and the adjunctive support to carry a patient through the procedure. There were no available growth factors like G-CSF to stimulate white blood cell production from stem cells and accelerate the return of the body's defenses. As a fellow on the transplant ward, I watched impotently as patient after patient developed overwhelming infections and died. The medication Elliott was taking—cyclosporine, to modulate the "education" of the grafted cells, so they gradually "learned" to tolerate their new home and not rebel in a tantrum of graft-versus-host disease—this too did not exist when I was in training. The ravages of this awful graft-versus-host reaction, with liver damage, diarrhea, and skin sloughing, were all too frequent then. If a patient survived, he was generally left incapacitated.

Elliott, my beloved friend, husband of Susan, father of Benjamin and Tikva, had been given back his life because of the stubborn commitment to research of physicians like Donnall Thomas. Science did change the world, fundamentally and for the better.

Elliott called me from Jerusalem three weeks after his return to tell me that Susan and his parents were planning "a survival party." Pam and I were invited, although they doubted we could come.

I told him we would celebrate in spirit from Boston, and toast the miracle of science that had returned him to family and friends.

"You saw it all along, Jerry. Your *choosh* was that I would make it."

I felt uncomfortable. I wanted to celebrate the triumph of medical research, not vague mystical intuitions.

"I don't know what my *choosh* meant, Ell. I did feel it, but perhaps it was just a delusion, a psychological mechanism to help me cope with the nightmare you were in."

Elliott paused and then replied thoughtfully.

"I've come to believe more in that mystical dimension, Jerry. Isolated all those days, my own cells forever gone, the stem cells of Michael growing into my new blood, I had a strange *choosh* of my own.

"I sensed it wasn't only coincidence that Anne Albright brought us together, but that she envisioned you as my brother, and then my two 'brothers'—you in spirit and Michael in flesh—saved my life. I felt a visceral connection to you, to Anne, to all the people who have loved and cared for me during my life. I felt this at the moment of the transplant. I felt as if all your spirits were being infused into me along with the marrow. As much as Michael's stem cells revitalized my body, your spirits breathed life again into my soul."

We left it at that, making these mystical experiences a part of the history between us, and moved on to talk about work-related things.

"I haven't figured out what I want to do yet," Elliott confided. "Whether it makes sense to continue at the *Bulletin* and on the lecture circuit, or do something different.

"I'm trying to understand what 'success' means in my life. That's not easy. It's a struggle. I've been thinking about how I measure success in light of what I've been through.

"When I couldn't hold a pen to write, focus my eyes to see, or even lift my head to speak, I realized that performing such simple acts then would have been a 'great' success. It's a cliché but true, that you don't appreciate what you have until it's gone.

"I learned in yeshiva years ago the question posed by the Talmud: *Eizehoo ashir?*—Who is wealthy? And the rabbi's response: *Ha sameach b'chelko*—He who rejoices in his portion.

"It wasn't always easy in the past for me to rejoice in my portion. But in my isolation room, as my new blood was being created, I was able to write my column again. And I *rejoiced* in doing it.

"You know my first article was about my leukemia and the transplant. After it appeared in the *Bulletin,* I was deluged with mail. So many readers wrote, not only wishing me a speedy recovery and sending words of support, but affirming how powerfully my ideas affected them. I realized that sometimes they do cheer you when you get on first base, that singles do count in the game.

"I have hardly lost my ambition. I still want to write a book of substance, of significance. But I see the reason for my ambition differently this second time. Above all, I have to find it satisfying, I should rejoice in it. I want to look inward, not outside myself, for a measure of its success."

I understood Elliott's struggle. The desire for greatness, to be recognized for your achievements, was an insatiable worm that gnawed at your consciousness, invaded your dreams. Who didn't suffer its effects? Driven to do more, make more, rise higher. But it was a fruitless climb because there was no real summit.

I knew this from my perch as a physician, witnessing the moment when the seemingly endless climb is abruptly, unexpectedly, irreversibly halted by the advent of life's end. As death looms, so much of the "success" that we have lusted for appears useless and vain.

There are, of course, lasting achievements in life. I thought of the success of Donnall Thomas. He was certainly driven by ambition, pushed forward by the desire to conquer nature's barriers and do what had not before been possible. And he had been awarded the Nobel Prize, science's highest honor. But that wordly acclaim paled before a greater honor—the legacy that he had created for Elliott and others like him who now could live.

"It's very hard to live by one's own inner standards, Ell."

"Probably impossible. But I'll try. And when I feel myself slipping back, I'll tell myself to reflect on how I felt during the transplant, how my life was so brutally constrained, how my days were literally numbered."

"Literally numbered?" I wasn't sure what Elliott meant.

"Yes. Each day on rounds, Jim and the nurses would number the days: day zero was the day my blood was destroyed by the total body irradiation. Then day one was the infusion of Michael's stem cells. Each subsequent day was numbered. It was a weird experience, to listen to Jim Fox count at my bedside and declare to the medical team: 'Today is day fourteen post-transplant, vital signs stable, no sign yet of recovery of the graft.'

"I was both terrified and hopeful—terrified because I knew Jim could be counting the last days of my life, but hopeful because it felt like he might be numbering the days of my second creation. And if I survived, I knew I would be reborn in a unique way, not like the infant with a blank slate, but with memory and insight from all that I experienced."

Elliott's words brought to my mind the verses from Psalm 90, a psalm of life and death. It is recited in my synagogue to begin the mournful service of *yizkor,* the service of remembrance of those loved ones who are gone. I saw myself then, standing deep in prayer, my eyes closed, seeking insight from memory. This time the words spoke to me not of loss but of gain:

> *The stream of human life is like a dream;*
> *In the morning, it is as grass, sprouting, fresh;*
> *In the morning, it blossoms and flourishes;*
>   *but by evening, it is cut down and withers. . . .*
> *Our years come to an end like a fleeting whisper.*
> *The days of our years may total seventy;*
>   *if we are exceptionally strong, perhaps eighty;*
>   *but all their pride and glory is toil and falsehood,*
>   *and, severed quickly, we fly away. . . .*
> *So teach us to number our days that*
>   *we may attain a heart of wisdom.*

Epilogue

DURING THE YEAR that I was writing these stories, a new story began in my life. My mother, then sixty-seven years old, developed breast cancer.

My mother has no special risk factors for breast cancer. She married young, at eighteen, leaving college in her first year to begin a family with my father, who had just returned from serving in the U.S. Army in Europe in World War II. My sister was born at the end of their first year of marriage; I and my younger brother followed in relatively short order. Breast cancer occurs more frequently among women who bear children later in their lives. Furthermore, we have no family history of breast cancer, and my mother did not take hormones before or after menopause. The cancer just happened.

Although she lives in New York, my mother wanted her care primarily to be at my hospital, in Boston. She said it was because I would direct her to the best surgeons, and she admired the efficiency and courtesy of the staff. But we both knew, without saying, that she was deeply frightened, and her fear would be lessened by being close to me.

I was frightened too. When my mother called me after the needle biopsy in New York, I imagined grim scenarios—finding that the cancer was not localized but widely spread; treating these metastases with intensive chemotherapy to no avail; watching her suffer and decline; tearfully reciting *kaddish,* the prayer of mourning, after her death. I forced myself to lock these morbid images away and focus on the step-by-step unfolding of her case. I knew I would be of no help to her unless I supressed my fear.

The primary mass was too large to be excised by a simple resection ("lumpectomy"), so a full mastectomy was required. During surgery, five mammary lymph nodes were found to contain deposits of cancer. Fortunately, it had not spread to other organs.

Given the size of the primary tumor and the number of involved lymph nodes, there were likely microscopic deposits of cancer remaining—despite the mastectomy. The chance of the tumor regrowing in months to years was high. Thus, treatment was indicated. Studies had shown, in cases like my mother's, that intensive four-drug chemotherapy given over twelve months reduced, but did not eliminate, the risk of recurrence.

My mother has always been one to speak her mind, and she did so upon arriving in Boston. She said my role was not to be her doctor, but her son. Nonetheless, as a son who was a doctor, she asked me to help interpret for her what was happening medically. She wanted, above all, to hear the truth, at all times.

Acting as her "interpreter" was hard for me, and at first I chafed at being put even in this minor medical role. I wanted just to be her son, to sit quietly next to her bedside and tightly hold her hand, far from the clinical details and decisions of her disease. But as the shock of her diagnosis and operative findings receded, I realized how much I could help, that my words of fact and hope had a special resonance for her. There was no one she trusted more.

We had long acknowledged a special closeness and a special conflict, probably because we were alike in so many ways. People often remarked how much I, of her three children, resembled her, the deep-set eyes and aquiline nose. We shared many habits and traits, from waking up well before dawn to begin the day to an obsession with order and organization. She had done most of the parental disciplining as I was growing, and I was a handful—rambunctious in elementary school and seeking independence at an inappropriately early age. There had been many contests of her will against mine.

My father, in a traditional role, had made most of the decisions in the family and my mother then implemented them. When he died, my mother's world shattered. During twenty-six years of marriage she had not been separated from my father for more than a day, and we, her children, wondered how she could reassemble her life. She was alone in our house in Queens, my sister married, my brother an undergraduate at Harvard. I was a second-year medical student at Columbia College of Physicians and Surgeons, and had been on my own since college. I brought my mother to live with me in Manhattan. Being together again took some adjustment on both our parts, but it worked to reestablish the nucleus of a family.

During those two years together in Manhattan, I began to see my mother in a different light. She had strength and endurance not apparent to me before. She sought a job as a secretary in one of the Presbyterian Hospital clinics. The hours were grueling and the stress on the workers considerable, but she persevered, applying her determined will and organizational skills to that chaotic and trying environment. She also made herself into something of a "class mother," hosting medical student friends of mine for home-cooked dinners even on evenings when I was on call and not in the apartment.

The strengths which I saw after my father's death returned with her current illness. After the mastectomy, as I held her hand tightly and talked about the upcoming chemotherapy, I was surprised by how strongly she returned my grip. Her eyes became moist but she did not cry, at least not in front of me. And she informed me she would not hide her diagnosis from others. Where appropriate, she would tell our extended family and her close friends that she had breast cancer, had undergone a mastectomy, then reconstructive surgery, and would be treated for a year with combination chemotherapy.

Her treatment is ending, two cycles left to go as I write now. The four toxic drugs have taken their toll, but my mother has weathered it.

"I make believe I feel better than I do," she confided after a particularly difficult round of chemotherapy. "Pretending for everyone else makes it easier for me—because I start to pretend for myself."

As I listened, I thought about how I too had begun to pretend. I had instructed myself to suspend thinking about all the negative outcomes—what purpose did it serve? And I told myself to assume the chemotherapy would succeed in fully eradicating the cancer and return my mom to a long and healthy life.

But in another way, we did not want to pretend, my mother and I. There were issues that we wanted to resolve, issues between us from the past and in the present. It was easier to air these now. The uncertainty of her condition, the unknown time remaining, had drawn us closer.

This year, in early January, I celebrated my forty-fifth birthday. That Saturday morning, I went to synagogue, accompanied by Emily, my four-year-old daughter. We walked through a gentle snow, Emmy measuring her small bootprints against mine.

We attended the preschool service, led by an animated teacher. I sat with a score of other parents in the back of the room, watching our children singing. Soon it was the time in the service for the children to tell their stories of exciting events that had happened during the week.

When Emmy's turn came, she stood proudly and announced she had spent the New Year's weekend in New York. Her blue eyes sparkling, she recounted the highlight of the trip.

"I saw my Grandma Muriel."

My mother had been strong enough to participate in family activities, it being the week before her next chemotherapy treatment, her blood counts normal and the effects of the toxic drugs largely dissipated from her system. Mom had spent a lot of time playing with Emmy during our visit. I had the sense of what a gift it was for my mother to know Emily and my sons, a gift that my father never had. I wondered how much of my mother's life would be shared with my children, how long and how deeply their time would be joined.

It was not just my mother's time that I pondered. I was now forty-five, a mere ten years younger than my father had been when he died. I prayed that my children would not suffer the pain and loss at an early age that I and my siblings had.

I began writing this book aware of the long shadow of my father's death, trying to understand how that event had given me the impetus and strength to do the work I do. As I close it, I look to the future, seeking lessons from the patients I have cared for, for my mother and myself, in how to live.

Acknowledgments

I AM FORTUNATE in having many friends who encouraged the writing of this book and critically assisted in its evolution. In the project's embryonic stages, Anne and Marty Peretz read several chapters and Anne passed them on to Maggie Scarf. Maggie led me to Suzanne Gluck at ICM, who took on the project with her unique energy and intelligence. As the work grew, Margo Howard, David Sanford, and Melanie Thernstrom lent their skilled hands to help me better shape my language and ideas. Charlene Engelhard, Liz Young, Arthur Sulzberger, Jr., and Arthur Cohen were especially forthright and insightful critics. I received important maturational feedback on certain parts of the manuscript from Caroline Alexander, Robert Brassel, Eric Breindel, Sally Button, Barbara Carton, Marilyn Chase, Roberta Fahn, Everett Fahy, Roberta Ferriani, Dan Gadish, Barbara Gladstone, Lenny Groopman and Yasmine Ergas (my brother and sister-in-law), Francine and Harry Hartzband (my in-laws), Young-sun Jung, Susan Kamil, Carol Kann, Larry Lasky, Merle and Yangja Legg, Rita Levinson, Robert McCleary, Ellen Murphy, Stephen and Georgia Nimer, Francine Pascal, Alexander Roesle, Stuart Schoffman, Terri Schraeder, Stephen Shea, Andrew Spindler, James Spindler, Brenda Star, Abe and Cindy Steinberger, Michael Ward

Stout, Andrew Sullivan, Abigail Thernstrom, John Thomas, Elizabeth Weymouth, and Debbie Zaitchik.

My mother encouraged me to write the Epilogue, believing it would help others to learn from her current situation. Each of my patients who is alive gave permission to their portrayal for the same reason. I cannot express how indebted I am to them for their courage and commitment. In all chapters except "Alex," certain personal details and circumstances have been changed to protect confidentiality. Otherwise, the stories as told are theirs.

Dawn Drzal, my editor at Viking Penguin, brought extraordinary understanding and professionalism to her guidance of the work. She knows how to shape a creation into its coherent form with insight and rigor. Barbara Grossman, Cathy Hemming, and Paul Slovak at Viking Penguin believed in the project and were essential to its fruition.

I am thankful to my family for putting up with what is often a consuming activity. Every draft was read by my wife, Pam. She knows me better than I sometimes know myself, and without her mind and heart, this book would not be. Some three millennia ago King Solomon asked, *"Ayshet chayal mi y'imtza?"*—A woman of valor, where is she to be found? I am blessed to have her with me, teaching me how to bring not only this work but my life to fulfillment.

Index

ABOUT THE AUTHOR

Jerome Groopman, M.D., is the Recanati Professor of Immunology at Harvard Medical School, Chief of Experimental Medicine at Beth Israel Deaconess Medical Center, and one of the world's leading researchers in cancer and AIDS. He and his work have been featured in *The New York Times*, *The Wall Street Journal*, *The Boston Globe*, and *The New Yorker*, as well as in numerous scientific journals. He lives with his family in Brookline, Massachusetts.